A LABOR OF LOVE

To Brick and Barbara,

May you weave only
love through your life!

Love and hugs,

Jim

9/23/06

A LABOR OF LOVE

Weaving Your Own Virgin Birth on the Loom of Life

Book Two: My Spiritual Awareness Series

Jim Young

iUniverse, Inc.
New York Lincoln Shanghai

A LABOR OF LOVE
Weaving Your Own Virgin Birth on the Loom of Life

Copyright © 2006 by James H. Young

iUniverse books may be ordered through booksellers or by contacting:

iUniverse
2021 Pine Lake Road, Suite 100
Lincoln, NE 68512
www.iuniverse.com
1-800-Authors (1-800-288-4677)

ISBN-13: 978-0-595-39931-4 (pbk)
ISBN-13: 978-0-595-84320-6 (ebk)
ISBN-10: 0-595-39931-2 (pbk)
ISBN-10: 0-595-84320-4 (ebk)

Printed in the United States of America

JIM YOUNG'S WEBSITE

creationspirit.net. The website contains additional creations to come through Jim Young, including collector-quality photography. Speaking services and classes dealing with his writings are also made available.

Acknowledgments

Each opportunity that appears to us seemingly out of nowhere offers us the choice to act out of highest good, the best in us—or not. No judgment is necessary, only discernment. The emergence of A LABOR OF LOVE is no different. Just after Thanksgiving 2005 I was asked to deliver a presentation to the Unitarian Universalist Fellowship in Eureka Springs, Arkansas. I was delighted to be asked. I felt privileged, actually. I have heard many splendid, enlightening presentations there and respect the fellowship's purpose, as well as their commitment to inclusion of people and ideas different from their own.

Just prior to accepting the invitation to speak, I had completed a manuscript entitled, "CREATION SPIRIT; Expressing Your Divinity in Everyday Life," and I was somewhat eager to share some of the ideas it contained. In preparation for the talk, I outlined some of the key points from that piece that I wanted to let out into the light of day. Under the title of "The Metaphysician Within," I was suggesting consciously going within to our Inner Authority as a way of replacing the largely unconscious means we normally use from past experience. During the preparation for "the day," I recalled the precise feeling I had while completing the last few pages of that previous manuscript. "This is the invitation to begin the next manuscript," I could hear myself saying. "And this is exactly what you must lead from," referring to the last issuance of that previous volume: "You Are God."

All throughout the preparation for the talk, the head of this new creature kept showing up. I'd fight it back, and it would wane for a while. Then it would show its face once again. And I'd shoo it away—again and again and again. Once I got the talk where I wanted it, I looked the new initiate right in the eye as a challenge to get on with it. Now the tables were turned—but not for long—just until after I had finished the presentation. The day after—early on a

Monday morning, I remember—I reviewed the outline I had used sparingly for the presentation and made several changes I thought would improve it. With that, I was about to check my e-mail when, with these same fingers on the keyboard, the new manuscript announced its desire to get on with it. Did it ever!

With only about five or six days off for good behavior during a three-week time frame, the first draft of this current offering spilled out onto these pages in complete form. Oh, the daily pillow and shower notes that appear to me from my Muse in the wee hours of the morning still reach inclusion in the manuscript with devotion, to be sure. But for all intent and purposes, it is finished.

Of course, as this one came to a close, the next began to appear in its infant stage. Actually, several of them have reared their heads! And at least one of them promises to be even more outrageous than this one has turned out to be. I'm not sure yet how, or even if, Christo Sahbays will return in one of them. But I'm convinced that if he himself doesn't show up, at least his spirit will be deeply felt. He is such a good friend that he wouldn't abandon me.

There is one other to whom I am ever grateful, and that is Dr. Pamela Finnegan, an inspirational novelist in her own right who has faithfully used her considerable editorial skills to hone this material into a more cohesive whole.

To whom is the real dedication here? It could easily be to the central character of these works himself: Christ Sahbays. He has been a continuing source of inspiration—and entertainment—for me. The dedication could just as easily be to The Unitarian Universalist Fellowship of Eureka Springs, AR. It was their invitation that focused attention on the closing of a door and the opening of a window to reveal yet another work. This book could well be dedicated to those who have supported me in this endeavor—and there are many. Through them I have received enormous support and inspiration for that which has opened my Life to a world I never had imagined—until now. But now I don't have to imagine it any longer. I am enjoying Life, as I never have before. Last, I could dedicate this offering as I have all creative work that comes through me, in part as least, to my family, to whom I heartily express my gratitude for all they are, and how that contributes to what I am.

Having given this theme ample thought, however, I have decided to dedicate A LABOR OF LOVE simply and reverently to opportunity itself. I am ever grateful for what opportunity brings me every day of my Life. Actually, I have learned that opportunity *is Life!* Life unfolds to reveal all that needs my attention each moment, offering me the choice on each occasion to see Life as multifaceted: either out of limitation, or out of complete inclusion, coupled with the creation spirit that expands the universe of meaning. Where this perspective has taken me by this time is to the understanding that there is only one choice that speaks to the highest good of all concerned. This choice is the Loving Way, expressed from the Truth that is available only from within. And what a treasure this Kingdom of Heaven is! For all of it, and to all who, and whatever, is included within it, I am forever grateful. Thanks to one and all that continue to rain such rich blessings on me in each present moment of this land of opportunity.

Jim Young

A Special Note: Should you wish to penetrate the veil of illusion around Life, you might well want to exercise the Spirit Noodles section at the end of the book. A series of spiritually-related questions and such appear for each chapter. If you consider these at the end of each chapter before going on to the next, your sincerity of purpose will carry you to great depths of meaning within. I encourage you to honor your divinity in this way.

The day of my awakening
was the day I saw
and knew I saw
all things in God
and God in all things.

—Mechtild of Magdeburg, female mystic

CHAPTER 1

The Return of Christo Sahbays

This is a story about coming home—coming home to our divinity—that essential Essence of God which we have abandoned through the process of domestication. This story really begins with the one that preceded it, *THE CREATION SPIRIT; Expressing Your Divinity in an Everyday World*; a story of an itinerant metaphysician from Northwest Arkansas named Christo Sahbays.

You will remember that we left Christo Sahbays after he wrote two penetrating e-mails to participants following a daylong retreat with them. For the most part, he had left them spellbound with his compelling focus on inner healing. In his first e-mail Christo briefly reviewed the major premises of the process for cleansing the old ideas and beliefs that serve as barriers to healing. In the second e-mail, very near the end of the first book, he leaped an inferential gap, risking losing both his credibility and his audience by suggesting that everyone *is* God. He was careful to quickly clarify that he did *not* mean that they were *a* god, or *the* God but rather, created as all Life is: with God as our very nature.

Since that time, Christo has written his former audience suggesting a day and a half affair on matters of the fearless heart. By continuing to cleanse the affairs of our fear-filled mind, he posits, we can finally arrive at a metaphysical place where we can see Life from a more wholesome perspective, which, in and of itself, is healing in its effect.

We arrive at the scene, somewhat diminished in size due to the natural falloff of attendees that can be attributed to a fearful mind that inhibits continuance on a plane, or in a direction, that seems to be too threatening to the old mindset. Nevertheless, undaunted by what some might say is a rebuttal of his teachings, he moves forward knowing the Truth of the matter. We now find Christo Sahbays ready to greet the participants, a crowd of around 2,000, housed in a conference center in Fayetteville, Arkansas.

In his usual humble fashion, he rises from his meditation stool stage-side and gently parts the curtains as he strides soulfully to the microphone. Christo begins reverently, as always: "Namaste, my dear friends. Namaste. Indeed, I not only acknowledge, but also enthusiastically celebrate, your divinity. I am so glad that so many of you have returned for this next leg of our journey." The humility with which he embraces the crowd is obvious, as is their warm response to his authentic presence. Through the power of a word—'Namaste'—the audience and Christo become One once again, as though they had never parted. Of course, the simple Truth is that they never had parted. One is One, after all, and is always just that way.

"Ah," Christo continues, "I can feel your loving Spirit, and I have missed being in your presence. But now we are reunited, thank God, physically that is. As you know so well by now, spiritually we have never left one another's company."

Christo can feel the crowd settling in for the long haul, and he listens carefully within to garner the next steps in the process of spiritual discernment. As usual, a knowing smile comes across his face, now a familiar treat to the audience, for it cements their feeling of Christo's authenticity. "All right then, let's begin by returning for just a moment to my rather stunning proclamation that you are God." Even though he knows that they trust him, Christo can feel a bit of uneasiness in the crowd when he uses those words, and he responds sensitively to it: "I know that this is an unsettling reference that probably cites itself in the pit of your fear-filled mind. What I want to do now is take you, rather, to the seat of your fearless heart, that precious space within where divinity resides. Where Truth reigns. So you can begin to see the light, that which erases the darkness that clouds your view. We instinctively know that darkness gives way to light and that ignorance gives way to Enlightenment, so let us begin with this leg of our journey together.

"Not so incidentally, by the way, I must confess that I left you all in somewhat of a lurch with my declaration about you being God. I did that on purpose. When we are engaging in meaning of this depth, it is wise, I have found, to discern quickly who is willing to leap the inferential gaps and who is willing to give up the old for the new, or is at least willing to consider doing so. Your presence here today is witness to your willingness to fathom the depths in order to arrive at Truth for you. And I applaud your commitment to Soul and Spirit.

"In order for us to move forward, we need to have a clear understanding of spiritual Life, Life in the world of thought: metaphysics. Even though we have discussed the meaning of metaphysics, of which Jesus was a master, a quick review of the term might be helpful. If I were to put a more whimsical face on it I might say simply that it all depends on your point of view." The crowd readily picks up on his disarming sense of humor, and the tension arising from the idea of they themselves being God begins to release.

"With a smile of anticipation on his face, which sets even more tension free, Christo continues: "If I wanted to play with it a bit more I might say that metaphysics is nothing but a colonic of consciousness where we cleanse our unconscious thoughts in order to live consciously. In reality, as we know, metaphysics speaks of the world, the *real* world, as spiritual; as a world of thought, which speaks as our perspectives on various aspects of Life. If we were to be strict adherents to its base meaning, we would attribute to metaphysics the principle of First cause. That is, that the First cause of any part of our divine Life is divine idea. The principle of First cause stems from the understanding we have that to begin rightly is to end rightly. Put simply, if I want to end rightly—where highest good is for me—I must begin rightly. I must begin with the only thought—a divinely derived thought, one lovingly created—that can head me in that direction. Then all I must do is be sure every step I take is in that same direction.

"In a metaphorical sense, if I want to weave a solid blue tapestry, I cannot arrive there by threading the warp with pink thread. So, because I want you to end rightly with a sense of your own divinity—your Godliness—by the end of the day, we must begin rightly with the single divinely inspired thought that would most assuredly take us there. That thought is a bit down the road, however, because I first want you to clearly see how we got where we are, so we don't repeat the same mistake of demonstrating mostly out of egoic mind, and end up in exactly the same place we were some months ago, rather than in divinity. To do otherwise is to demonstrate the definition of insanity: making the same decision time after time thinking it will produce different results. As we begin, then, I want to take you to the threshold of your own metaphysician within. When you arrive at that threshold, you need not fear, for you can be assured that you will be ready to step over that threshold on your own.

"In this regard I'm reminded of that which is attributed to Jesus. You will recall from Scripture that Jesus was supposed to have said to his apostles that when he left—which most have unfortunately been taught to mean that when he died—he would see to it that they were fitted with a spirit. 'The Holy Ghost' this spirit has been named, the Paraclete—'the inner guide' Jesus called it—upon which they could continue to lean for the Truth of living. I am here to tell you that this was not the meaning of Jesus's admonition. If we understand his meaning to be 'spirituality,' as we must take Jesus and our notion of God, for this is one of Jesus's greatest teachings, then we take his words to the seat of metaphorical meaning. By doing so, we could well understand his statement thus: 'You have been leaning primarily on me for your understanding. It is time I weaned you a bit. If I don't, you will have missed the purpose of my teaching, which is that you can find real meaning for you only from within yourself, where God resides. In this way, whenever we are apart, you have the means of going within for all the guidance you will ever need. It is upon this thread, this principle, that you find your own divinity, rather than attributing divinity only to me and some god external to your own."

The crowd seems to gasp collectively, almost come to a stunned silence. Christo gives this rather abrupt translation time to settle in. Then he repeats the key phrase to punctuate its meaning, so it can penetrate the armor that might formerly have made such penetration impossible. "By going within, you have the means for all the guidance you will ever need. Is this profound, or what? All the guidance you will *ever* need. Not by leaning on some outside authority, even one like Jesus, but by going within to your own divine guidance. Wow! In that single teaching he erases the potential for the lie that external authority and validation are our saviors. Only our inner authority and validation is that: our savior. Indeed, that which saves us from ourselves is found only within. In that single teaching Jesus also erases the possibility of codependence, that unhealthy means of holding one another hostage to our perceived needs. What an extraordinarily wise teacher was this man, Jesus!

"Even though we have barely begun our day together, I want to give you a short break so you can fathom the depths of meaning from Jesus's admonition, for that meaning forms the foundation of our work together here today. The real Truth of the matter is that it forms the foundation for living a compassionate Life passionately. Without this understanding firmly implanted, our work together today will be much more difficult. So let's take a fifteen-minute break and we'll reconvene promptly at nine o'clock. I'm sure you have already located the restrooms and places for refreshments, so by all means make use as you see fit."

With this brief introduction, Christo Sahbays has indeed set the stage for what he instinctively knows he has to follow. He returns to his prayer stool with a smile in his heart, warmed by the receptivity of the gathering. Sipping his tea and munching on a ginger snap or two, he relaxes before the next session is to begin. He had learned long ago to let INspiration and INsight just be, and awaits their infilling with great pleasure and gratitude.

Several of Christo's closest followers come to him with feedback from their survey of the crowd. It simply affirms what he already has discerned with his finely tuned receptors. The crowd is indeed ready for the next big steps in understanding the nature of their own divinity. Carefully setting the stage with an element of desire is part of being an authentic teacher, after all. Christo is also pleased that his aides are demonstrating their own growing awareness of what is transpiring, simply by listening within for the real meaning of their observations.

CHAPTER 2

Cleansing the Unconscious

The time of arrival has come, both literally and figuratively speaking. The insights and enlightenment that now fill him to overflowing refresh Christo. Once again he approaches the stage with grace and abundance. The participants seem comfortable in their understanding of the framework Christo has provided. He can feel their receptive energy, even if they haven't entirely absorbed how going within relates to divinity.

Christo begins once again with reverence for his audience: "Namaste, my friends in Christ." Before he can continue, Christo is greeted with a hearty, "Namaste, Christo Sahbays. Namaste." Christo, humbled by this display of affection and respect for his divinity, reaches out his right hand, with his left hand embracing his heart, and sends a burst of unabashed loving energy out to the participants. Time stands still in this simple embrace, a heartfelt hug of its own making that seals their relationship with trust. This is a telling signal to Christo, for it says that he has their full confidence and can continue from the depths of his being without encumbrance. "Thank you, dear ones, for your loving energy. This in itself is a sign of your divinity, even though on some levels you are still not yet ready to accept this about yourselves."

He continues in the wake of this wondrous connection, wanting to set the stage for the process of reaching Enlightenment through the teachings of the Master Jesus. But he feels he needs to make a distinction, just to be sure he does not misrepresent himself. "By now you know that although my spiritual foundation is Christian, no one could truthfully say that this is so in the traditional sense of the word. My spiritual focus is on the teachings of Jesus, the loving

Spirit, or divinity, the God we are that informs without fail only for our highest good and the highest good of those around us. Nowhere have I been able to find in the scriptures Jesus's proclamation that he came to this planet to save us. The distinction for me, however, is that his teachings certainly do save me from myself—time after time after time. When I go within for the Truth that comes through INsight—not physical sight—I am led to Enlightenment, which allows me to transcend my old ways for the new.

"Because I left you out on a limb with the inferential leap to your Godliness, your divinity, I want to slowly trace the steps from domestication to revelation, but in a different way from that used in our earlier time together. At some point I will reinforce some of those earlier elements, but for now I wish to begin anew. You deserve no less than a fresh start, so strap on your seat belts and get ready for the ride. I won't wear you out by traveling too far before giving a respite, so worry not. Just sit back and drink this in and be refreshed by it. There is nothing that I will say that you don't already know. It's just a matter of reminding you of your own Truth. I just love Wordsworth's conclusion in this regard: 'God lends us to one another this way.'

"Let's begin this leg of our journey by dealing with the greeting 'Namaste' for just a few moments. Most translate this as acknowledging the divine *in* you. The deeper meaning is that I heartily acknowledge and celebrate the divinity you *are*. The holiday season we are in right now affords me a marvelous analogy to demonstrate the difference between the two meanings. Saying that I acknowledge the divine *in* you is tantamount to my jovial neighbor coming over to me the day after Thanksgiving and saying that he acknowledges the turkey in me—when he'd really like to tell me that I *am* a turkey!" Christo chuckles to himself as the crowd giggles at his silliness. Still, it is immediately obvious that his analogy has hit home. "See the difference? Either I am the turkey in me, or I *am* the turkey, but not both. Having it inside me doesn't make me that. Nor does my being that put it in my tummy. They are discreetly different. When we apply the same principle to divinity, we have it right. We *are* divinity, meaning all of our being is divine. We don't just have a piece of divinity in us somewhere.

"By now I have absolute confidence that you all have an intellectual grasp on the greeting 'Namaste' and its implications for our divinity. But why is it that so few of us use this greeting? Is it simply because it is counter to our culture? Just so we can see for our own information, how many of you *do* greet those you meet with this precious word?" Just as Christo suspects, fewer than a hundred people raise their hands in response. "Let's continue this survey for a bit and see where it takes us," he rejoins. "How many of you refrain from using 'Namaste' as a greeting because it is unfamiliar to those with whom you use it and you don't want anyone embarrassed?" About half of the participants raise their hands. "And when you answer this next question, you can ignore your last response. In other words, the answer to this question and the last one don't have to be mutually exclusive. Now, how many of you don't use it because you don't yet feel comfortable with either your and/or another's divinity?" Nearly all the hands in the audience raise, most rather reluctantly. The answer is clear, the reluctance notwithstanding. "That's exactly what I sensed was the real answer. In varying ways this is precisely why we are going to deal with this throughout the day. So we can loosen that grip on self-image enough to acknowledge and accept—and hopefully even embrace—our divinity.

"Well, if we don't *feel* divine, how come? If we simply go within, where we *do find our divinity*, then we can then easily not only identify with the divinity we are, but we can also take ownership of it. Is this the only way we can be in touch with our divinity? I think not. However, there is much that clouds our view. These clouds are contained in the veils of illusion about ourselves that prohibit the light from entering. In order for darkness to give way to light, for ignorance to give way to Enlightenment, we have to part these veils, the layers of limitation that envelop us. My purpose in this segment is to rend those veils, so you can not only see your divinity, but also see new ways of exercising, of demonstrating, your divinity on a more conscious level.

"You know from our last meeting together that we have the choice of exercising either unconscious or conscious thought as our way of Life. As the apostle Paul told us, when as a child we thought as a child and behaved as a child. But now we are more mature, so we can think and behave as an adult, one who is more mature in understanding metaphysical Life. Before we move to the more mature discernment of meaning, however, it is helpful to review our childhood pattern of dealing with Life largely according to external authority and affirmation, and also from the seat of unconscious application of Life's meanings. By first remembering our childhood we can have a better chance of avoiding the same mistakes we may have been making. Again we have the meaning of beginning rightly in order to end rightly.

"Let's take a quick look at how we began in our youth. Unless we do begin rightly, we are, at the very least, going to be a house divided—our house being the container of thought through which we look as we engage Life. The division will be between unconscious and conscious thought. It will be evidenced by whether we obtain what can be discerned as Truth from the authorities without, or from our divinity that speaks to us from within. So now I want you to pretend with me for a bit.

"As we have said in the past, Life is little more than metaphor, the purpose of which is to inform us spiritually. The late, beloved Brother Roger of the Taizé spiritual community in France unfurled a marvelous revelation when he said, 'Childhood images remain the loom on which events are woven and rewoven.'

"What marvelous imagery with which to begin! Many of you may not know the vocabulary associated with weaving, so I'll describe the process enough to give you an ample idea of how it works. In order to weave, we must have a means of threading our yarn, the threads of which will form our tapestry. The threads that are firmly stretched vertically on the base of the loom form what is called the warp. The threads that are woven across, over, and under the threads of the warp form what we call the weft, or woof, as it is sometimes called. The warp is the foundation that Brother Roger speaks about, our metaphorical threads of childhood meanings through which we weave Life as it comes to us.

"On a very important related note, most people think that experience is the circumstance or event or happening that crosses our path as we traverse the planet. But what experience *really* is is nothing more, or less, than the way we *view* what comes before us. Reality for us, then, is not the actual happening, but how we choose to view that happening—how we choose to 'experience' it. When we look at the event of experience in this way, we stop being a victim of Life and instead take full responsibility for how we see what comes to us. When we finally make the inferential leap that all of Life is Gift, and come to understand the validity of that approach, then we will have found our Heaven in earth. By the way, the spiritual reality of that phrase is not Heaven 'on' earth but, rather, Heaven 'in' earth. It's Heaven—divine, Loving thought or idea—made manifest in material form, which is earthly in nature. Thus, the expression is more properly said: Heaven 'in' earth.

"Here are several more examples to clarify the difference in experiencing the idea of 'experience.' Two people can see the same 'accident' and provide entirely different stories about it. Two lovers have a quarrel, and each provides a unique rendering thereof. A married couple lives in Boston but view the pros and cons of living there from entirely different perspectives. In each instance, the person has chosen how to see the event or circumstance using the only lenses he or she has available to look through. Hence, they experience Life in precisely that way and only that way—until and unless they come up with a new perspective, a new set of lenses that can assist them in transcending the old way of seeing. As an early hint to you, perhaps INsight is that way.

"Having said that, I'd like to point out to you that from now on, every time you hear me use any term that can be associated with divinity, or be thought of as another synonym for God, I want you to see it embellished with an upper-case letter which starts it. Soon, you will get the idea, if it is not already imbedded in you, that all of Life is sacred.

"It is also important to understand in the beginning of this conversation that in whatever ways we choose to view Life, it is those that will become habitual in nature. It is also true that we are reluctant to give up these ways unless we have more desirable alternatives to consider. Let's look at the habits of thought that come to us in childhood, one at a time, and see what their impact could be.

"Children are like wet cement: whatever falls on them makes an impression of some kind. Indeed, whatever falls on them can make an intellectual, emotional, physical or spiritual impression. When something, a simple understanding, for example, falls without other emotional or spiritual encumbrance on a child, it usually isn't very heavy. It barely merits a single thread on the warp of our loom. If that something that falls on us has some additional elements that accompany the intellectual impression, like a strong emotional and/or physical component, for example, that merits a larger thread. Or, if we want to keep it simple, it merits at least several threads of that nature. Using color as an example, if something makes only a light impression, it merits only a single red thread. But if that something that falls on us is compounded, it may merit ten or a dozen threads of red on our warp. So those red threads will show more abundantly in the weaving than if the impact had not been as great. It's the difference between having a light, fluffy feather making an impression on us, and having someone stomping on our neck wearing a pair of combat boots. From the winces on some of your faces, you get the idea, I'm sure.

"Okay, now let's look at some of those other threads. They're not only threads made up of negative imagery. *Whatever* falls on us makes an impression. So the loving, warm, and fuzzy things also make an impression. Hopefully, each of you has far more of the warm and fuzzy than otherwise. We know, for example, that when a child is in the womb, he or she is influenced by the energy of both parents. The mother has greater influence in some ways, to be sure. But the father also contributes by his attitudinal energy: his obvious love of wife and child to be; if he really wants the child or not; how he treats his wife overall; even how he feels about himself and even his work-Life. The mother influences the child in vastly wider realms beyond these, for example: by her attitude; if she 'feeds' her unborn with loving words and strokes and with comforting music; with her own healthy diet and exercise regimens; by her use of drugs, alcohol or tobacco. Each of these impressions forms a thread, or more, on the warp of that child's loom—upon which he or she will weave Life.

"Now, the child comes out of the womb, and how is it greeted? The very first thing that happens is that the doctor spanks the newborn in order to 'jump-start' this human machine. 'There, this is for nothing, now wait until you do something!' can be the way this is felt. This reminds me of a story about the baby who is born at home. The father is at work when the mother's water breaks unexpectedly. She calls 911 and the EMTs arrive just in time to deliver the baby. The one who delivers the baby strikes it on the bottom, making it cry a little. The little eight-year-old brother who has witnessed all this shouts out: 'Good! Spank him again. He's got no business crawling up there and making my mommy miserable!' A little humor helps even in these occasions it seems.

"At birth the mother and father usually greet the baby with great joy and acceptance. Indeed, for the parents, just the sight of the baby renders the judgment that it is angelic, divine. This may or may not last long, but whichever it is, that will be the impression that creates the pertinent thread for the warp. The same is true about the impressions left on the child's Soul by siblings and peers. It all has some impact.

"As I take you through this process, which is largely about the unconscious nature in which we travel on this planet, I'm going to use mostly those images that have negative impact, just to exaggerate the exercise for affect. If you can't identify with these examples, and have more positive ones, by all means use those. This is your tapestry that you are preparing to weave, remember, and not mine.

"In early childhood we are cuddled, stroked, and even fed when we appear to be hungry, even though we may have been crying to have our diapers changed instead of because we were hungry. We are picked up and cradled when we appear out of sorts. But soon our mother seems to be paying attention to others as well as to us, and thus is not as readily-available to our needs. We begin to get the impression—and take on the fear—that if we don't take control of our lives, we won't get what we want when we want it. So we learn about 'Life as control and manipulation.' And along with this, comes the fear of being controlled and manipulated. And the 'control freak' is thus born.

"Then we start having limitations placed on us: what we must eat; when and how much; the fences that are put around us in the forms of gates and cages; and all the yeses and noes. From this we learn about Life as limitation and lack of freedom. And we learn the fear of losing both.

"As we get older, we are told that 'big boys don't cry,' and 'big girls don't express anger.' We soon get the message that expressing our feelings is just not what is done in this family, particularly if we rarely see the gods of our youth, bigger than Life itself—our mother and father, of course—not exchanging feelings or intimacy of any kind. From this we learn about 'Life as lacking feeling and intimacy.' It doesn't take a lot of imagination to see how this lesson could play out in Life.

"Perhaps an example provided by scripture will make sense here. I've told you this story before, but as G. B. Shaw says, 'I like to quote from myself; it adds sparkle to my speeches,' so humor me for just a bit if you will. It will make an important point in this context. You will recall the story of Jesus healing the man by the waterside at Bethesda. As the story is told, Jesus asks the man what he wants. The man says to Jesus that he couldn't get anyone to take him to the troubled waters. Jesus is reported to have said, 'Pick up your bed and walk around.'

"If we were to translate this metaphorically instead of literally, we're liable to come up with something like this. By the way, the stories of Jesus' healings always seem like instantaneous healings have taken place. But the suspicion is that there was more conversation taking place than indicated. Of course, the full conversations couldn't be included because if the Bible contained all of what really transpired it would have to be many pages longer than it now is.

"It is likely, however, that once the new realization took place, the new perspective took on other meanings. Then the shift within—we call it INsight—was immediate, so when we are told of the 'healing,' it looks like what transpired happened in but an instant. Anyhow, I offer this as but another rendering.

"I can just hear Jesus saying to the man who asked to be healed: 'You know, you have made your bed and I could just as well let you sleep in it.'

'What ever do you mean?' responds the man.

'Well, you have made the decision to live vicariously, even voyeuristically, I suppose. As you travel the stream of Life—the metaphor for feelings, the emotions of Life—you are afraid to live what you feel within yourself. I understand that you would more than likely feel guilt or shame for doing so, but it is time to look at your Life differently now. You're an adult, after all, not a child any longer—and not only age-wise, but hopefully also spiritually. You are *not* your feelings, and yet a part of being in this body is for you *to* feel them. Feeling your feelings is part of what it means to be human, to be alive on this plane of existence. By denying your feelings you become numb, deadened to them.

'Let's take anger, for example. My bet is that you were made to feel guilty if you confronted anyone in anger, if you displayed anger in any real way, actually, and largely because either your mother or father, or both, were afraid of exposing their own anger. Now let me ask you this: When you do you feel some levels of anger, and the need to express it because it's tormenting you, what do you do?

'Hmm, I guess I look for some safe way to expose it, somewhere and in some way that I won't feel guilt or shame for doing so.'

'Yes,' Jesus rejoins, 'just as I thought. I'd be willing to bet that when you have a lot of anger stored up that you start to press someone else's emotional buttons to get them riled up. You press and press, knowing precisely how to do that out of Life experience, in order to survive your feelings. You've become really skilled at it. In this way, you get to live your anger through them. Is that not so?'

'Wow!' exclaims the cripple, 'I would never had seen that all by myself. Now that I think of it, I do a similar thing with fear. I want someone to take care of me like my parents did. But from this different perspective I can understand that I can go either to fear or refrain from doing so. It's my choice completely. I don't have to depend on anyone else to do it for me—or to make me feel guilty or shameful if I do. I can see now that my behavior has crippled me emotionally and I am grateful to be healed of this one. It's bigger than I was willing to admit.'

'You did a nice job of transferring the example of anger to the way you live fear through others. Enlightenment works wonders. Well done. Now that you know the issues, you can change how you deal with them. The nice thing about Life's choices, about making our bed, is that we can change one bed for another, or even just change the nature of our bed clothes,' says Jesus. 'We can cast such infirmities aside, and walk in a different direction. We can change the way we think and take on a different perspective, exchanging it for the old. In this way, our blindness to another way is healed. We can hear, that is, understand, a different meaning. We awaken from the deadened feelings we have hidden from view. And in the process, we will have healed our guilt and shame and become alive again. In fact though, you really haven't been healed at all. What's really happened is that you have just allowed the veil of illusion, the untruth about feelings in this case, to be parted. This act alone allows you to see yourself once again as you always have been: divine. You were blind but now you can see. You were dead but now have been resurrected to Life anew—been born again.'

"You see," says Christo, "it took a little while to bring the man to a new perspective, but his 'healing' was instantaneous. I'm sure that you do this same kind of thing regularly with those who come to you for help: by listening in the full presence of compassion, and leading them to the threshold of their own inner knowing, which arrives instantly as INsight. It is from INsight, not from what we see outside of us, that Enlightenment comes to us. With Enlightenment we transcend to a new Life from the old. This solitary act of Loving presence renders you as a metaphysician and divine, all in one. Perhaps you've just never thought of your divinity—or metaphysics—in this way.

"Let's continue just a bit longer to wrap up this warp of unconsciousness. As we get older, we begin being judged for things we do and say that don't appeal to our parents and siblings and others along the way. From this we become accustomed to 'Life as judgment and guilt.' Based on the example set by others, it doesn't take us too long to begin blaming others and ourselves for simple mistakes. When we add to that the punishment that is handed out, we learn of 'Life as punishment.' The sad part of this one is that it is heavily laden with emotional and spiritual impact, and such renderings diminish our Soul. Because these feelings are so deep, so profound, we begin to do anything to avoid the pain, including lying. And so the world of the lie ensues. The fear of pain is that great, and many of us will do anything, including lie, in order to avoid it.

"Then, when we get old enough to display some behavior that can even remotely resemble something sexually uncomfortable for us, our parents or other family members, we are gifted with the debilitating feeling of shame. Yes, guilt and shame are so strong in their impact that they become the gifts that keep on giving. This reminds me of something that might help relieve a bit of the shame syndrome. How many of you have heard it explained that a Freudian slip is founded in latent shame surrounding sexuality now expressed?" They all raise a hand in unison. "Well," instructs Christo, "perhaps this will help correct that misunderstanding. More recently it has been determined that a Freudian slip is not that at all, but rather something you wish you had said to your mother but were afraid to." The crowd joins in laughter, and the tension about all these childhood inflictions is lifted somewhat. Christo heads down the road to conclusion, knowing he has to reinforce the point with enough depth to have lasting meaning.

"We're almost home free now. Somewhere along the way we get the understanding that we must depend on external authority, any external authority, for our own validation and authority on almost any matter. Unless our parents or others teach us that it is only from within that we can really know Value and Truth, we will be stuck forever in the hands of others. We will be forever-wounded; both by their judgments and by their erroneous advice about how we should live the Life they want for us, rather than on advice about what is best for us. Of course, just as in previous cases, unless we understand the 'withinness' principle, we will do anything for external validation and to obtain the information we think we need in order to live a happy Life. If this illusion were true, however, how is it we end up feeling so hollow? So unfilled? So lacking in purpose?

"We soon get the idea that we must be less than divine. Less than perfect, meaning to most, less than, period! Otherwise, Life wouldn't feel so futile. The fear then becomes one that says that unless I work hard, I won't be good enough. This is the Life of the overachiever, unless, of course, he or she concludes that it all just isn't worth it and becomes an underachiever instead.

"Last, we come to understand that, 'my innocence has abandoned me. My angelic, divine image has abandoned me. My freedom has abandoned me. Eventually, even my family and friends have abandoned me. And because my parents were like gods to me at one time, even God has abandoned me.' Think about the magnitude of the loss of security bound up in all this. This can blossom into the fear of loss and abandonment and a need for security. The latter is often expressed by looking for someone outside oneself to provide security, represented all too often by financial security. Thus the proverbial 'gold digger' and 'sucker' are born.

"What generally happens in Life is that what we see as children is what we come to think Life is supposed to be. So in order to feel comfortable, we continue to select circumstances and people who repeat this drama. Or, even more perverted in its nature, we see Life exactly as we saw it as a child for the rest of our lives, no matter what the reality of it might be. In a phrase, we are doomed to repeat it—unless we change how we see it. As Dr. Wayne Dyer says, 'When we change the way we see, the things we see will change.' How clever—and how true—all in one.

"The truth of the matter is that all of these are what are called 'take-aways.' All of them are untruths, illusions that take away from the Truth about Life and our place in it. They drive us further and further away from the inner knowing of our divinity. In a way, this is the ongoing definition of crucifixion, the means whereby we kill the Truth of our divinity. It is only by changing the nature of our perspective, by awakening to a new one, that we are resurrected to Life anew, more than likely being the meaning Jesus meant to convey to us."

Sensing an intervention within, Christo pauses for a moment. The participants have learned to recognize this slight tilt of the head, the slightly turned up corners of his mouth, and the ever-renewing twinkle in his eye. They respond en masse with trusting anticipation—trusting that even greater Enlightenment is about to come their way. And they are not to be disappointed. "Thank you for your patience," Christo begins. "I have some related views to share with you. My original intention was to deal with this after our next break but it seems that it is to be shared now, so we can complete our initial take on the warp upon which most of us have woven our lives.

"So far, we have dealt mostly with those unconscious threads that seem to find their way onto our warp, almost as though we were totally unaware of their presence. Of course, as we matured in our ability to think and feel and discern the difference between illusion and the reality of our spiritual Life, we began to make some different choices. Some of us have learned to use that which felt bad to us to instill a vow that we'd never 'do that' to anyone else. That's all part of growing up, spiritually at least.

"Now I want to add to our warp some of the threads that mix unconscious with conscious application on our parts. These come from the disparity between what appears to stem from the teachings of "the church" and the teachings that come from Jesus himself. Listen carefully as I present these in juxtaposition to one another. Compare them to what you think you have heard as you grew up in the world of theological mythology.

"Dear, dear, Christo; now what have you done?" Christo says in mock self-chastisement. "Apparently I didn't listen to the conclusion of this offering before I leapt ahead of myself. Let me slow the train of thought down just a little so I don't lead you astray. 'Theological mythology:' whatever do I mean by that term? I'll put it this way. We all carry in our seat of understanding various stories about Life. Whether we are a Christian or not, or even an atheist or not, we carry imagery pertaining to God, and about Jesus. Such imagery is largely developed from our view of our parents, so strong is that bond which helped paint our inner theological landscape. In other words, we carry an image of God that may look like an angry and vengeful God, one that will judge and punish us, that validates us and determines our entry to heaven or hell. This imagery comes about primarily from how we see our parents, but also from what 'the church' has taught us, indoctrinated us with, the church being *the* supposed external authority. This is the God of the Old Testament.

"Or, contrarily, if we had mostly warm and fuzzy relationships with our parents, and they taught us to go within for our own authoritative Truth and validation, then our God would look much more like the God of the New Testament. So let's now look at some of those teachings and discern their impact on our lives.

"For example, the church teaches that Jesus is divine and that we are less than divine. We are original sinners. Jesus, however, teaches that all is and are divine. 'Man is made in the perfect image and likeness of God,' he says. The church wants us to believe that Jesus and God, by their divinity, are separate from us. Jesus asks us to believe that we are all One; never separate: 'I and my father are one.' 'We all are brothers and sisters, I in them, they in me.' The church talks of saving society. Jesus tells of forming a society of savers: 'If you believe in me, then you, too, shall do these works; even greater than these works shall you do.' The church informs us that we are our brother's keeper. Jesus teaches that you and I are our brother's brother: 'I am my brother's brother. We are one. I am in him, he in me.' Yet again, the church tells us that we are mere mortals, finite and imperfect. Jesus tells us that we are immortal, infinite, and perfect: 'Be ye perfect, even as your God is perfect.' The church sets itself up as the authority on matters of religion and family and Life. Jesus, on the other hand, tells us to go within, to our inner authority—not without—for our Truth and for our validation: 'God is within. Go to that still small voice within for your Truth. The God within knows of all which you are.' The church emphasizes the Life of Jesus as God and his death and resurrection, and teaches about what he did. Jesus teaches how changing one's perspective can change your Life, can heal you, make you see and hear the Truth found within, so you can change your perspective and change direction, repent and sin no more.' And last, although there are many more which you can add on your own, the church tells us we have to work hard to get into heaven. Contrarily, Jesus tells us the Truth of the matter: that we already are in Heaven by our divinity, that we feel and come to know that we are in heaven when we live from the perspective of our divinity. 'The Kingdom of Heaven is within you.'

"There, now just think what our lives must look like when we combine all those more or less unconscious, externally-derived, threads of our warp with these erroneous religious teachings. At the stage of development at which we took these on, after weaving our warp with these threads—and others like them—we are still like wet cement, remember. But now, at this stage of our lives, we're just all mixed up and hardened. Indeed, we live using hardened thoughts and beliefs that become our psychoses and neuroses. In our warped mind's eye (pun intended) we have woven a tapestry that is largely about fear and misconception. This one we can truly say represents a tapestry that came from our fear-filled minds. Is it any wonder we're so mixed up?

"As we look at the warp, we should understand that every time we weave something through it, that something takes on the coloration, the texture, and the flavors of those warp threads. If a Life circumstance or personality trait matches a bunch of those same kinds of threads from our warp—and we have not yet resolved that concern or issue within us—then our relationship with that concern or particular relationship will take on a 'charge' of energy. We will feel ill at ease, discomforted, painted with inharmony. If we are fearful of dealing with it, or feel that we might be somehow judged or stigmatized by getting professional help in dealing with it, then we more than likely won't do so. Thus we are doomed to repeat the erroneous thinking until we do take the steps necessary to reshape our perspective about it, as well as about ourselves.

"Just so you don't go to the break with the heaviness that may be trapped in you from this rather arduous review, let's see what we can do to release some of it. Think with me for a moment about how certain events of our lives have been woven across some of these charged warped warp threads within us. Close your eyes and find just one thread that seems to be very strongly represented in your warp. Or perhaps one impression that is so dominant in its impact that it is represented by scores of threads. Now take just one incident that seems to elicit an internal response of some magnitude, an event that triggers a highly emotional response within. Just sit with that feeling for a moment or two. This may strike you on a deep level. Let it go just deep enough where you can recognize the feeling, but no more than that. What we are striving for here is to be able to discern the feeling, not drown in it. We want to become familiar enough with the feeling to be able to recognize it when it arises yet again. We'll deal with larger aspects of this treatment later on."

Christo gives just the right amount of space around each bit of guidance in order for the participants to create the desired inner imagery. "Now," he continues, "see yourself without those same threads on your warp. Look at only those that have the warm fuzzy appearance. Once you have successfully done this for yourself, let that same impressionable incident come back into your Life. This time deal with the incident without those debilitating threads, those deeply emotional, highly painful memories, being present. What do you now feel as this Life incident passes through you? Again, simply sit with it for a few moments. Drink it in until you are informed by it."

As is his custom, Christo wisely waits for all this to settle in. By now, because of such treatments in past sessions with him, the participants are mostly available to themselves in order to readily retrieve such meaning without making it part of their being. Their discernment has grown to mean only: 'What wonderful information this is that takes me to INsight and Enlightenment and on to transcendence over my past debilitating impressions.' After a few minutes Christo resumes. "Okay then. Open your eyes and give yourself adequate time to arrive back home, here in your divinity." Christo sees that the glow of understanding has permeated the gathering. As others 'wake up' to the present moment, it is easily seen that the collective wisdom is growing exponentially as they look around, seeing what by now has become a familiar glow of self-affirmation. "Ah, let this feeling sink in, this feeling of meaning. Let me ask how many of you are now able to see the impact of unconscious impressions, and some conscious ones to be sure, on the way we view Life?" Nary a hand was left in one's lap. "Wonderful!" Christo exclaims. "This is a very difficult thing for us to do as humans. Yet, in just one simple display, you have seen it for yourselves.

"Another great thing about what transpired in just the last few moments is that you have also gained the knowledge of how to do such cleansing for yourselves. For the time being, however, I dare say that you will not have difficulty any longer with an episode similar to what you have just cleansed from your midst. For you have parted the veil of illusion about those images and have returned to your divinity. There may be an ever-so-slight blip still on your emotional screen but with just few more exposures, it will be gone forever. This may seem rather arduous—to clean each out one by each. What we have identified just now is a short-term solution to emotional upset. We'll discover a long-term care process later in this session. What we'll focus on will be a simple way of seeing those same old scary things in a dramatically new way.

"What we also are doing here is developing the ability to effect exactly what Jesus admonished his apostles to do: learn to go within to the source of your own Truth, rather than to rely on me for Truth all the time. Be assured that you are doing very well in demonstrating exactly what Jesus asks. Quickly, now, you are becoming the example that teaches."

Christo takes a long, deep breath, testing his Inner Authority for the next step. Hearing nothing new, he continues: "That's probably enough to deal with for now. For one, I could feel some of those same heavily-laden threads within me during that simple exercise. Knowing that this must also be true for you, all I ask is that you refrain from judging yourself for what you feel, or for how that feeling got there in the first place. I also want you to know that there is a simple way for you to change all this to the good. A hint for how to effect this change comes from that earlier reference from the apostle Paul, to paraphrase: 'when as a child we think and act as a child. When as an adult it is time to think and act as an adult.'

"For now, just give yourself some space to let this have its proper meaning for you. Don't over-think it. Merely let meaning come from within. Look for the INsight, not the intellectual explanation. Said another way, merely ask, 'I wonder what meaning all this has for me?' Then wait for the answer. By now you know how quickly it will come. We will reconvene in 20 minutes. Addio."

Once again, Christo has discerned with indelible clarity that the participants are exactly with him on this road to recovery. He also intuits that the reminders of the "warped" lives they have led have impacted many of them emotionally. He will prepare to be responsive to their need during the break simply by listening within, just as he has instructed others to do. When he reaches his stool, he removes his jacket and folds it like a pillow, and then lies down on the floor for a little snooze.

When some of his followers awaken him some fifteen minutes later, Christo is completely refreshed and obviously in tune with what needs to be done next. His followers affirm his earlier insight that many of the participants are feeling somewhat emotionally spent. Christo responds with a knowing wink, as though to say, "Well done, my friends, well done. This is good discernment."

CHAPTER 3

Sowing the Seed for the Virgin Birth

Christo approaches the stage with an aura of compassionate confidence. As he casts his eyes over the crowd, he flashes a warm smile and casts gentle waves of Love their way. "Namaste," he begins, reinforcing yet again the Truth of their divinity. "It appears to me that many of us have learned to fear our feelings. Now is the time to come to a different perspective on such things. And this is the place where you can be absolutely safe in doing so.

"Yes, it's really okay to feel those feelings. Really feel them. And safe," he assures them. "It's just that some of us don't really know how quite yet. This is how the divine learns about such things, and about what to do about them. In a phrase, just sit with them and savor them while you do. Fear them not. Embrace them in gratitude for what your feelings are teaching you. Furthermore, understand that most of what you are feeling is not a matter for which you have to take responsibility. For your feelings have come about and been stored mostly unconsciously, mostly from observations and impositions from without. You don't have to be at all concerned about setting them free. With what we will now learn, the cleansing will come more effortlessly than you might think. At least, it will feel that way. They seemingly will come out of nowhere, and vanish quite the same way: harmlessly.

"Based on how we've been taught, the natural response to what you now see as your warp would be to remove each untoward thread of the warp, one by one. This might seem so even for those of you who have been able in this brief moment to see how your Life has been touched and informed *by* that warp as a healthy act of kindness.

"Visualize with me, if you will, the back of the tapestry, where the threads can be seen more in their rough form. Just think what a job that would be to extract each thread of the warp, one at a time, so none will impact your Life any longer. In the first place, it would be some kind of sadistic God that would have you take responsibility for using such an arduous process to remove something implanted largely from outside oneself. Secondly, we have been provided, through the example and teachings of Jesus, with a much simpler way for clearing such things from out midst.

"Close your eyes once again. I'd like you to take as much time as you need to bring into focus that loom upon which we have threaded the warp. Use a little discernment here. Find those threads that correspond to the warm and fuzzy, the nourishing things that have lovingly made an impression on the Soul. Make them any color you like. Enjoy the colors and the feelings that are generated from such fond visions. Take your time; we're not going anywhere soon. Savoring requires letting go of time and space, so grace can show its face. I'm a patient man, so just s l o w down and let yourselves really be with this vision for a few moments."

Christo assesses the gathering and it is clear that most, if not all, are now being at peace and joy over this part of their youth. The smiles that light their faces tell it all. After a few minutes, Christo interrupts: "Okay, now let's locate some of those other threads. Let's make their colors dull and dark or pale and neutral, depending on their impact on our lives. Choose whatever colors fit with your feelings about each of them. If you find threads representing judgment or blame, identify with the feelings you have when you touch these. If you find threads of punishment or abandonment, likewise take a moment to be with these—just long enough to make contact with the feelings that correspond to the threads. Continue for a few minutes and identify the rest of the warp, not exhaustively, but just long enough to acknowledge the elements and the feelings that correlate with each. Be careful to avoid sinking too deep into those feelings or you could come out of this quite depressed." Again Christo provides ample time to ferret out the feelings felt, so the process of discernment can become clear.

"Now, return to the warm and fuzzy threads for a moment and then—slowly—but surely—step back to obtain an overall impression of what kind of warp was formed in your childhood. Then give yourselves an opportunity to feel that general impression. Is it rosy, for example? Mostly gentle and nourishing with just a hint of discord? Is it largely dark and ugly? Just discern which. Don't beat yourself up with it. Or even celebrate the good feelings, for that matter. What we want to celebrate is the development and honing of your ability to discern. All that's necessary then is to just get a general picture and feeling about it," Christo concludes, again pausing long enough for the visualization to take hold.

"I know this may be difficult for some of you to handle emotionally. But if you'll stick with me through this exercise and the one that will follow, I think a great deal of good can come from them. Keep your eyes closed. You're still sitting on that bench in front of your warp. You now have a good idea about what your warp contains and how it feels. Now, find just one incident with another person in your Life that has troubled you, that has made a significant impression on you. Very carefully, begin weaving that thread through your warp. See where it touches the gentle and where it touches the not-so-gentle threads on your warp. Feel the change in feelings as you traverse this exercise. If the incident you chose has a particular bent to it—let us say, feelings of abandonment—watch particularly carefully when this thread from the weft touches that same thread on your warp. Abandonment meets abandonment is what the intersection represents. Sit with that feeling and imagery for just a few seconds, just long enough to get an idea of its impact on your soul," Christo says, pausing yet again for the effect to take hold.

"Now, this is critically important: feel this feeling to the depths of your Being. See where it resides within you. Is it in the pit of your stomach? Or do you find in your abdomen? Or is it around the side to your buttocks? Does it appear as a pain in the neck or as a strain in some part of your back? Just feel the feeling and determine its location. I want you to take what you're feeling—all this meaning you have obtained from just this one intermingling of the threads from your warp and weft—and know that this is what we most often hide from in order to avoid the pain associated with it. I also want you to know, without a shadow of a doubt, that instead of being a pain producer, this connection constitutes that simple feeling of inharmony or being lightly ill-at-ease with a particular feeling. If left unattended, this feeling is the prod that elicits a strong reaction towards someone who, in this case, triggers a feeling, of abandonment, for example, in you. But now you know that the only purpose of this 'charge of energy' is to alert you that you have some unfinished business to complete. But this unfinished business is not with the other person, as formerly believed, but within you.

"As a child," Christo begins to explain, "you would have sparked at that person. Your ego would have told you to protect yourself from those feelings. And you would have reacted, perhaps harmfully, towards that person. Now, however, you take this feeling as a simple sign, a friendly warning from your ego that is but a call to clear out that which you have disowned for all these years. As you sit with this intersection then, replay the incident and those feelings. Instead of retreating to your childish ways of handling it, however, simply greet the feeling as a friendly gesture, and wave a cheerful 'thank you' to your new friend, the ego. Fully acknowledge this gift with all the gratitude you can muster, and then let go of it. In any way that works for you, give it up. Let go of it. Have full confidence that you are free from that old way now. Get up from that old way and walk in a different direction. Cast that old bed of thought aside. Repent and sin no more.

"Your conviction, the faith you have placed in the inharmony you have felt when immersed in feelings of abandonment, has shifted through to INsight and Enlightenment. You have parted the veil of the fear of abandonment, and you are now able to return to the proper view of yourself: as the divinity you always have been, and as you always will be. The feelings of disharmony convert to a celebration of your Truth once again. This is good work you have done, folks! I think you now have a clearer idea of how to discern inharmony. Just as important, even more so, you now know how to reclaim your divinity.

"I think you are now ready to see how this same process works with others. This will make it easier for you to make the transition from the old to the new. Be assured that you are well on your way up the stairs of transcendence.

"I shall begin this next idea of cleansing with extending our story about the man beside the pool at Bethesda to another situation, one I feel confident will be familiar to one and all.

The person who was taught not to express anger in any form can give a rather impressionistic example. And furthermore, that it was improper to confront anyone about essential differences. You've all seen this scenario played out, I'm sure. Let's say it's the woman in a couple who has taken on this burden, largely unconsciously I might add. It was made clear to her that expressing anger is just not something a cultured woman does. She's feeling anger over something that happened at work. It festers and festers, and yet she doesn't feel comfortable expressing her distress at work.

"The inner question, then, becomes: Where *does* she feel more trusting about sharing some of this? As is the case, the answer is found in the form of her sensitive, loving spouse, who is always there for her. But she doesn't really know how to deal with her feelings of anger, by now having the impact of inner rage. This is just too big to take to him, directly at least. So along the way one evening, her spouse says something to her that sets her off—something that normally wouldn't have set her off, by the way, but her heightened sensitivity simply is waiting to be triggered by an innocent remark. You have all seen someone who looks like an accident waiting to happen, I'm sure. Well, she is like that in her current emotional state: she's an emotion waiting to explode.

"She responds to her spouse's innocent comment with an accusation loaded with guilt and shame, which just happens to be his 'ouch' point. Before he catches himself, he barks back at her. She, in turn, presses his guilt and shame buttons again. The heat has now been turned up a good bit. He again responds but catches himself this time, and declares a 'time out' to relieve some of the pressure. But she needs relief *right now*! Not later. Which, of course he knows not of, although he's getting suspicious, because he knows he hasn't done anything to warrant this kind of treatment. Anyhow, out of her cloaked need to rid herself of this suppressed burden, she presses his guilt and shame buttons yet again, those same buttons that have enabled her to keep her rage at bay until now. This time he loses it and explodes, yet without demeaning her personally. But she takes it personally, which justifies the spewing of her guts all over the room in response. She doesn't do so to the degree he supposedly has just incited her to, mind you, because that would have taken her back to her (erroneous) belief in the guilt and shame connected with this course of action. So scream and holler she does. Just as far as her 'justifiable homicide' will allow. And, of course, when she is finished, she has to label her spouse as the Dr. Jekyll and Mr. Hyde, in order to safeguard her own behavior and self-image as one who 'certainly knows better.'

"Interestingly," Christo continues, "this could just as easily have been an example Jesus used with the man at Bethesda. Does this example sound familiar to any of you? Raise your hand if this explanation has touched you with any sense of familiarity." Again most of the hands go up immediately, many accompanied by a smile that attributes a sense of: 'Oh, yeah, that's one that rings a bell loud and clear.'

"Now I want to tell you my favorite story from real Life," Christo continues, recognizing a golden opportunity to whet the appetite for a greater measure of meaning. "This comes from a rather recent happening, one that may well bring even greater clarity for you. This story refers us to what a particular part of our warp might look like in real Life. Detached from it as you are, it may be easier once again to gain new perspective that you can apply to your own Life.

"Some time ago I was visiting with a dear friend in Greece. We had taken his then 94-year-old mother to dinner around 10:00 in the evening and returned home about 12:30 in the morning. Believe it or not, she walked back with us, some dozen blocks or so, with arms linked to ours on either side of her. It was charming, to say the least, and she was such an elegant woman, appearing much younger than her ascribed age. Anyhow, we tucked her into bed and proceeded over to my friend's apartment where he poured some ouzo, which we took outside onto his balcony overlooking downtown Athens. He began to tell of his woes at work and I quickly fell into compassion for his pain. When he finished he inquired about what was new in my Life since we had last been together. I pondered his query for a moment and a flash of a recent memory came into view. 'Oh,' I responded, 'a friend of mine back home just got his sixth divorce.' Now, all of you, before I tell you the rest of the story, please make a mental note of what you just thought and felt as I spoke of the six divorces.

Christo pauses for a moment to allow this capture and then continues with his usual passion for Life, expressed as deep compassion. "My dear friend took a sip of his ouzo and, looking up at the night sky, rejoined with a most profound declaration—stretching out the spaces between each word for affect: 'Isn't that just wonderful!'

'Just wonderful?' I reacted. 'Didn't you hear what I said? He just went through his sixth divorce!'

'Yes' he said, 'I heard you correctly. Isn't it wonderful that six different women could have loved him enough to marry him?'

"*Now* what are your thoughts and feelings? This is a rhetorical question, to be sure, but sit with both and distinguish between the before and after. Was there a difference? Has your perspective changed any? This alone would be enough of a story, but that's not the end of it. At least not in terms of its major impact on my friend back in the States. As soon as I landed at the airport in Atlanta I called my friend and told him the story. When I delivered the punch line I heard a gasp at the other end of the line—and time became pregnant with pause. I waited for what seemed like hours and finally said, 'Richard, are you there? Are you okay?'

'I'm here.' he said, obviously groping for words, 'I'm just searching for the words to describe the remarkable feeling I just had when you shared this different perspective. I'd never heard anything like it before.'

'Suddenly,' he continued,' I felt this huge load lift off my shoulders. Your friend's perspective let me see myself in a completely new light. I had buried myself in guilt and shame. You see, in my first marriage, I came home from work early one day and found my wife in bed with another man and immediately felt guilty and ashamed, and I took all the responsibility for what she did. If only I had been better, had done something to change what I was. Plus, my mother used a lot of guilt and shame with me as I grew up. To make matters worse, I was the first in my family to have been divorced. You can just imagine the judgment I felt. Yes, my guilt and shame stopped me dead in my tracks, and crippled me in my closest relationships.'

"'How do you feel now?' I asked."

'I feel so relieved. Like the burden has been lifted completely from my shoulders. I can see now where I went wrong. And I suspect that if I don't continue to take on guilt and shame that my relationships will be healed. I guess you could say I've risen from the dead. Thank God.'

"At that very moment, not only was he healed—able to see his own divinity again—but he was relieved of his blindness and from being crippled because of it. Indeed, he had risen from the dead, and continues to live Life renewed. At the same time, I came to realize the words of Jesus when he said, 'If you believe in me (meaning "my way"), you shall do these same works; even greater than these you shall do.' My earlier thought that I would have to go through a series of wisdom schools in order to help heal anyone left me completely. Simply by understanding that being there for someone, sharing their Truth with them, is all that is necessary for someone to be relieved of a debilitating perspective about themselves—and thus their Life around them. As we now know, our perspectives about Life, no matter how we arrived at them, are the lenses through which we see and use to cope with Life. Now all we need to do is to learn how to really *live* rather than to barely cope—and we're well on the way to this discovery.

"One last part of that story needs to be told, although more may unravel in the future. At any rate, as we were finishing the conversation, you know what voice spoke from within me. It was as though someone had opened my mouth for me and spoke these words for me: 'Richard, you speak as though you were divorced from all those women, but from whom were you really divorced?'

"There's another long pause—and then," 'Well...uh...well, me, myself, and I. That's three divorces right there,' he joked. "Right there and then I knew he was going to make it through the rest just fine. When 'Madame Humor' enters the picture, it's all but over. The immense tension that surrounded this major misperception surely had been released.

"'Okay, then,' mySelf seemed to say for me once again, 'and the most important aspect you had divorced yourself from by putting your faith, your belief, in your self-image of guilt and shame?'

"A pause of much less duration ensued this time." 'Oh, that's an easy one. I had gotten so wrapped up in the perverted image of myself that it blinded me from going within for the Truth of the matter. Oh, yeah, I had divorced myself not only from my true self, but from my God within.'

"How does this fit with you, folks? How many of you were touched by this one?" Just as before, most of the hands raise in full acknowledgment. Christo continues: "And how many of you could track your impression and imagery shift from the time you originally heard me tell you about the six divorces and on to how they had been treated by my good friend in Greece? Did you feel the shift in perspective?" This time Christo was a little surprised by the unanimous declaration. He had suspected many would have felt it—gained meaning from the shift in perspective—but this unanimous declaration now told him that all the participants were indeed ready for what he had come to know was needed for the next phase. "Ah, good for you!" he declares with abundant enthusiasm. "Now we're ready to deal with the process Jesus gave us for dealing with our unconsciously-derived warp which has been threaded on our Life's loom.

"It seems clear to me that every one of us would want to get rid of all these erroneous impressions from our past. What we have been taught is that we must work hard to ferret out each one, one by one, in order to clear ourselves of such debris. And unless we do, we will indeed continue to be crippled by them. These so-called psychoses and neuroses will continue to haunt our daily existence. What a negative model we have adopted! It's the Old Testament rearing its head once again. Unless we change, bit by bit, to meet some externally imposed expectation, we will be limited in our capacity to be healed—and we will be eternally punished until we do. What was it the Apostle Paul told us? 'When as a child we thought as a child, behaved as a child?' But now we are adults, more mature, and so can think and behave like an adult. Just keep reminding yourselves that we're talking about our spiritual condition here.

"What might this look like?" you ask. "Well, we have taken the first necessary steps by reviewing the major influences on our Life's perspective. By now, I suspect we won't be eager to repeat those same influences. Of course, you have properly concluded that you want to get rid of the old warp so you'll be cleared. If we look at the tapestry carefully, we will find thousands of connections between one thread and another, between one thread of our warp against each thread of Life that has crossed it. And if you are as ancient as I am, that's a lot of crossings!" Christo teases. "But, thankfully, we're not going to unravel the past this way: thread by thread. There aren't enough Lifetimes to do so. Instead, this time, we're going to go back to Jesus's teachings and apply them to our craft of weaving our Life's testimony. So, metaphorically speaking, of course, just slide your loom of the past to one side and joyfully pull a new rig in front of you. Let's see what we can do to reconstruct your Life by beginning rightly. Indeed, it is time to throw away that old bed and walk in a different direction. Ladies and gentlemen: IT IS TIME TO REPENT!" Christo chants loudly, to the glee of the crowd. They are really with him now. Christo can tell.

"The old way provides psychologists and MDs and counselors with a livelihood. We ought not to disparage this fact. In fact we ought to give this potential its full accord until we can go our own way within. My point with each of you, however, is this: it is time for us to go within with precision, with absolute resolve. And with our conviction placed in the Truth that comes from our divinity. Such conviction about our divinity makes our divinity faith-expressed. Acknowledgment of our divinity, and our ability to extend from it, is the First cause that creates only in that same image. Unless that stream is broken, that's the only direction the stream of divinity can flow.

"Indeed, the time has come for us to extract our faith from illusion and instead place it in Truth. *THIS*, my dear friends, is beginning rightly. And the only place that Truth can come from is *where*?" Christo teases the audience. "From *where* do we get Truth?" he shouts? 'From within,' returns the answer. "Where?" Christo challenges again, much like a pompon squad elicits a response from a crowd at a basketball game. This time he is amused by the strength of the response: 'FROM WITHIN!' "Where?" 'FROM WITHIN! FROM WITHIN!' the participants play with him. "You are so delightfully bright and wise, all in one!" Christo plays back. The crowd is nearly in evangelical form by now.

"*Now* you are ready. Let's think back to the teachings of the church *vis a vis* those of Jesus. If we really think about it, all those of Jesus boil down to just two declarations. The first is that we are rendered divine by our Oneness with God and with one another. The second is that we have a process for rending the veil that clouds our perspective on Life and prevents us from seeing the reality of our divinity. This is beginning to look pretty simple, isn't it?

"Jesus gives us only two things to focus on in this regard: our divinity and a process to reveal our divinity in perpetuity. That sounds a lot less complicated than what we've been used to using doesn't it?" Christo gauges this understanding by the numerous nodding that has caught his attention.

"What Jesus is really telling us is that the *only* threads needed to form our new warp are the threads we call divinity. Yes, you heard me correctly. The *only—the only*—threads we are to use are those that come from a perpetually-invested perspective of our divinity. You never will find anywhere in scripture where Jesus tells us to undo all those unruly threads of the past. No, Jesus says to us—now listen as you've never listened before: 'ye must be born again. Be as a child.' In order for us to repair ourselves, to return to our divinity, we must begin all over again. We must begin in a different way: by taking on entirely new impressions. By creating an entirely new perspective toward ourselves and Life as it appears around us. Indeed, we are to be born again, so we can begin anew, in the innocence of a newborn child.

"'And this time the *only* thing I want you to remember,' Jesus seems to be saying, 'is your divinity. At all costs, divinity is your nature. I want only for you to return time and again to your divinity. Until you know you *are* divinity. And that your neighbor is *likewise* divinity.' What wonderfully healing energy comes from this declaration of Truth! Yet most of us are still so uncomfortable with this idea of divinity that we are fearful of declaring it even with a simple greeting like 'Namaste.'

"'This seems rather radical,' I can hear you saying. Yes, it is radical. So is throwing your bed away. So is walking in an entirely different direction. When we feel lost, either spiritually or materially, we need to find our way home. This reminds me of the story about a young devotee who asks his guru for directions to Mecca. Literally, the youngster is asking how to get to the site of Mecca. But the guru knows better, and answers spiritually with a conundrum: 'Simply be sure that every step you take is in that direction.'"

Christo is pleased with the amused response of the participants. There is no doubt that they are on the same page of the hymnal. "Yes," he continues, "right is radical. Just like quitting smoking cold turkey. Is being radical courageous? Having the thought—hearing the intuition—that one ought to quit cold turkey, indeed takes courage. It is courageous to think that a different direction is absolutely necessary at this moment in your Life. But from then on it isn't courage that is necessary. It is simple obedience to the Truth that this is for one's highest and best result. Now we are to follow this same path: being courageous in our perspective in order to change direction. And this is to be followed only by obedience to the Truth that the new way, Jesus's way, is right for us. Why? Because it is for our highest good. You have heard me attribute this wisdom to Dr. Wayne Dyer before: 'When we change the way we see, the things we see will change.' Never has this truism been more relevant than now.

"I am touched by the lack of this perspective in our society, so much so that I have concluded that one of the greatest sins—if not the greatest—is our failure to see the divinity that lies unexpressed within all. It's akin to leaving this body with our own music still left unexpressed within us. Now, together, in this moment, we have the opportunity to come to the place where we can both acknowledge and celebrate the divinity of all. So 'Namaste'—said or left unsaid—is our motto. Our mantra. Namaste is to be demonstrated. It is to be lived with regularity. As we become more and more aware of our own divinity within, Life without becomes more and more divine at the same time. And soon divinity is all one views. Divinity is all one lives. As within, so without. As in heaven, so in earth. Whatever we cast into the ocean returns to us sure enough.

"So Jesus says to us: 'Heal thyself.' Following this statement comes the commonly held calling—but unfortunately most always misrepresented: 'The Lord helps those who help themselves.' The reason I say the latter is most always misrepresented is that often the tail end of statements like this one are chopped off because people don't know what they mean. Rather than penetrate to the full Truth, they are happy going their own way, which is usually the quick and easy way. In this case, the easy way is always helping ourselves and expecting God to enter the picture only because we have worked our butts off to solve our dilemma of the day ourselves, in order to justify our control over the matter.

"In the process, we almost always neglect to look for God's discernment, which can come only from INspiration, INsight, and Enlightenment. Therefore, the statement should more properly be understood thus: God helps those who help themselves—by going within for help. How do I know this is true? Because Jesus taught me so. 'Go to God within. Not I, but my Father (God) within, does and says these things. Ye must be born again.' Where? In your perspective, which can come *only* from within, where INspiration, INsight, and Enlightenment—the wisdom of our divinity—reside.

"There also are other callings to go within. Jesus isn't our only inspiration in such matters. If you are touched by poetry, for example, listen with discernment to this marvelous gift to us from Robert Browning's poem, 'Paracelsus':

> Truth is within ourselves; it takes no rise
> From outward things, whate'er you may believe
> There is an inmost center in us all,
> Where truth abides in fullness; and around
> Wall upon wall, the gross flesh hems it in,

This perfect, clear perception—which is truth.
A baffling and perverting carnal mesh
Binds it, and makes all error; and to know
Rather consists in opening the way
Whence the imprisoned splendor may escape,
Than in effecting entry for a light
Supposed to be without.

"Reinforcing this, of course, is Jesus' own admonishment to his apostles when he declared the need to go within on their own instead of depending on him for every spiritual understanding. This is the idea of the Paraclete, our divinity, speaking to us. Jesus makes the same plea to all: move from the perspectives of your fear-filled mind to the Truth of your fearless heart, the seat of the divine. When we repent and walk in this new perspective, we move from a Life of appearances to the Truth of our divinity; from working endlessly at transformation in order to proceed from feeling 'less than' to being something more, bit by endless bit. Oft' times, when we finally have reached the end of our rope, we let transcendence simply be. By beginning rightly as divinity, we arrive, at last, at the top of the ladder of Life. We accept nothing less than the Truth of divinity as our perspective. Yes, when we change the way we see, the things we see will change. We engage Life and move beyond our past—not by undoing but by living divinity always.

"Here we have yet another opportunity to correct a saying attributed to Jesus. As we know, spiritually, metaphorically and metaphysically, sayings can have other meanings for us beyond their literal meaning. For example, consider the saying: 'I am the way, the truth and the Life.' Unfortunately, the most popular interpretation of this statement is that Jesus himself is the way. Only Jesus is and knows Truth. That he is the Life. It is through Jesus, literally, that we must traverse. Unless we can turn this literal meaning into metaphorical understanding, however, how would any of us be able to pull off such a thing?

"Turned around in a renewed perspective—reframed if you will—is Jesus not really saying to us something more like this? 'The way I am teaching you is the way to Truth. It is this knowing that makes you free to express Life Truthfully, instead of only coping with Life by expressing over and over again your illusory patterns.' Said another way, 'the way to Truth is by going within, where you will find the Truth about Life, real Life, not the imagined one you have been exercising.' How many of you can feel the shift in meaning taking place here?" Christo really doesn't need to ask this question, for almost everyone is nodding in the understanding that is pouring through them now as he speaks these words. Attentive to the crowd's energy Christo realizes it is becoming more and more the case where what comes out of his own mouth is being heard akin to "The Word," if not as "The Word" itself.

"Jesus is saying to us," Christo continues, "that by engaging Life with such a process—and knowing without a shadow of a doubt that this process is the essential activity of our divinity—we are afforded the riches of the Kingdom: all the INspiriation, INsight and Enlightenment that comes from being a true heir of God, made in God's perfect image and likeness. In order to enter this new era, this time around we now give up our old treasures garnered from the more unconscious paradigm we used when we were children. By giving up our old treasures, we are afforded our own process of Truth-finding, which sets us free from past burdens so we can celebrate while living divinity in all.

"Divinity is the gift that Life simply is. Isn't this the story of the young man who asks Jesus what he must do in order to follow him? Jesus's response is simple and clear—when we see the metaphorical, metaphysical, meaning: 'Give up all your treasures and follow me, my way, instead.' In the story, the man—unfortunately for him—chooses literal meaning of what Jesus is telling him: that he must give away what he owns. By treating Jesus's entreaty literally, he misses Jesus's wisdom entirely. We need not miss the Truth of this statement's meaning now, however. Spiritually, we are now adults and can think and act accordingly."

Christo pauses momentarily for one of his characteristically obvious "checkins." "It has just dawned on me that some of you may be hearing Paul's admonition as one dealing with us in our relative state of chronological age. As we now know, of course, chronological age is nonexistent in the spiritual world. The spiritual world is both infinite and immortal. Remember that Jesus admonishes us to deal with God's entire Kingdom spiritually, metaphorically, metaphysically, even though he didn't use these exact words to say so. However, it is only when we deal with such terms in these varied ways that we are able to gain their deeper meanings.

"I don't need to belabor this point, so I shall get right to it. The reference to children and adults is one regarding spiritual immaturity and maturity, not physical or chronological intent or fact. When we were mere yearlings in spiritual understanding, we thought that way. We behaved that way. But now that we are more mature in our spiritual understanding—in a way, for example, which renders us and all else divine—isn't it in our best interest to think and behave from this perspective rather than our more spiritually naive one? This is what Paul is really saying to us in terms we now understand to be the principle that underpins our existence in the spiritual world." The glow that stems from INsight and Enlightenment is now showing transcendent meaning all across the arena. Christo is glad once again that he has been obedient to the call.

"I see that you are at the threshold of your own Truth, and before I give you the nudge that is sure to take you across the threshold so many of us seem reluctant to cross by ourselves, I am going to suggest we take a short breather now. Reluctance is perfectly natural given the circumstances. Now, however, we are adults, completely mature enough spiritually to take this radical step into a very different presentness with our divinity. So, let's reconvene in twenty minutes and see where we go from here. Addio. Hmm," Christo pauses. "I guess I forgot to tell you the meaning of that word the first time I used it. 'Addio' is a Greek greeting which is used to convey between friends that one looks forward to their return to loving companionship, but until then now leaves you 'with God:' ah-deeo. So, Addio, my dear friends."

His closest followers quickly approach Christo as he leaves the stage, indicating that all the signs point to the readiness of most of the participants for the next highly-penetrating episode. Some of the followers seem more than a bit concerned that all of the participants might not be ready, however. When they tell Christo of their fear in this regard, Christo responds with a pricking of their conscience: "Ye of such little faith," he proclaims with a twinkle in his eye. "What makes you think that just because someone might *appear* not to be ready that this is the truth of the matter? Besides, must all *be* ready—and at the same rate? It's their bed they are making, is it not? Having said that, however, fret not. By the time the day has ended, you will see the group in quite another way." Of course what Christo means by this is that it is perhaps the followers themselves who are merely projecting their own insecurities onto the crowd. He smiles inwardly knowing the Truth of this insight. Promptly he refreshes his speaking voice with some warm tea and honey and then pauses for a few minutes of inner reflection.

CHAPTER 4

The Virgin Birth Unveiled

Christo awakes from his simple means of refreshment, both spiritual and physical, and walks softly to the podium. This time he takes a different route, one not as direct as before. Instead, he traverses among the crowd and exchanges words while exuding his Love for them and Life itself. Christo is indeed charismatic in the best sense of this term, and his energy seems to penetrate all as he meanders eventually to the podium. The crowd doesn't stir as in the expected reaction to a rock star, for example. No, it's more of an inner thing. The participants simply drink in Christo's Loving essence, and it overflows through the entire setting.

As Christo reaches the podium, he emphasizes his appreciation for them by placing his left hand over his heart and reaching out his right hand, spanning across the arena in the quiet hush of full acceptance. Without prompting, some individuals, and then more, and more, mimic Christo's energetic gifting, until the entire arena is exchanging loving energy in abundance. When Christo senses that this is the moment, he lets the sharing come to a natural close. He begins thus: "I cannot tell you the meaning of 'Namaste' more clearly than you have just witnessed. I thank you with all my heart for giving this meaning to yourselves and for celebrating it with and for others. I have full faith that you are now *in* your divinity rather than being reluctant to even acknowledge it, as before. Bravo!

"As I said just before the break, I see you right at the threshold of your own Truth, living your divinity. So I now want to provide for you the way Jesus taught us to *be in* our divinity always. The process is a very simple one. It's one way that can be *your* way—*your* Truth—and *your* Life. From the subtle shift in energy that I just felt in you, I know that you understand what Jesus meant when he said, 'Follow me. I am the way, the truth and the Life.' Again, bravo! I am so proud of you and pleased for you.

"As I said, this process of divine discernment is a simple one. It is important to digest and assimilate the understanding that simplicity gives you enough room for yourself. If Life is too crowded, you certainly don't have room for self-expression. And when we do not leave ourselves room enough to express fully what we are we begin to die on the vine, the Lifeline that takes us to the seat of our very being.

"This simple process that I'll now share with you is the antidote to such suffering. It definitely will not only leave room for yourself, it also will create sacred space around your heart so you can be in continual touch with your divinity that's just waiting to be expressed. This process has only three steps to it. The precursor to the first step of beginning rightly—so we can end rightly—is to keep this as simple as it was designed to be. This is my only admonition. The process is so elegant that it has only a single kind of thread available for use. Divinity is the only kind of thread we are to allow onto the warp we are going to fashion anew. And divinity is golden. From this moment forward, there is no other thread in sight, none else available for our use. *NONE! PERIOD!* Nor will there *ever* be.

"The weft thus has only divinity that it can touch as it weaves its way through the numinous fabric of the newfound warp. To use a mixed metaphor, this new warp becomes the lenses through which we will view Life from now on; if we just make sure every step we take is in this direction. Indeed, Mecca, the birthplace of a faith, is the sacred ground upon which we walk.

"The very first step in this process is what you might not fully expect: 'Namaste.' 'You're not serious!' you say. 'We've come all this way and all you can tell us is that saying Namaste is the first step?' Yes, that's *exactly* what I'm telling you. I told you it was a simple process, didn't I?" Christo says with a smile beaming widely across his face. "You seem aghast with this humble offering, but yet most of us are still uncomfortable with saying 'Namaste' with conviction, so uncomfortable are we with placing our unfettered conviction in the Truth that all *is* divine. So, dear ones, 'Namaste' it will be." Christo pauses with his right hand cupped behind his ear, gesturing rather dramatically in order to obtain the desired response. Actually, he is only baiting the gathering in order to make a very important point. A weak "Namaste" returns from the crowd. Christo mimics with an even weaker, "Namaste." Again he cups his hand behind his ear, teasing them once again. This time the gathering responds with a more spirited, "Namaste." Christo tempts them further, this time without even saying 'Namaste,' but rather by cupping his hand behind his right ear again and really leaning towards the crowd, giving the impression that he still can't quite hear them. This time, they catch on fully, and really let Christo have it full force: "NAMASTE! NAMASTE, Christo!" Christo laughs uproariously, followed with, "Hah! Got you again. When will you ever learn?

"Each of you can shout 'Namaste' to me just fine now—but can you yet say it even ever-so-gently to yourselves? And *mean* it?" The question cuts to the quick. By their response he knows the point has struck home. "Wow! We can be tricked into saying 'Namaste' to someone else, without yet even being able to acknowledge divinity in ourselves. We can call a baby 'divine'. During courtship we can call our lover 'divine.' We can even call a particularly sumptuous dish 'divine'. But can we call ourselves that? Can we yet call ourselves 'divine' with authenticity and conviction?

"*THIS* is *precisely* why the first step is to accept and celebrate our divinity within. So I say to you, your first charge is to practice saying 'Namaste' to yourself every time you see your reflection in a mirror or window. I encourage you to also practice saying it to yourself every time one of those old perspectives pops up in your head as well as during the normal events of the day. You may not feel divine at first. Let's face it, there is so much imbedded within our perspective about Life and us that has taught us just the opposite. Just remember the phrase: right is radical. Look into your reflection everywhere and see the face of God, the Christ in you: your divinity. And then bid yourself, 'Namaste.' This bit of Hinduism is magnificent in its power to return us to our Truth within.

"If you still have difficulty identifying with divinity, just remember what one of the characters in *Catch 22* said: 'there is no established procedure for evasive action. All you need is fear.' Look fear straight in the eye. Then walk straight through fear to the other side. Continue saying 'Namaste' to yourself at every turn. In the same way say it to all you find on the other side of fear.

"As part of this first step, when you begin to feel comfortable with your own divinity, flip the process around. By that I mean practice using 'Namaste' with everyone—and *every thing*—you come in contact with, moment-by-moment, day-by-day. Even though you may be very comfortable with your own divinity, at first it may be somewhat difficult for you to greet people publicly with 'Namaste'. So begin, if you must, by saying it privately, within. The 'withinness' will soon nudge you in its ultimate feeling of safety to look beyond your fear of rejection to the Truth of your being, and all that inhabits the planet in kind. Suddenly you will find yourself saying it publicly, without notice. What a gift it will be for all concerned! You will see for yourselves very soon now.

"What has actually happened as a result of this first step coming to fruition? What master lesson from Jesus are you demonstrating as you greet and treat all with the essence of a most loving, 'Namaste?' If anyone thinks they know, please raise your hand." Christo waits for a response, even a timid one, but none comes. "Don't be intimidated by the question or humiliated by a lack of response. It's no wonder none of you think you know. Your natural reluctance—we can even call it our natural ignorance without guilt or shame by now—is clearly due to the high degree of indoctrination to the contrary.

"Now, in this moment, let the answer be known. The only clue I'll give is that this is exactly what Jesus meant when he responded to the one who asked him, 'Jesus, tell me what laws are the most important to follow if I am to be one of yours?' And just how did Jesus respond?" Christo looks out over the gathering, assured that they knew what was coming next; the brightness of INsight and Enlightenment is that strong. "I can see that you know with indelible clarity. Of course, his response was to boil down all 617 laws of the Torah and the Ten Commandments of the Bible to just two: 'Love God with all your mind, heart, soul and strength.' And, 'Love your neighbor as yourself.' By developing your capacity for exercising this first step with clarity and conviction, you actually are placing your newborn faith *only* in divinity, the same divinity that is in everyone and every thing.

"Here, once again, we need to be careful about how we visualize Jesus's response to his inquirer. If we just shift the meaning even a slight turn of perspective here, we get a mighty different picture. By keeping the understanding as it is normally received, we keep God outside ourselves. We must love this entity called 'God' out there, the old meanings say. If we can bring ourselves to that point, then we must learn to love our neighbors and ourselves likewise, as separate entities. But Jesus taught us that God and we are One. That *all* is One. He taught that God is within each of us, not separate from any of us. This then takes on the meaning that God is within all. *Is All*, actually. What Jesus really meant, at least as I perceive it, is this: 'Love Godliness with all your mind, heart, soul and strength.' Said yet another way, 'find and love Godliness, divinity, with every Loving thought. With all your heart, be in the Loving Spirit. With all your conviction, your faith expressed, meaning with all your strength.'

"You see, many of us think we are being Loving when if fact all we're doing is exercising infatuation with Life and one another. We become infatuated with

Life in this trade or that one. With this person or that other one. We become infatuated with the *idea* of someone or something. But we rarely really *commit* to it—or to them. Jesus worded his admonition the way he did so we would see the difference between simple infatuation and real Loving. It's the difference between using something or someone to titillate our fancy as opposed to jumping in with both feet and living it to the depths of our being.

"Think of it this way, if you will: In order for you to take infatuation to the level of genuine, authentic Loving, you must take it from your head—as a mere fanciful thought—and put it into your heart, where real meaning resides. Exercising infatuation is making a mockery of real Love. It is an illusory form of the real thing, a mere facsimile of the genuine article. It is only when you take Loving into the depths of your heart, where divinity resides, that you commit all you have to it—without end. Love is not genuine until it is expressed from the heart. When you can bring yourselves to do precisely that, you will feel and know and exercise the divinity you are in all its glory, to the benefit of all, not just for yourself. This represents passion turned outward as compassion. And all win by inclusion

"When we see Jesus's words from this perspective, our task becomes one of simply Loving all day long or, as I like to say it, 'making love all day long.' Thus Loving, no matter with whom you meet or in what circumstance you find yourself—no matter whether with sentient being or not, becomes the return to our most natural state: as Lovers of the first order. The reality of truly Loving is to Love from the heart *ALL THAT LIFE BRINGS US! NO MATTER WHAT!* Doesn't it seem more likely that when we can see whatever Life affords us from our seat of Loving genuinely and authentically, that we learn to *know* that *all* is divine? That we will recognize and celebrate what divinity really *is* rather than fearing what it's *not*? Or what *we* are not? We'll deal with some of the issues that may make you reluctant to do so in a moment. But for now, merely let this first and most important step sink in."

Christo pauses at some length before dropping the bombshell he has in store. He was going to save it for the end of this section, but his most recent "reading" of the situation tells him to give the gathering some time to absorb what has just transpired before going on to then drop the bomb abruptly. "Do so now," is the message he hears. As one to faithfully demonstrate obedience to "the Word from within," Christo waits for what to some feels like an inordinate length of time.

Then, seemingly suddenly, he startles all with this proclamation: "What you are witnessing in yourself—at this very moment—is the magnificence of a virgin birth." He then pauses for another seemingly long period of time—for affect, of course. Since it is the holiday season, the impact of his declaration is even more shocking.

After a bit, he dares to enter the seeming fray. Before he begins, however, he takes another reading of the gathering. What he has just conveyed is seen by many to be heresy: "Has Christo lost it in the complexity of the holiday season?" "Does he have some issues with the virgin birth he hasn't yet resolved?" Christo hears these questions and apparent castigations, and many others, emanating from the audience. The shift of energy is dramatic, to say the least. It goes from being totally engaged—almost married, actually—to an abrupt feeling akin to abandonment. Being Christo, he faces these reactions head on.

"I can see you are quite shocked by this declaration. Especially because this is the holiday season, I suppose you are even all the more shocked by it. You'll be much less shocked when I ask you once again to recall that in this setting together we are dealing with Life metaphysically, metaphorically—not literally, linearly, physically. Surely you don't think I meant that you are performing like the Virgin Mary. Or are you? Permit me this explanation as part of the continual construction of the foundation for our work together.

"What has just transpired in the investigation of this first step of our new approach to Life? When I coupled our new approach with your take on my comment regarding the virgin birth, you still heard it literally, didn't you? I don't even have to ask this of you to know that it's true. It's only natural this early in the process that this would be the case. The initial response is one that comes from the more familiar ways of Life. This same kind of response, based on your past beliefs and related feelings, will show its face from time to time until you have fully adopted the new path for your Life's journey.

"What I mean, in metaphorical terms, in a metaphysical sense, is that you have given birth to a new brain child. This representation of the virgin birth is new thought, at least one that's new—or virgin—to you. It's a new perspective on Life that is unadulterated, fresh, uncontaminated, unalloyed, and not at all connected with how you would have thought about it in the past. What is this virgin thought? I Am Divine. I Am That; I Am. And so is everyone else That. They Are That. There, now, that's not so bad is it? My proclamation really isn't heretical after all, is it? I haven't really 'lost it' in the complexity of this holiday season, have I? From this description of the virgin birth to which each of you has given your all, you can understand that I really don't have issues with the virgin birth, do I? I hope you don't now, either."

Christo pauses rather lengthily again, listening carefully to the Word from within. The signs are telling yet again: the tilt of his head to one side, the now almost impish grin on his face, and the huge twinkle in his eye. You can almost hear the crowd say in unison: "Okay, let the other shoe drop—whether we're ready for it or not!" Christo hears the clarion call for more and responds faithfully to his charge.

"Yes, you know I'm about to drop the other shoe. And while I'm not saying that Jesus wasn't born of the Virgin Mary, I can say with authority—the authority of metaphysics and the power of the metaphor—that the baby Jesus represents a metaphorical virgin birth. That which he came to teach is so foreign to our understanding of what Life is and can be about that the Truth about this dramatic shift in perspective is virgin to our ears. Life's new meaning is virgin in origin when juxtaposed with that which previously was given to it. His teachings that all is One, and that this One is within—not without—and that not just God and he, but that *all* are divine was absolutely contrary to the understanding of scripture in that day, and remains so for many still today. Indeed, his teaching was new. It was fresh. It was unadulterated by literality. It was uncontaminated by fear. And unalloyed with anything of any kind. It stood alone as Truth, divined from within. It *was and is* the Truth *we* now find within, the source of Truth that presents and remains timeless. So there you have it: a new story of the virgin birth. And you have your own virgin births to take home with you to prove your case!

"The interesting part of such an exercise in metaphysical exploration is that, at least in this case, you have come to the understanding that all of Life is about virgin birth: hearing the salient divinity coming from within in the form of new meaning for you; thus changing perspective about Life *for* you, so you can really live according to the gospel of divinity that Jesus brought to our understanding in the only way real understanding takes place—by example, through the example of penetrating Life stories. As Albert Einstein put it: 'Example isn't the main means of influencing another. It is the *only* means.' And thus do we know Truth: by example.

"The last conclusion to be reached during this first step, then, is not to only Love divinity, but even more important, to always come *from your* seat of divinity. By coming *from* our seat of divinity, we give evidence that all around us and we *are* divinity. The final act, therefore, allows you to follow the main premise of all that has gone before. The idea is not to see mortal man or so-called material substance as the perfect image and likeness of God. Rather, the idea is to see the likeness and image of God *instead* of mankind and supposed material substance."

Christo is struck with yet another insight. By now, the participants are reading Christo's moves on the fly. In anticipation of his next declaration, they seem to be leaning forward en masse. "I see you are anticipating my every move now," Christo gleefully responds to their body language. "Yes, there is one last point to be made here. I always thought that shoes dropped in pairs. But here's a third 'Ahah!'" he exclaims. "Such things come in threes. Death, it is said, comes in threes. So, here is another death from which we can be resurrected: the death of yet another misconception. It is a misconception born out of our disposition for dealing with Life literally and physically.

"The misconception is this: we have come to believe in birth and death as physical configurations, as natural happenings. If we take the meaning of birth and death spiritually instead—that is, metaphorically—then does it not suddenly become the Truth that it is ideas and thoughts that come—are born—and outworn thoughts and ideas that die—leave us? The process of idea creation that is available for manifesting endlessly affords us our True abundance. The infinite supply of creative energy abounds and enriches. The First cause perpetrates the first effect. Beginning rightly leads to ending rightly. When we're finished with such treasures, we let go of them and place them behind us. We forgive and forget them. We let go of them and let God replace them with yet another—and still others. We experience metaphorical birth and death, so we can resurrect ourselves to receive anew yet again. This is infinitely so—throughout eternity—which gives us our immortality."

Christo has their attention with this seemingly outrageous claim. Yet the energy he is reading from the participants is not that of alarm or utter disbelief. Rather, it is one of deep contemplation and quick acknowledgment of Truth's profundity. He continues, "Yes, my dear divine ones, new ideas are born. New INsights pierce the veil of illusion. New forms of Enlightenment plunge us to the depths of meaning. All such newly born entities automatically render dead on arrival that which has been transcended. In the process of exhibiting spiritual behavior we are resurrected to express Life anew from the seat of one or another virgin perspective. It is feasible, then, to speak of the cycle of Life—the Life of the spiritual within—as the dying of the old—the no-longer-usable ideas and thoughts and beliefs—and their replacement by the Enlightenment that arrives through each new virgin birth. Indeed, we could very well summarize spiritual Life like this: there is death and renewal, but the

Life of virgin birth lives forever. Hence we have the meaning of prosperity, immortality, and the infinite way all in one fell swoop.

"Okay. Are you ready for the second step in this three-step process, or do you need a break?" He feels the gathering is divided in its current desire, so he asks straightforwardly, "How many feel the need for a break in order to absorb your virgin birth?" It is clear by the massive show of hands that it indeed is time for a break. "Well, that's pretty clear. So let's take a twenty-minute break and refresh ourselves for steps two and three. And I promise, no more bombshells this time. Well, no more big ones at any rate." He concludes with that boyish, almost impish grin on his face, which puts the gathering further at ease. They are nearly over being emotionally shocked, although the meaning of "virgin birth" itself has taken on its stunning Truth for them.

As Christo leaves the stage, he weaves his way back through some of the crowd, making himself available to quell the uneasiness of those who still need it. Overall, when he returns to his stage-side stool he is convinced that he has heard the Word properly, and followed It to Its end. "Not a thing to be concerned about," he could hear himself saying as he takes a long drink of water to slake his thirst on the physical level. On the spiritual level, his thirst is regularly quenched, as is the thirst of the gathering.

CHAPTER 5

Judge Not, Lest Ye Be Judged

Christo returns to the podium with the everlasting smile that adorns his face and heart. "Namaste, dear friends. I respect your divinity and Love you deeply, and always will. Even if some of you couldn't wait to get to your cell phones to tell someone you had just given a virgin birth!" Christo's humorous treatment of the potential for lingering unsettledness brings the crowd to instant relaxation around this issue, and this is exactly what Christo intends. Although he wants them to understand the seriousness of the work at hand, he wants also to emphasize that it can be fun and entertaining as well. In a word, the work is serious, but he admonishes them by example to refrain from taking themselves too seriously.

"I think you're about ready for step number two now." He pauses momentarily to check within so he won't miss the guidance that would take care of questions or concerns along the way. In this format, with thousands of people, it would be next to impossible to respond to need in any other way. Christo has already committed to himself, however, that following this gathering today he would begin to conduct smaller sessions around the region, mostly to provide settings where people could vent their concerns and fears, thus freeing themselves for more virgin births. In this way, he confesses to himself, yet again with pleasure for the humor that shows itself within, folks will come to understand that virgin births are appropriate no matter what the season. "Indeed, virgin births are the reason for every season," Christo chuckles as he hears it said within.

Having made a mental note to convey this expanded approach to them, Christo launches into the explanation of the next step in the process. "The second step of this three-step process is what I call practice, practice and practice even more. Even though practice is a necessary element of the first step, as well, this phase takes you to a simple way of letting your concern about the old warp fall by the wayside with very little effort on your part. The only real effort is in developing awareness of Life around you. Now that you will have become more and more comfortable with your own divinity, and that which forms all your surroundings, practice watching Life. Not judging it. Simply watching Life. Observing its contents and discerning within what it brings to you for your highest good. Step two is about becoming more and more aware of Life around—and in—you. If, when you come into contact with someone or some circumstance—or even some thing—that could have set off your inner alarm in the past, you do not hear or do not feel any resonance within about it, then you more than likely have eliminated that portion of your old loom. Seeing divinity instead of error often does that without any additional effort on our part. Indeed, changing the way we see does cast a new light on what we see. This is real in its demonstration from our new seat of divine perspective.

"The reason you are to practice from this seat of awareness is to develop and finely hone your discernment for what's happening within you as Life weaves it way through your new warp. The purpose of both steps one and this one is to become conscious of this connection between Life and our view of it. If, then, rather than a particular event, circumstance, or person having no discernible effect on you, you feel a sudden 'charge' of energy about it—feel some disharmony within, or ill at ease—then this is a tip to stop and notice. In the parlance of parental warnings when we are about to cross a street or the railroad tracks: stop, look, and listen. Remember this: what we are looking to build and strengthen here is our discernment about any discord between what we know is Truth about all of Life in its divinity and how we might be responding to the appearance of something that is an illusion: something other than divinity.

"The tack to take then, always, is to begin any encounter, no matter how simple or complex, by saying, 'God is divine.' 'I am divine.' 'He or she is divine.' And if there is some disjuncture involved, then begin again with this same declaration, but add only this: 'However, this is not.' What is actually happening in such instances of discord is that the person or circumstance is a gift to point out to you the discord you have within you. It's really not about the other person at all. What's really happening is that your ego is calling for you to defend. But if you already know the other as divine, what's to defend against? It's like having ill-perceived thought. Our purpose is to reduce all impact to thought. 'Why?' you ask. Because, have you ever heard of an incurable thought? Not any more. Not after all you've come through to this point.

"So as you take this gift, let's decide to call it something that will put a different face on ego-demand. Instead of your usual response to ego, to snuff it out or kill it—or be totally dominated by it as before—you decide to make your ego your friend. When you feel discord, which is a signal, your intuition is speaking to you, telling you to look for the ego waving the red flag that says 'Pay attention to this!' Again, simply declare: 'God is divine, I am divine, he or she is divine; this thought about that appearance I'm translating is not that.' Just that simple. No judgment. No fear. No guilt or shame. Just a clear declaration of something that is not divine.

"Take this then as a clear sign to go within in the spirit of awe and wonder. Stop, look, and listen for what's happening within. Don't judge it. In a straightforward fashion, just say: 'I wonder what this is about?' Then just get out of INspiration and INsight's way and wait for the answer to show up. Keep in mind that it is metaphorical language that informs. When you take yourself within, it is tantamount to knocking at the door of understanding that is always open to you. Your Muse, INspiration, will be there waiting for you as always. Waiting for you simply to show up, so she can take you to INsight and then on to Enlightenment.

"By INspiration then, through your Muse, you are led to INsight. Darkness gives way to light—ignorance to Enlightenment. And *voilá*! There you have it—just that quickly and that clearly—your answer arrives and, believe me, you will stand in awe of its power to return you to your most natural form of divinity in a split second. It will work exactly as in the story of my good friend in Greece. That's why I used a story with such impact, so you could apply it within for your own use as well. In a nutshell, what has happened in this portion of the process is that you have taken yourself to the seat of Loving creation in order to adopt new imagery for the warp of your loom.

"A brief explanation is in order. When I said the answer would arrive quickly, I mean that in the same way INsight arrives: seemingly out of nowhere. However, if you are one who is unaccustomed to going within and/or of letting go, then it will take some practice "showing up" at the doorway to the Kingdom. Rest assured that this need not become an arduous task, unless you make it so. Simply show up, declare your wonderment, and then be patient. Your answer may not come at that moment or even while you wait. It may show up in the middle of breakfast, or while walking your dog. It matters not when or how it shows its lovely face. It matters only that it does. You can rest assured that it will, without fail. Always.

"Another clear warning is warranted, this time from Scripture: 'Judge not, lest ye be judged.' What this characteristically has meant to people is that if you judge others, judgment will come back at you somehow. It is sometimes thought of as instant karma: 'what goes around comes around.' Whatever you cast as your bread out onto the waters comes back at you. On it goes. Of course, as you now expect, there usually is a hidden 'however' associated with this use of Scripture. Again, think of it metaphorically, as having meaning within, in our perspective of what we have made Life to be and then laid it against what is Truth. Here is another way to think about it: because divinity is *all*, whenever we judge something or someone outside ourselves as needing to develop their most natural state, divinity, then we're at the same time denying our own divinity. As we judge another, so are we that judgment.

"Where and what you are judging in another is that place in yourself we call denial. It is the disowned part of your perspective that you are being alerted to examine. What a magnificent gift this is! All we need to do is pay attention to, become aware of, some dissonance within and then let it be a devoted friend who takes you to your seat of clarity: divinity personified. Just know that when you judge, it's automatically indicating to you that you are judging yourself, not another. It's also the marvelous gift that says that you have a need for judgment—you need to judge—so you can come to this place of discernment and make a necessary modification in your perspective. How do I know this to be true? By way of observation, simple observation.

"Follow me here and now. Here's a fun and easy way to keep tabs on judgment. Point your index finger at someone sitting across from you, so as not to potentially disturb your immediate neighbor. You're liable to get hit across the head with somebody's purse if you do that! Now, with this simple gesture, what you have just been put into contact with is the most important law of all God's laws," Christo says with tongue in cheek. "At least as far as this process of cleanup is concerned."

Still with tongue in cheek, Christo continues, "This most important law is the Law of Three Fingers. Play along with me now, for just a moment longer. Look carefully out along the index finger you have pointed at someone, as though you have just declared some judgment against him or her. Look v-e-r-y carefully now." Christo draws it out for dramatic affect. "What do you see coming *back at* you? Yes. You got it right: *three* fingers, three *big* ones. This is a handy form of shorthand that says: 'Whenever you point a finger at someone, that pointing says that the real consideration is three times stronger for our self-denial.'

"Simple law, isn't it? And it's a very useful one at that. I'm sure you all have heard the admonition that anything you need is no more than three phone calls away. Well, the same is true here. Not only is your judgment of another telling you that you really need to look much more seriously within yourself. This built-in alarm system is also telling you that your INsight and Enlightenment are only, at most, just three solid points of wonderment away. I'll give you an example showing how this works in a few minutes, so fret not.

"When we have mastered the use of the Law of Three Fingers, we can move quickly from the declaration of 'You make me angry as hell!' to one that says, 'It feels like hell when I come from anger,' to one that tells the absolute Truth at last: 'What is it that I've disowned inside, in my imagery about myself?' Then, just as Jesus told the man at Bethesda, give it no thought; don't try to figure it out. Merely ask, 'I wonder,' and then let it be. Although the appearance of anger may trigger your inner denial of it within your emotional being, don't buy into it. Just release it to wonderment and awe and return to divinity as quickly and completely as you can. Cast your bed aside and walk in another direction.

"This place within is what Jesus referred to as the kingdom of Heaven. Listen carefully now, with ears to hear the metaphors and their application to our Life as a metaphysician. When Jesus is asked about Heaven, as in Matthew 13:31, he responds like this: 'The kingdom of Heaven is like a mustard seed, which a man took and sowed in his field. It is the smallest of all the seeds, but when grown it is the biggest of shrubs and becomes a tree, so that the birds of the air can come and shelter in its branches.' What are these seeds of which Jesus speaks? They are the seeds of thought: new, divine, ideas. Every one of them is divine, and the potential source of a new virgin birth. The only thing that can reduce one to something that appears not to be divine is how we look at it. If it appears to us as not being divine, is it not just like someone's fear of abandonment triggering that which we have denied in ourselves—a red flag waving to get our attention—so that we are alerted to take it within for discernment? Therefore, isn't the idea that appears to be lacking also divine? You can bet on it! With your money or mine.

"Regardless of how they appear, we cast them out all day, and all night, long, mostly unconsciously. Is Jesus not telling us here that the kingdom of Heaven is the kingdom of ideas—the endless stream of divine ideas consciously derived—that is Heavenly? And that each is akin to the mustard seed, which grows and grows and grows—just as ideas do—until they transcend the idea into material form? As long as we place our conviction in them, abide by our faith in them—with all our mind, body, soul, and strength—they are sure to flower. And what about the birds of the air? Is this not just another form of metaphorical symbolism we use to speak of other thoughts—spiritual forms, flights of fancy—that adorn and find shelter in this metaphysical Life? Be sure to sit with this one when you get home and see where it takes you. You see, if we read this parable literally, it goes nowhere. But when we read the parable metaphorically while sitting in the lap of metaphysics in order to discern its more Truthful meaning, it works wonders for us.

"Earlier I said that I wouldn't drop any huge bombs on you during this part of the process. But you can take a slightly smaller one or two can't you?" Christo's infectious smile overtakes the audience once again, and he can sense their anticipation. So he lets loose with these. "If you're like most people, from time to time you show concern for prosperity, or lack of it. Well, when we speak metaphorically, we change our perspective on prosperity from one that deals with material prosperity—like having lots of green stuff to line our pockets—to one that helps us understand that the real meaning of prosperity has to do with the prosperity of ideas. No one I know who has ever gone within to consult with the teller at the bank of divine ideas has ever really been broke. It is this bank, with the infinitude of ideas as its only currency, which provides us with *real* security. Here we are again at that door. Just knock—just show up in other words—because the door is always open to you. Be not afraid. 'The kingdom of Heaven is at hand,' it is said, so closely at hand that we can always find it within. And so are all the treasures of this Kingdom that pave the way as manna from Heaven.

"Oh, come on! You want the other shoe to drop on this one, too?" Christo chides the gathering, fathoming their expectation. "All right then. How many of you are comfortable with defining infinity, really comfortable? It's perfectly okay if you aren't, or can't, by the way. The term infinity has such mystery connected with it that I wouldn't blame you one bit if you couldn't come up with one....You just knew I had a 'but' to insert here, didn't you? But now that you are becoming masters of metaphorical conversion, it could just slip out, and that would be okay. Make a mental note of your definition in this context, one that just happens to fit our discussion about the kingdom of Heaven." Christo pauses for the record to be made. "Ready? Okay. Here's the 'but': ideas are the infinite source of divinity that lead us to our highest good. The supply is endless, completely endless—and absolutely infinite in nature.

"Could anything be more true? I think not. Now, with a show of hands, how many of you were right on the money with this explanation?" En masse, the class had scored a perfect A+. "Just as I thought. See how talented you are, especially when you take yourself to the seat of divinity within? Let me ask this of you: How many of you can feel your theological mythology reshaping itself? Raise a hand if this is so. Go within to make this determination, not simply to your intellect. How many of you are feeling a shift?" he concludes. The response comes more slowly this time, not because there is reluctance, but rather because the participants are, in fact, using the discernment process they have been learning more and more about. As a result, hands rise slowly, but surely, until the entire arena is aglow with affirmation. A sense of peace abides in the wake of this acknowledgment.

"How wonderful!" Christo concludes about his survey. "This takes us to the end of the second step of the process. I'll only add that when you go within, use your spirit of wonderment to turn things around in your field of perspective. You're not going to judge yourself for anything that comes up any longer, so play with the process. Have some fun with it for goodness's sake. For *your* goodness's sake!

"Looking at the old tapestry is akin to seeing through the glass darkly. In the new, in the form of our virgin birth, darkness gives way to light. Ignorance gives way to Enlightenment. Time and time again we midwife virgin birth as our salvation: the new perspective that resurrects the Truth of our divinity, and of all of Life. In our old perspective—thinking and behaving as a child—we are filled with thoughts of fear, abandonment, judgment, and punishment, among others of like nature. Is this not the message of the Old Testament once again; the message that has us warring within and without, using our precious energy merely to *cope* with Life?

"Then, as now, it's still a matter of what's within is that which demonstrates without. In our new perspective, from the principle of divinity, we find the familiar landscape of the New Testament. Our new landscape is witnessed by a Life filled with grace after grace from our Kingdom of Heaven, lived passion-ately as compassion personified. Indeed: as in Heaven, so in earth.

"While we're at it I might as well disarm the mythology about alchemy. This simple transcendence from the old to the new is akin to taking the perspective which formerly weighed us down, the hardened, heavy perspectives, and let-ting them be transformed in the wisdom of Enlightenment, the golden threads of our new warp on Life. Once again we have wisdom at our doorstep, simply by exercising our natural tendency, natural for now at least, to convert the old to the new in order to transcend the material misunderstanding in favor of the metaphysical Truth. Yes, alchemists we are. And it is alchemy that we will have exercised on a much more frequent basis now that we know the process. Actually, we have been exercising alchemy all along, only not so much on a conscious level. Now at the next break, be sure to call your friends and tell them of your new wizardly talents." The smile is so wide and bright on Christo's face that the gathering is completely light in all meanings of that word now. "Add that to our continuing status as one giving virgin birth," tempts Christo, "and you're going to be quite a luminary around town.

"Yes, right is radical. At least it seems that way. But that's only because we haven't been accustomed to dealing with Life as Jesus would have us create. But now, as adults…well, you can complete that sentence by yourselves. Radical is learning to see all as the divine it is. It is radical is to know Love for what it is. For example, we often hear the meaning of the word 'love' divided into unconditional and conditional love. This simply cannot be. How can conditional love be Love at all? There is only Love—or Loving—and everything that is not. Just like there is divinity and everything that is not. In both cases, however, we see only what is, and use the appearance of what is not to get us back to Love, that is, to divinity. Give all else no thought, for the rest is nothing but a detail."

Using his discernment, Christo asks the gathering: "Can you handle the last of the three steps in this process or do you need another break? How many need a break?" Nary a soul raises a hand. Their thoughts are elsewhere, to be sure, so transfixed are they by this message, this provocative process. "Well, I need a brief respite, so why don't you take yourselves into a short meditative exercise of your own doing, and I'll be right back."

Christo wants to be sure that he is clear on the next steps. He has gotten so caught up in what has been coming out of him that he has neglected to reflect, as he knows he must. He takes a slow walk to his stool, and by the time he reaches that point his INsight has informed him of what direction he must now take. Immediately he returns to the podium and respectfully gives the assemblage a few minutes to complete their individual meditation sequences.

He begins with this: "Thank you for your indulgence. Frankly, I got so caught up in what was transpiring, I needed just a few minutes to check in 'you know where' before continuing. Now the way is clear. All it took was letting go of where I was at the moment, so INsight could speak to me without a veil of any kind separating us. My Muse, she is a jealous lover, and she likes a clear path to me," Christo says with that familiar twinkle in his eye. There is a return from the gathering that affirms the same in them, which tells Christo that they are becoming more accustomed to their own divine connection within.

"Let's now move on to the third and final step in this process. Ready or not, here it comes! Once INspiration, INsight, and Enlightenment have done their job, take just a moment to bid a proper farewell to the old. When many of us transcend to a new way of thinking, even a new way of Life, we sometimes ignore the necessary act of grieving. Even if we are moving to something that is clearly better than what is past, grieving is appropriate. It is not necessary to dwell on the past. It is only necessary to honor it. When you really think about it, why would you *not* want to honor something that you thought was right for you at the time—that very thing that has helped get you to where you are in this present moment? When you do take just a brief time to rejoin it in homage to it, you may have some emotions rise within you. Honor this, as well. Thank it all. Express your genuine gratitude for the gift it all is. Then simply let it go. If any guilt or shame shows up, honor these, too. Then let them go, just as with the other. As Jesus has told us: 'give it no thought' any longer.

"An important part of this step is also to turn things around that you once erroneously attributed to someone else. If, for example, you thought that someone else was unavailable to you, or was incapable of intimacy, turn that thought around to reflect the Truth about such an appearance. The Truth is that when we take responsibility to deal with what comes our way, a judgment such as, 'He's simply unavailable for me,' is turned around to 'I'm not available for him.' And if we turn it around one more time, we more than likely will come to another aspect of the real Truth: 'I'm not here for myself.' Then the guilt and angst and shame fall away. In the process we also move from thinking of ourselves as a victim to taking full responsibility for how we see what Life brings us. We then are afforded the opportunity to see the real giftedness that shows up repeatedly through simple contact with others. In another portion of this session I'll explain this more fully and give you an opportunity to see how you can apply this to your own inner Life.

"I hear another shoe waiting to be dropped, so let's do it now. This part of the process deals with what has given root to two expressions: 'forgive and forget' and 'let go, let God.' With regard to the first, 'forgive and forget,' most of us have been taught to forgive even our most grave offender, and to forgive ourselves. We are told that forgiving is more important for us even than for the other, because it frees the bonds that tie the past and us to another.

"If we place this idea within the current context of letting go of our warped past as it comes up for release, then we get a slightly different take on it. All, and I do mean *all*, of those threads that come up for release are, now listen carefully to how this is said, for—giving—up! Yes, we are to simply let them all go, honoring them first, of course, for their contributions to our Life. The second part of this expression deals with forgetting. While it may seem unlikely that you'll really be able to forget all of what has transpired, what forgetting really means is that these are, listen closely again, for—getting—on with your Life. Yet another way of thinking about this is to recall some circumstance in Life when you expressed or carried out what seemed like a harmless thought or action with another and were quickly humiliated by your own word or deed. And you rush to apologize. Your best friend let us say, responds with a simple: 'fagidaboutit already!' What such a response tells you is that this wasn't as important to the other person as it was to you, and it therefore releases you to move on—to let go of it.

"I can hear some of you saying, 'Yes, and Jesus said to forgive 70 X 7.' Yes. And no. 'Yes,' in the sense that what he meant by this is, 'as many times as necessary.' This is an interesting use of metaphor. But 70 X 7 equal only 490, and while that may seem like a large number of times to forgive something or someone, it isn't really that large. It seems more likely that what Jesus said was 7 to the 70th power. But how does one say that in Biblical text in a way that most would understand it? That is a slightly more sophisticated form of arithmetic. Believe me, 7 to the 70th power is an infinitely larger number than 490. It's almost off the scale. And, of course, you will recognize the number 7 as the perfect sacred number, indicating that his was a spiritual message, not a material one. That is to say, that Jesus was referring to forgiving within us, which says nothing about forgiving another. But when we forgive ourselves due to a new perspective, forgiving another for a new understanding of their circumstances frees one in forgiveness just as easily as forgiving oneself. In fact, it's automatic. As long as we're acting out of our divinity, the fact of the new meaning we give to something a person does or says is an act of forgiveness: it is based on a new way of seeing something and setting the old free, thus forgiving it. As long as we are acting from our divinity, forgiving another is just as simple an idea as giving our own no-longer-useful imagery away. And just as easy to implement—as long as we see all as divine. In this sense, then, how could you not forgive another divine entity and then fagidaboutit? In actual application, what used to torment us in this regard is set free from that which binds in pain. It just *happens* as a result of INsight, Enlightenment and Transcendence doing their jobs, along with letting it happen on our part, of course. Loving intention sends the old on its merry way.

"Well, it is clear, is it not, that the same kind of thing applies to 'let go and let God?' It's identical in its intent and demonstration, absolutely identical. Why have two phrases to suggest the same thing? You've heard it before: God says the same thing in various ways, so those who need to hear it in a way that brings meaning to them are afforded the unique expression of Word that does exactly that. So, let's just for-give and fagidaboutit—or let go and let God, whichever way works for you. In either case, it is just as if Jesus were standing before you and saying: 'Pick up your bed and walk around.' 'Give up the old and begin anew.' 'Repent, and sin no more.' 'Unless ye are born again.' 'Be as a child.' So now we can add to this array of terms meaning repentance these two phrases: 'forget and forgive,' and 'let go and let God.' How charming.

"Well, that's it! I told you that this is a simple process, dictated by none other that Jesus himself, although most would be hard-pressed to find it in the teachings of 'the church.' That really doesn't matter. The only thing that *does* matter is that it has meaning for you and that you practice this process until the cows come home. I'll put that last admonition differently if you will permit. Actually, I'll put it differently even if you won't permit!" Christo teases the gathering. The energy throughout now feels like the deep, cleansing, Loving energy that envelops a small gathering of dear friends, adorned with as much fun being expressed as possible.

"I suggest that you do this on the basis of a forty-day trial run. You will recall Jesus's trip into the desert, which lasted for forty days and forty nights. He did that to clear away his demons. Or at least he did it to clarify and clearly establish a process for dealing with the old habits, the more unconscious, youthful threads of the warp: those beliefs and ideas that needed to be cleared out before he could see himself and all else as perfect divinity expressed. 'Get behind thee, Satan' is exactly like 'forgiving and forgetting' or 'letting go and letting God' in its principle form. So give yourself these next forty days to put Satan behind you, the satanic means of holding you back inside the old perspectives, so you can move on and create your Life anew.

"Some of you have expressed concern along the way—call it what you will, a fear I call it—that if you commit totally to this process of living divinity as your purpose in Life that you will lose your individuality. In Truth, it's quite the contrary. By living primarily unconsciously, we follow the dictates of outside authority, the strength of outside validity and opinion. Such authority is geared to make us all alike, in everyone else's image for us, so they can sell us what they will—for their benefit. In their own way, they would have us do what they will for us, so they can control all we are and do. This *old* way of coping with Life largely out of unconscious motivation is what breeds homogeneity. The old way does not permit or even encourage finding your own power within, which can be manifested only through your unique character. I recall that in prayer one day this same concern came up and the response from within was simply profound: 'What comes through you is unique to your ability to demonstrate it. If this were not so, it would not show up as it does.' So worry not, my friends. Simply be what you so beautifully are, now and always.

"Well, now, go within with me for a few reflections. Close your eyes and envision what this tapestry could look like. First envision yourself threading the warp of the new loom. What do the threads look like? Are they made of lead or of gold? If you are choosing gold threads, then you are well on your way to your new way of Life: to being born again, being as a child, in all innocence. Good for you! Now, just thread the entire warp with these wonderfully brilliant threads of gold. Up and down, up and down, up and down, up and down. As you do this, pay attention to how you feel and what your surroundings look like. Is there any music playing? Does a sweet glow envelop you? Do you feel joyful in your task? Is your mind at peace? You are recreating the foundation, the principle elements, of what will become your legacy to the world. So as you thread the warp, each time you place a thread on the loom think within: 'God is divine, I am divine, all is and are divine; God is divine, I am divine, all is and are divine; God is divine, I am divine, all is and are divine.' Let this become your mantra, not only as you thread your warp, but for all of Life. Become so conscious of this mantra that whenever anything or anyone comes into your Life, you say that same mantra: 'God is divine, I am divine, all is and are divine.' Commit to doing this and see what happens to your demeanor and your perspective on Life. Get ready to become aware of all the gifts Life has for you. That's really the point of it all: to recognize all of Life as gift. Life is nothing but divine gift, beginning with God—exercised through you—as well as through all. Actually, Life *is* all—not just *in* all. Then, when you feel or see something that appears to be lacking divinity, when it has a 'charge' for you, it will be clear that this is not real. That it is only a figment of illusion. Really, it is a gift of illusion from your friend the ego, an illusion that is asking to be let go now. It, too, wishes to move on, just as you want to.

"Hold with me for just a bit longer. Just sit with your vision for a moment more and see if you can look far enough into the future in order to find the tapestry that will have been created on your new warp. Can you see the brilliant golden threads all throughout the weaving? Isn't…this…simply…divine! This is not simply an exercise in envisioning something. This is prophecy—prophesy stemming from beginning rightly! Yes, rather than beginning as we used to, we are now afforded the opportunity to begin anew, be born again, as a child. But this time Life is beginning rightly for us. And the tapestry we will leave as our legacy will be finished rightly. Okay, you can finish this prophetic visualization as you like. Then bring yourself back home to your divinity in the present moment. Or should I say: bring yourself back home to your divinity in each moment that is a present? And to think that in just one day you've given virgin birth and become a prophet as well. You are wizards at work, you are!

"Well, as you look around, what do you see? How do you feel? What kinds of thoughts arise? Just sit with this feeling for a few moments." As usual, Christo waits patiently in order to provide enough time for the reality of this newness, this divinity within—for the Kingdom of Heaven—to show its face in earth. After a few minutes Christo continues in highly reverent tones: "Now, which would you rather witness day after day? This? Or what you had become familiar with as the past witnessed over and over again? Or the fear that it would? The choice is yours to make. Unless I miss my guess, you're well on your way to being born again. You are well on your way to coming home once again—and again, and again, and again—without end. Yes, this is what it means to come home. Coming home is not about coming home to God or Jesus when this material Life ends. It's about coming home to your divinity time and time and time again. So you can live *this* Life *as* divinity. Yes, you're home at last, in the kingdom of Heaven. And you can be here absolutely any time you choose.

"During this holiday season, let me reinforce the idea of the virgin birth, but not as something disrespectful to Mary or Jesus or Joseph or the Christmas tradition. Just as Jesus did, you have given virgin birth; you have brought to Life a new perspective, new for you at least. This new perspective sees the divinity of all. This meaning of divinity is a new gift for you: fresh, unadulter-ated, unadorned, uncontaminated, and unalloyed. It is virgin in its origin for you. Each of you has created this virginal perspective in your very own way, in the way only you could. In this way, too, you are midwives for virgin birth, just as Jesus was, and Aristotle, who used metaphysics in a similar fashion. This new way of thought begins with First cause—a divine idea—and it manifests itself in the image and likeness of this divine idea. Just as we have been created as us but in the image and likeness of that divine idea. You are divine creators in fulfillment of your prophecy. In the end, this reformulates your theological mythology: from one predominantly created out of unconsciousness to one created out of divine consciousness. Indeed, this is divine! As *you* are divine! As *all* are and is divine!

"Just so we are abundantly clear about what happens when we engage Life this way, I want to reemphasize that what we're really doing is not healing at all. Rather, it's simply pulling aside the curtains—the veils of illusion—and revealing on the screen of our egoic nature the erroneous ideas and thoughts that manifest as dis-ease or dis-harmony within. These represent the curtains of limitation, if you will. When they are parted they leave revealed what is already there, what always has been and always will be there: our divinity, our perfection. No more need there be torment founded in illusion. Just divinity personified. The grace we receive when this occurs we call healing, when in fact it's just returning us to our original state of divinity. This, my dear friends in the Christ, is the Law of First Cause. And the Law of First Cause can only render its exact likeness or effect. Beginning rightly is ending rightly—always.

"Just to complete this present to yourself in summary fashion, what you're being asked to do is to step out a little further in this direction and exercise the forty-day trial run—with a full money-back guarantee if that's what it takes. However, you may well excel in its use before then. You and you alone are the best judge of that. Trust your Inner Authority to inform you when you've completed this portion of the process. This process of living divinity, an eternity of perpetual virgin birthing if I may, has only three steps: engaging and marrying divinity; practicing discerning between the images of divinity and illusion; and forgiving and forgetting or letting go and letting God. Think of the challenge with confidence and with these words from the apostle Paul ringing in your heart of hearts one last time: 'When as a child, we thought as a child, behaved as a child. But now we are adults, and we think and behave as adults.' From Jesus we hear: 'I am the way, the truth and the Life.' And, 'Ye shall know the Truth and the Truth shall make you free.' Face your demons, these mental habits of the past. Get them behind you: 'Get behind me, Satan!' Indeed, 'Get behind me, erroneous thoughts. For I will *not* let you pull me down from my divinity.'

"Speaking of erroneous thoughts, some have criticized this process, this way of reframing Life, on the grounds that it represents the demonstration of absolute denial. Not so. Here's where the naysayers go wrong. They say that if one only looks at Life through what the naysayers call 'rose-colored glasses,' that one is deluding her or him. There are things other than Love, divinity, and God out there. And some are quite evil and vile. Well, yes, there are some who *behave* in evil ways, predominantly because they see themselves—first and foremost—as 'less than' divine, and they project this lowly feeling of self out into the world in varying degrees.

"On the other hand, when we weave our lives on the warp of divinity, we see even those who exhibit evil in their ways as divine. This allows us to always Love them, even as we hold them accountable for their actions. Added to this is our response to their acts. Formerly, using our unconscious warp, we would have used the layered inner response as a reason to club them. We would have taken their action personally and thus felt the need to defend ourselves or take revenge. Now, however, using the warp of consciously-derived Love as divinity, we still listen to the resonance within to see if their behavior is triggering our need to cleanse that same entity from within ourselves. Now we do it not with rancor but rather with Love in our hearts.

"This is not denial. This is Love at its best. We begin by Loving ourselves, by letting go of the personal nature of someone else's need to provoke or be heard. By letting go, we free ourselves from the bond of separation and all the pain that separation engenders—the pain that makes us want to strike back for the hurt it causes. Instead, we are free to listen with compassion. We recommit to being there for another in need. By so doing, we Love our neighbor as we Love ourselves: as the God in all, being all. Is this denial? Hardly. This is using Life to inform us of anything we indeed *may be* denying, so we can forgive and forget that which is diminishing and destroying us within.

"As we let those gremlins of our past go, as we give them away, we open space to be filled with what?" Christo feigns a question. "These spaces await the Truth of our divinity to infill. The more we let go of those childhood issues, the more and more room we make for divinity. You will find, I am sure, that once you commit to traverse through the eye of the needle, walk the straight and narrow, such cleansing will be your second nature. Before you know it, you will again be filling regularly—most naturally, I might add—with the Truth of divinity. Water seeks its own level. In this case, divinity seeks to infill to its own level. It surely will, and without fail. If this results in seeing through rose-colored glasses, so be it. Life is indeed lovely as a rose; even it appears as one that is wilted. But with rose-colored glasses, we still recognize even it as the gift it is. This we cannot deny. Are we home free on the accusation of denial now?" Christo asks in earnest. "Raise a hand if you are." Affirmation buttresses Christo's own sense of completion.

"This is more than enough to digest for now. Let's take a half-hour break this time. It's time to rejuvenate the body as we have the Soul. Be sure to drink ample amounts of good clear water, just as we have been drinking spiritually for this time together. Additionally, provide your body with some healthy nourishment, just as we have been nourished by our Spirit with meat the earth knows not of. When we return I sense it will be time for me to take you through real Life examples of how the process of inner reflection can be simply divine. Then, we'll move on to other examples of how you can use this Life 'out here' for your spiritual development 'in here,'" Christo says while gesturing to punctuate his intention. "Addio."

As Christo leaves the podium, he feels a state of revelation has been reached for almost all. Then he takes a second reading and realizes that indeed for all this has been achieved, even if at differing levels. When his followers arrive with that very feedback, he affirms their accurate discernment. All is in place for the next steps on this journey of divinity.

CHAPTER 6

Life As Metaphor

Christo feels as though things are on the right track and that the assembly is ready to move forward with grace. "Namaste, dear ones." Once again, before Christo can utter another word, the gathering responds in unison with a warm and cheerful, "Namaste, Christo. Namaste!" The arena fills with Loving embrace and smiles that adorn both heart and face. "Thank you, dear friends in Christ," responds Christo. "I can feel much less reluctance in your energy now. To me, this says a few very important things. First of all, it tells me that example works. Secondly, it tells me that the seemingly trite expression, 'fake it 'til you make it,' isn't trite at all. It, too, works. I hasten to add that by that I don't mean that Namaste is trite or that you are faking it. It just means that we come to authenticity by practice, even if we're not totally comfortable with that authenticity. It's like a little league pitcher being taught a new way of releasing the ball from the mound and not fully having grasped it before he has to pitch again. By just *doing* it, the successful new delivery appears much sooner than expected. Well, I'm here to tell you that your delivery is improving—and very fast! I am so pleased for you! Third, it tells me that you are willing to do what is necessary to move on in your Life. Not just move on, but also move on with a refreshed perspective on Life. This, too, is wonderful. Now let's build on your willingness to fully participate.

"Just before the break, in the presentation of the three steps of our process for living divinity, I briefly mentioned the potential for 'turning around' previous impressions in order to accept ownership of them for yourself. This is key to releasing the old for the new. If you stay in denial of the real Truth about an appearance, how can you let it go? It's like someone expecting you to rid your-self of the straw in your hair when you didn't know you had straw in your hair. 'What straw in my hair?' would be your initial thought, if not a spoken reply.

"At this point, then I want you to perform a miracle on yourself. 'Oh, here he goes again!' I can hear from you. Yes, here I go again. But none of my requests has failed you yet, as far as I can tell. So all I ask is that you follow along with me this one more time and see where our journey takes us.

"As I begin telling you this story about a conversation that took place with a dear friend I'd like you to role play it within yourself. As you hear me ask ques-tions of her, ask them of yourself. See what effect this has on your understand-ing of the process. I will prompt you along the way, so this will be rather simple. The key for your understanding will be for you to listen carefully not only to my telling of the story and the prompts I will give but, even more important, also listen carefully within for insights and Enlightenment to show their faces. Ready?" Christo realizes that they are not completely so, but by their nods he also knows that they are willing partners in this marvelous gift Life itself just is.

"First of all, this story actually took place over a few weeks. But I'm com-pressing it to save a little time. I'm also telling you this so you know that although we may have something 'working on us' within for some time, the INspiration and INsight and Enlightenment which perk to the surface are instantaneous. It is probably fair to say that this is exactly as Jesus's healing practice operated as well. The stories were compressed, and in this compres-sion it seems like all of Jesus' episodes involving healing took place all in one conversation—one very brief conversation. See now with me if this story cor-relates with such a translation of the works of the Master.

"Here goes. One beautiful Sunday morning, I ran across one of my friends. Let's call her Jane, although she's hardly plain Jane. Well, Jane looked mighty glum to say the least: washed out; slightly disheveled; shoulders drooped; sad eyes—you name it. We greeted one another as usual, with a hug and smile, although hers was rather limp on both counts. 'How are things going in your Life these days?' I ask. Rather reluctantly, Jane responds with, 'Okay—I guess.' 'Are you really okay?' I ask. 'Well, no, not really,' she answers as her shoulders droop even further. 'Want to talk about it?' I inquire. 'No—well, I guess we already are, aren't we?' Jane rejoins. I acknowledge her need and focus my attention completely with her, listening intently to every word while also pay-ing close attention to her body language.

'Well,' begins Jane, 'it's this relationship I'm in. Like all the others, he's just not there for me.' Jane then goes on to begin explaining that he works long hours and spends some time with his friends, and generally just isn't there for her. She then begins to tell me more about the relationship. Suddenly she returns to his unavailability by blurting out in the middle of a sentence dealing with a completely different aspect, 'He's just *not* available, *just like my father wasn't available!*'

"Now, test your feelings and thoughts at this moment. Is anything sounding or feeling familiar? Make a mental note of anything that appears as we continue, but stay with the story so you can gain a full appreciation of its impact on you," Christo encourages his listeners before resuming his story.

"With that, Jane continues along as though she hadn't even said that he was just like her father. 'Wait a minute,' I say. 'Did you hear what you just said?' 'No. What did I just say?' Jane asks in utter amazement. 'You didn't hear what you just said?' I query. 'No. I have no earthly idea what you're talking about.' When I heard the words 'earthly idea' come out of her mouth it was hardly difficult to understand where her mind was. 'Well,' I say to her, 'you said that he is not there for you, *just like your father was not there for you.*' 'I said that?' Jane says in disbelief. 'Yes, you did say that. Do you mean it?' Jane reflects for all of a split second, and rejoins with, 'Without a doubt. He's just like my father.' 'Does this say anything to you about what could be happening here?' I ask. 'Hmm,' she says, 'I think probably, but I'd have to give it some more thought.' 'Fine. This is yours to take meaning from. I'm just a mirror. And sometimes just a prod, so you can look within for your own answers,' I say. 'Yes, I know that,' Jane nods, 'and it's very helpful. I can already feel something loosening up, so let's keep going.'

"Jane goes on a bit further, only reinforcing in my mind that there's something going on here that's not what she thinks it is. She's pointing an accusing finger at her male friend quite frequently, with more than simple vehemence. Jane reaches a point where she seems to be running out of gas. She has dumped a rather large dose of emotions out into the world, and I hear from within that a certain simple shifting of thought would be helpful to her. You know me. I obey the INspiration and INsight, trusting fully that somewhere down the line it will be right for her.

"'Jane, might you consider a slightly different approach to solving this problem?' I ask. 'Sure, I'll try anything. I'm ready to even move out if I have to. I can't take any more of this!' It feels like she's about at the end of her rope, sort of like an alcoholic hitting bottom. I use her present demeanor as an opportunity to follow the rather drastic approach that has come to me; drastic in the sense that it's 180 degrees away from how she's looking at it.

"'Jane, in a word, how do you feel about this relationship when you see him not being there for you?'

'In just a word? Hmm, it's tough to put it into just one word…but…yucky. That's it. Really yucky!' I smile inwardly at her use of the word 'yucky.' 'Isn't that a little girl's word?' I think to myself.

"'Jane, can you be absolutely sure, without a shadow of a doubt, that he's not there for you?' 'Of course I'm sure!' she shouts in my direction. 'Didn't I tell you that's what's happening? Didn't you listen to me?' 'Yes, I heard you,' I say, being careful not to take any of her emotions personally, 'quite clearly in fact. That's exactly why I asked you the question I did. I hear you saying that you *feel* like he isn't there for you, yet could there be another explanation for what's going on?' 'No,' Jane shakes her head vehemently, 'there cannot be another explanation for this. He's just not there for me, period!'

"'Let me ask you this one more time. Jane, can you be *absolutely sure, without even a shadow of doubt* that he isn't there for you?' 'Well,' she says, 'nobody can be *absolutely, positively* sure of *anything.*' 'Good! Now, how about just a little more truth?' I ask. Jane looks puzzled, but blurts out, 'Sure. What can I lose? Go for it!' 'Okay then,' I say, 'I want you to close your eyes and think about him without the thought that he's not there for you. Can you do that?' I ask. 'I'll do my best,' she says, and I can feel her give it the old college try. 'This is difficult,' Jane murmurs. 'My feeling that he's not there for me keeps trying to come in.' 'That's okay,' I say, 'don't fight it, just watch the negative thought go by and soon you'll be free to think of him the way he was before you thought he wasn't there for you.' I wait patiently. In a fraction of a minute I see a delightful smile come across her face. 'Hmm,' she says, 'that's nice.' 'What's nice?' I say. 'Him. He's nice. *Real* nice.' Jane says admiringly. 'Jane, does this feel better to you than when you think the thought that he's not there for you?' 'Are you kidding?' she retorts, 'There's no comparison!' 'You're sure?' I ask. 'Yes, absolutely sure,' Jane argues.

"'Jane, I ask, 'can you see any reason to drop the thought that he isn't there for you? Before you answer, be clear that I'm only asking if you see any reason why you might. I'm not asking you to give it up. It will come and go when it or you pleases.' 'Oh, yeah, for sure!' she exclaims. 'I'd love to be able to do that.' 'Would you now? Really, would you?' I tease. 'You bet your bottom dollar I would!' she proclaims. I know now that she's willing to venture even into the world of the unknown to get this behind her, if at all possible.

"'There's a way that can happen,' I tell her. 'How? Tell me! Quick!' Now Jane shows not only her willingness but her eagerness as well. 'Okay,' say I, 'but first we have to discern a bit more truth here. Can you handle that?' 'I've been handling a lot worse than that, so let's do it,' she says approvingly. 'Okay then. First let me say that I agree wholeheartedly that you have been dealing with a whole lot worse than that. Let me ask you a few questions that could well reveal that to you. The first question is: Are the patterns of behavior for your father and lover similar? By that I mean did your father and does he work long hours, for example?' 'Yes, and when he got home he paid attention to my mother, who demanded it of him. My other sister, too, so he didn't have any time for me.' 'And in a word, how did this make you feel, Jane?' I ask. 'In a word? Why yucky, just like I told you before,' she responds. 'Think carefully, as an adult now, Jane. How did this make you feel?' 'Yucky! Just yucky!' she proclaims strongly.

"I just waited with a knowing smile on my face. 'What's wrong?' she asks. 'Nothing,' I respond. 'I'm just waiting to see if you heard yourself this time, that's all.' 'Heard what?' she asks. 'How you answered that same question—both times—not just now.' I say no more; just wait patiently for Insight to arrive. Time is pregnant with pause. Now while she reflects I can almost hear the wheels of progress turning in her head, and I tell her not to think about it but just let it come up from within. With that, I can see that she relaxes, and almost immediately after she lets go of the struggle the effects of INsight show on her face. 'Oh…my…God!' she shouts. 'That's the same little girl in there speaking now, isn't it?' 'Is it?' I ask simply. 'Only you know for sure.' 'Yes,' she responds without further thought, 'that's exactly it. I can even feel the same feelings when I think that thought!' she exclaims.

"'Well, Jane, is it just possible that you took your father's work habits personally, and his attention to your mother and sister, as well? And is it also possible that you adopted the view that this is just the way it is supposed to be?' 'Oh, sure, that's exactly what I did,' she responds in new awareness. 'And I'll tell you something else, too,' she continues. 'Because he wasn't around I never got to see him enough to have an intimate relationship with him. And I wanted to be close to him so badly.' I quickly ask, 'Was there a modeling for an intimate relationship anywhere at home, even in your mother and father's relationship?' Jane retreats to her childhood memory, taking time to reflect honestly, responsibly. 'No, not really—Daddy was so tired when he came home late from work every day that he didn't seem in the mood for anything, let alone an intimate conversation—or for anything else so far as I could tell, even if Mommy demanded it. He was just too tired, I think. So he couldn't win, no how. Wow! Does this ever begin to look different now!' Jane acknowledges.

"'I'm sure it must. Just remember that you are now looking at all this with an adult mind. But then you weren't an adult. With this new information, can you describe what that imagery that you have carried forward as Truth for you represented to you? In a few words of Jane the child, how would you describe your father?' Jane didn't hesitate one iota: 'Although I didn't know these words then, the feelings are the same. I'd use 'unavailable' and 'lack of intimacy' as two of the biggest feelings I had. And still do.' 'Can you feel the emotion when you use those words?' I ask. 'Oh, yes, I sure can!' says Jane, quickly placing her hand on her solar plexus. 'Especially because these thoughts are so emotionally laden, can you see where you just might have carried the image forward that *all* men are unavailable and lack capacity for intimacy?' I ask. 'Yes, I actually can,' Jane responds thoughtfully. 'And you know what?' she continues, 'in retrospect all the men I've been with have been—whoops—looked like—that to me. Wow. It's all about how I've been seeing them, isn't it? I need time to let this all settle.'

"'That's a good idea, because there could be more to it. It could get confusing as to whether you have attracted the same kind of men into your Life time after time until you could 'get it,' or whether you were just looking at the circumstances with young Jane's heart and her emotional eyes. But that can wait for now. You're now able to let that come to the surface with clarity when you're ready.

"'Before we quit, though, if you're up for just a small clincher you can use on your own, I'd like to leave you with it.' 'Sure,' Jane responds, 'I can handle that—I hope!' 'I have full confidence that you can, and quickly, with real meaning at that.' I confide. 'When we began, Jane, you said that he wasn't there for you. Is that correct?' 'Yes, that's what I said,' she says hesitatingly. 'Well, I'd like you to turn that thought around. Flip it around 180 degrees. Reverse it completely.' 'You mean…I'm not there for him?' she asks bravely. 'Exactly. Are you there for him, Jane?' I prod a bit more. '…No. Oh, gosh, I almost answered in my little child voice. I almost said, No, why should I be here for him? He's not there for me! Goodness!' 'Yes, goodness,' I say. 'And now, as an adult?' 'No, I'm not there for him, because that little girl inside me won't let me be—until now, that is.' Tears begin to well up in her eyes. 'It's all okay, Jane. There's nothing to feel guilty or shameful about. This happens to all of us in one way or another. The good news is that now we're adults, so we can think like one. And it's perfectly okay to feel anything you want in this regard. That's part of owning it, and then grieving its loss. Even though it didn't feel healthy, it got you to where you are now. So simply thank that little girl and her imagery and let it go. Give it no more thought.'

"'Just one more request?' I ask rather sheepishly, not wanting to push on too far. 'We've gone this far, why not? This is something else!' 'I asked you to turn your original image around and you did that perfectly,' I lead her. 'Now do it just one more time. Take the last one, that you aren't there for him, and flip it over once more.' Jane looks puzzled, thinks for a moment, and then seems to freeze in the next. 'Let go of it,' I say. 'Just say something like, I wonder how I'd do that and let go of it.' Jane suddenly goes blank in a state of letting go. Just as suddenly, the light that casts away darkness comes in like a flash. 'Oh…my…God!' she screams. 'I'm not there for *myself*! My God, that's absolutely true. I've been so busy pointing fingers at him that I haven't been seeing and handling my needs like an adult. Woe is me!'

'One more step?' I could hear myself ask. 'Sure,' she says. 'Might as well.' 'Okay,' I say, 'here goes. What is it you've always wanted for yourself? What is it you always wanted to be, but haven't given to yourself?' Jane looked off into the sky, to her internal bank of images. After a time she responds with, 'I want to be completely irresponsible for once. I've been so responsible for everyone else, I just want to be responsible for me for awhile.' 'Jane,' I suddenly ask, from where I know not, like someone else is guiding all this, 'is there something you haven't told me? Like, is something ailing you physically?'

"Now tears really well up in her eyes, overflowing down her cheeks. Pensively she confesses, 'Well, yes. There is: I have a lump in my breast.' 'No wonder all this is coming to pass!' I think to myself. 'Jane,' I begin, 'is it any wonder what's going on here? Is it any wonder that you're given this opportunity to clear out what's really troubling you?' 'What do you mean?' Jane asks. 'Well, do you remember my saying that right is radical?' Jane nods in acknowledgment. At that moment I couldn't believe that I was about to say the guiding thought that had just entered my mouth. 'Jane, in what other connection have you heard the word 'radical' used?' She reflects for a moment, pondering my query. Suddenly, she is struck by INsight. 'Oh, no: I'm not going to let that happen,' she reacts. 'I'm not going to let it get to that stage. I'm not going to let anyone do a radical on me.' 'Well, Jane, let me put it to you this way: Either you are going to have to do radical surgery on yourself—on these beliefs that have kept you from drinking the milk of human kindness for yourself—or you'll have radical surgery physically. This gift has come to you in order to dramatize the issue, the appearance of something large and dramatic enough so you will finally see it for yourself. The choice is clearly yours. How we see our Life inside is how it manifests outside, so here it is, both emotionally and physically. Now that you're taking care of the emotional aspects of it, please get the proper physical care. Make that commitment to yourself right here and right now.'

"'Wow!' Jane responds. 'I know what I can do physically, but what can I do about it emotionally? And how?' 'Just as it is telling you to: do your own radical surgery. If you were thinking one way about Life, what would be the radical response to that? Turn around and go exactly 180 degrees in the other direction. And then be sure that every single step you take goes in just that direction. It will take single-minded conviction in that direction to erase the old for the new. I know you well enough by now, Jane. You are absolutely and totally up for it. Go for it! How does this INsight make you feel?' I conclude, looking into her tired, but resolved eyes. 'Wow! What a Sunday school lesson this has been!' she declares. 'And how does that feel?' I ask once again. 'I just told you,' Jane responds even more thankfully now, 'Wow! What a Sunday school lesson!'

"Fast forward now to a couple of weeks later. I run into Jane again and she looks like a new person. 'How's it going?' I ask, knowing that this answer will be a lot different from the one a couple of weeks ago. 'Oh, my, I don't have enough time in the day to describe it all. Let me just say that I have freed myself—and him—of a lot of burdens lately. I am now taking care of myself quite well, in lots of the same ways he does actually. Like going out with my own best friends rather than putting all that on him. What a difference growing up has made. And I'm planning the trips I've always wanted to take. I feel so free now. Free as a bird. All these new ideas have made me free. I just *love* it.'

"I won't prolong this any further, only to tell you her answer to the last question I asked, which was: 'Well, Jane, with all that's going on in your Life now, in a word, how would you describe your relationship—and him—if that can be done in just a word.' 'Oh, that's easy!' she proclaims. 'In a word: it's divine, simply divine!' End of story—except that she's also thankfully on the road to recovery physically as well.

"This was a rather lengthy story, but I watched you as I told it and I could see lights going on everywhere in this arena. What I'd like to do now is take a short break to let all this settle in, and to give you some time to discuss this with anyone you wish. A few of my helpers will be making themselves available to answer any questions. But mostly I just want them to assess how well you're deciphering the main messages from this story. When we return, I'll use that information and add some of my own. You can adjust your perspective as need be but don't do it for me, for my assessment is about how I see things. Yours is not to replicate mine, but rather to come home to the seat of your own perspective, and to be sure you can use this simple process without putting too much pressure on yourself. Most of what you'll be going through in Life should be much simpler and less stressful than what I've described. 'Why do I say that?' Because you have just rethreaded your warp, and as such things come up against those golden threads, it will feel more like they're just melting away, rather than feeling like Jane's tasks that had to be overcome. Let's take a 30-minute break. Addio."

Christo returns to his stool and decides to take some refreshment, especially in order to ground himself. He sips some tea, and nibbles on a few nuts and some fruit and cheese, with a bit of dark chocolate thrown in for good measure. Then, for just a few minutes he goes within peacefully and waits for what he knows is there to guide his way. His body immediately relaxes and when he opens his eyes he feels completely refreshed and aware of the next steps. He recognizes that this gathering is turning out to be much more like a weekend intensive retreat, without the full capability to deal with people individually. It strikes him in this awareness that he must begin a series of smaller regional retreats, where people's concerns, questions, and individual development can be more easily dealt with. There and then he commits to this tack, and makes a mental note to announce this new leg of the journey before they part company at the end of the day.

CHAPTER 7

Turning Deeper Meaning Into Common Meaning

Christo is ready to surge on to the next leg of the journey. Knowing the importance of reinforcement in the learning process, he is committed to walking the gathering through the process, showing them how simple it can really be. He rises from his prayer stool and, instead of parting the curtains that separate him from the stage, he walks in through the side entry, gracefully greeting people with his generosity of Spirit. Even with this, he arrives back at the podium at the prescribed moment and greets all with the usual: "Namaste, divine ones. I can tell that more and more of you are willing to allow divinity to be your state of character now, so I call you divine ones with more than just an element of Truth ringing through that phrase.

"Let's use the next few moments to quickly review the three steps of the process that will take you to divine simplicity. If you are faithful in your practice of this principle of divinity, you indeed will find your Life simplifying before your very eyes. Those things and circumstances that no longer belong in your Life will fall by the wayside. The same is true of people who no longer need to be there in your surroundings. And the illusions of your memories and thoughts of tomorrow will give way to the only thing you can *truly* live: now. The present. Yes, you will soon find yourself in a Lifestyle that will enrich your Soul Life beyond your imagination. You will find clarity around your purpose and the marvelously rewarding means for fulfilling your purpose, moment by moment. You will take on the glow of the divine being you are. You will even look and act more youthful, filled with enthusiasm for Life you have never before witnessed.

"If you will permit me yet another rather dramatic example of such radical change, I think it was Deepak Chopra who spoke about the importance of demonstrating what you came to Earth to be. He was interested in the decisions people made when they were told they had a terminal disease and had only a few months to live. In his study of this question he found that some merely accepted the diagnosis and, sure enough, they left their body precisely as predicted. Another cluster accepted the diagnosis, but fought it with all they were worth, thus shifting the end date, but moving to another plane nevertheless. The third group, however, was stunning in its response. These people chose to totally ignore the diagnosis and, instead, declared that if they only had a particular time left on this planet, then they were going to do precisely what they had always wanted to do with their lives. And they did! What happened with these people? They lived happily ever after. As I recall, their so-called terminal disease went into permanent remission. Just as Jesus had admonished those he 'healed,' they gave it no thought. They went on and lived the purpose for which they came to Earth. There is no sadness to report in these cases: joyfully, they invested their lives in releasing the music that had been waiting within to be expressed. What a difference a shift in perspective can make. Is this extraordinary or what?

"Dear divine ones, is it not true that we all have an arrival date for transforming to another form? Not in a metaphysical sense, our spiritual sense, but in the mortal lie that must one-day cease? Why, then, would each of us not want to live our purpose rather than living the lie we have come so decidedly to believe instead? My plea to you is to follow your purpose beginning right *now*, at *this very moment*—or at *the very latest*, when you awaken tomorrow morning. It is living your purpose, your unique demonstration of divinity that gives you your glow of being fully alive: that which unleashes your enthusiasm for Life, your youthful spirit and countenance, along with unparalleled energy and spark. As we now know, this all comes from living your Life authentically and genuinely as divinity. When you live from this principle Life comes with abundance of Inspiration and Insight, clarity of Enlightenment, and a transcendence that renders that which has crippled us nonexistent—all in a seeming flash of a moment.

"The way in which I related the story of Jane was perhaps more complex than need be. However, I took you into sufficient detail only to show you the depth of meaning that emits when the process is used thoroughly. In Jane's case, she was not yet as informed as you are, so it is likely, although probably not always so, that you won't need to be as detailed in your exploration of the unexplored. Here are the three steps expressed in absolute simplicity. I will then use them to reduce my conversation with Jane to that same simplicity.

"The first step, you will recall, has two complementary parts. First, expand your self-concept, your perspective on Life, in order to accept your own divinity with conviction. Second, expand your definition of divinity to include everyone and everything. As you bring this commitment to yourself and all of Life, it may be useful to think of yourself as becoming engaged with the idea of divinity. Just as in other fruitful relationships, engagement leads to marriage. In this case, engaging the Truth of divinity leads you to marriage with the principle of divinity. You then apply the principle to what you have been married to all of your Life. Life cannot be simpler than this.

"The second step, then, follows closely on the heals of the first: using similar means of practice. The practice in the second step applies to paying close attention to any feelings of disengagement from your newfound depths of divinity: feeling ill at ease for any reason, inharmonious with your surroundings, or emotionally charged by a thought, feeling, circumstance or happening. This step is tantamount to befriending your ego and using its flag-waving skills to lead you within for discernment.

"The third step is again related to practice. This time practice is applied to for-giving and for-getting, to letting go and letting God; it is about not holding on to the past. Not *anything* from the past. Unencumbered in any way, you can then move forward with dispatch.

"Now, with these three steps in place, let's see what you received from Jane's story. My assistants have provided me with a summary of what they heard you discussing about Jane's case during the break. I'll summarize that for you so you can complete your own inventory along the way. Remember, the importance of this exercise is not that you must agree with my perspective on it, but rather that you come to clarity within yourself about how you can easily apply the process of going within for help.

"All right then. What's the first thing that happened? Jane wore the face of her issue in public so she could draw to her the help she needed. Each of us does the same thing. All we need to do is learn to pay attention to that face ourselves, using that face we put out into the world for our own discernment. By the way, the face is just an image representing how we feel, look, and reveal ourselves by gesture, posture, tone of voice, and so on. But then, you know this already, don't you? So Jane was struggling with her issue. She had seen the ego's red flag wave and was stirring for an answer. Her slight offering that she was willing even to move out on her lover was the key to her choice of the moment.

"When she ran into me, her intuition told her that it was safe for her to divulge her problem to me. Actually, she began by obeying when her intuition told her to put on that face as a means of working through her issue one way or the other. You can do the same simply by knowing that it is safe to trust your-Self, your Inner Authority, for all the answers you need. Now, one thing I know about Jane that you wouldn't, at least not at first, is that she knows her divinity quite well. Just like the rest of us, though, she forgets from time to time that she and all the rest of Life is divine.

"Once she let herself come into contact with her divinity again, by her willingness to consider other perspectives, she found herself in the lap of INspiration, INsight and Enlightenment. Eventually she came to transcend her childish perspective for the more mature one, leaving the old behind. Time and time again you could sense her freedom from the old bursting forth in INsight after INsight. Indeed Enlightenment was burning brightly. And a good deal of darkness gave way to light.

"My use of the 'turn it around' sequence with her is something you might not have thought of, but that's perfectly fine. You know it now, and it is a very good way of finding where the real responsibility for Truth lies and then exercising that to good advantage for all concerned. So I suggest you incorporate this contribution into your self-explorative process. If you wish a more comprehensive understanding of the principles involved—although it is highly unlikely that you'll need to be more explicit with yourself than what you've already heard—then have a look-see at Byron Katie's enlightening book, *Loving What Is*.

"In the end, by continuing her commitment to Truth in this situation, Jane returned to the Truth of divinity and declared it thus. When we engage Life this way we are quick to return home to divinity in precisely the same fashion. One cautionary note: don't push yourself too hard too fast when using this process, especially at first. If you do, you'll more than likely slide back into largely intellectual treatment of the issue and thus avoid the deeper meaning for yourself.

"We all can hide behind the mask of intellectuality. But wisdom lies within. Just ask in awe and wonder and be patiently aware of the answers as they flow most naturally to you. Be assured that this is so, and they will. In very short order.

"Finally, Jane gave up her old thoughts about her father and home situation, particularly as they relate to her father not being there for her and his apparent lack of intimacy. Of course, she also had to give up that imagery which she had carried forth to paint her world of relationships with men. Was she successful in doing so? Was she able to complete the radical surgery she set out to do? I think we would agree that she has, as least as far as we can tell. It will be interesting, now that she has largely healed her thought process, to see how long it will take for the tissue in her breast to be cured.

"So, in this story about Jane, you have had the opportunity to see how this process works with another person. I suspect that—with just a little practice—you also could practice this process with others. The important thing now, however, is that you learn to do it within for yourself—one step at a time, with only one story to complete as it shows up.

"Well, how did you do? Raise your hand if you are reasonably comfortable with the meaning this has for you." Most all raise a hand. "Good! The completeness you have achieved doesn't surprise me at all. It is obvious that you have committed to grow in this direction. Because of your convictions, you are now moving very quickly towards mastery for yourself.

"What is happening here is akin to these admonitions: 'turn the other cheek'; 'love your enemies'; and 'love your neighbor as yourself.' In each instance—the cheek, your enemies, and your neighbor—you find those wonderful reminders telling you to look within so you can clear out the old thoughts and set them, and yourself, free. No wonder is it that we can come to Love them. They all lead us to the Truth within which does indeed make us free!

"Is it any wonder, then, that I say that Life itself is simply the gift it so beautifully just is? Time after time after time, Life gifts us with the understanding that all of it is the Word—the symbol for something that is showing us what is for our highest good—and that we can find that something simply by going within for the Authority that informs us thus. If we make just a simple inferential leap, then, we can arrive at the space where we come to understand that what we find within is the First cause, the gift of Life's offerings: the Divine Essence of Life that is God ItSelf. Every happening becomes a story we can read for that purpose. Yes, all of God's offerings, gifts, and stories, are those that are birthed for our highest good. It's learning to read them in the tongue of mystery—the metaphor—that which sets their Truth free. The cycle of Life is thus complete. So we can begin, gloriously so, yet again.

"Those of you who haven't quite grasped this, or at least to your satisfaction, don't be at all concerned. I'll have my assistants pass out a brief outline of the process of 'turning it over' so you can reinforce your potential in this regard. Furthermore, I'd be willing to bet that if any of you is willing to expose even a minor concern to your travel mates on the way home tomorrow, that you'll have given yourself enough coaching to be well on your way.

"This is probably as good a time as any to inform you of a decision I made during the last break. It is becoming more and more apparent to me that it might well be helpful if I made myself available to you in small enough group sessions for some role-playing and in-depth meaning to prevail. So, beginning right after the first of the year a schedule of such happenings will appear on the web-site so you can know when and where they'll be available. Don't be concerned about cost. Just as we've done with our two larger sessions, the principle of a just donation will apply. You're doing fine in that regard.

"At this point I'd like to engage in a little story-telling as a way of providing more food for spiritual development. You will recall from our last meeting together that I used some parables to explain the metaphorical mechanism for obtaining meaning. I will continue that approach after our next break but for now I want to share a few personal stories to awaken you to the kind of entries you can expect to find in your own lives from now on.

"My purpose for heading in this direction is straightforward. I want you to ingest enough examples from scripture and real Life so you can become familiar with the means of using Life as a metaphorical tool for looking *within* your own Life. In each instance thus far—with the story about Jesus and the man at the pool in Bethesda, for example, and the one about my friend with the six divorces, and this latest one about Jane—in each instance the issue or concern was a metaphor for what had happened within the person. The 'what had happened' was that they had adopted a framework, a perspective on Life, a particular attitude about Life if you will, that had crippled them in some way. In most cases they were crippled or deadened on several levels.

"The signature of this pattern, if I may put it this way, is that what they are seeing on the outside is but a symbol, a metaphor, for what's happening spiritually on the inside. Spiritual Life has to do with our thought process, our perspective, about how we are looking at Life. It is the endless infinite gifts of Insight that feed the process of reframing our perspective that we then use to clarify that which lies unresolved within. What is the only purpose of that clarification? To return to our sole, and soul, purpose of expressing the Truth of our divinity through all we are and do, no matter what.

"I will begin with a few cases from my own daily Life, very simple ones, to show you how I have used what was happening outside myself to inform me about how I was living my spiritual Life within. And about how I was looking at Life in the moment. Then I will move on to a further exploration of some of the parables and other Scriptural references from the Bible. What I want to stress with you as I begin is the absolute importance of understanding that whatever comes to you through this process of going within is a virgin birth. It's a birth of living your Life from a perspective different from the one you formerly used to influence how you manifested your Life. My friend with the six divorces had a virgin birth in how he saw himself without guilt and shame. The man beside the pool in Bethesda had a virgin birth that made his living vicariously no longer a legitimate choice. Jane had a virgin birth that erased the diseased pattern that had darkened her experiences with men. Now I'll give you some less complicated examples.

"About a decade or so ago now, during a trek across the Milford Track on the south island of New Zealand, I had a rather serious tumble, rolling almost over the edge of a huge chasm alongside the path descending what are called the Southern Alps. Not only had I cracked my skull on a boulder and torn open my knee against another, but my ego was badly bruised as well. I was furious with myself for letting it happen; 'so careless was I,' or at least, so I told myself. As I picked myself up and continued the descent, much more carefully now, I asked for another way to see what had become a rather arduous task, given my frame of mind and soreness of body and pride. Simply by wondering what another perspective might look like, one showed up with such clarity and power that it startled me at first. What had come forth was a clear image of a pack mule. I could see the mule putting one cautious step in front of another, carefully testing the stability under foot before proceeding to the next. In a very short time, I found myself *as* the mule, emulating that same caution. I immediately gave up the perspective of myself as an angry, ego-bruised, self-deprecating nut case in favor of the example I followed the rest of the way down that mountain.

"I arrived safely at the bottom of the mountain without further incident. And the lesson I had learned was more than worth the slight price I had paid to learn it, soreness notwithstanding. Well, when we hit the bottom of the trail down the mountain we landed at the foot of another trail that was a mile or so long, and it was covered with sharp shards of shale as far as I could see. I could hear moans and groans of anguish coming from everyone both in front of me and behind me on the trail. Yet again I asked for a way to get me through this—any simple imagery I could use to erase the perspective of a potentially painful conclusion to this otherwise magnificent journey. Just as before, an extraordinary image came into view.

"As I took my first few steps down that darkened lane, a thinly-clad native Indian appeared off to my right, as a vision, of course. He was a little taller than I am, with long dark hair pulled back, and dark sparkling eyes. And he was lean and strong, walking alongside in his bare feet. He had a sly grin on his face, as if to say: 'You palefaces are too much! Use a little common sense here.' Then he delivered the crowning blow, a simple instruction that corrected the entire situation. He smiled a sly-looking smile and said directly to me: 'Let the moss be your feet.' I looked to either side of the path and noticed for the very first time wide beds of rich green moss, as soft and deeply-matted as my living-room carpet back home. I smiled back at my friend just as he disappeared and thanked him every step of the way to the finish line. I shared these two stories with my now ex-wife and our friends at dinner that night, which just confirmed my craziness in their view. But I knew better, didn't I?

"Here, in just two simple stories, you see what can be done when we really want to give our control over to a better way: to a different perspective that can make Life easier on all fronts. In both cases, I had taken on a negative attitude that was undone, so to speak, with a perspective that carried more Truth than the position in which I had placed myself spiritually at the time.

"Now I'll provide you with two other personal examples, more comical in nature. At least, they first appeared comical to me. They both have to do with my automobile informing me of my warped, or at least temporarily hidden, perspective on Life. Yes, I know," Christo laughs, "you think I've really lost it now, by using my talking auto to inform me about my inner workings. But what happened is true. I'd like you to consider that our automobile is a metaphor for what happens as we are transported through Life. Now that's not too farfetched is it? At least not symbolically speaking. I have for a long time said that you can tell more about the current situation of someone by looking at what's happening with his or her car than by most other ways. Personally, I think that anything we have in our possession is preciously divine, so we ought to treat it like we would the supremely divine. So I keep my car clean, mechanically sound, and physically conditioned. If you run into someone whose car looks like a garbage can inside, you can be sure that his or her inner means of seeing Life is also cluttered. If they're always running into trees or bumping into other objects it tells you something else about their spiritual outlook. I can see that dubious look on most of your faces. But there are enough of you with that knowing look in your eye to encourage me to go on with this. Convinced or not, you will now receive the first story.

"Last year I began to notice that my car's front tires were spinning as I pulled away from stop signs, or even when pulling slowing out of a parking space. After a few episodes of this I checked my tires and found that they were getting pretty bald. So I purchased new tires, thinking that the problem would be solved. Well, I was wrong, and disappointedly so. The new set of tires had cost a good bit of hard-earned money, after all. And yet there I was, with my tires still slipping and sliding—at least until I figured out the real message.

"Now don't get me wrong here. I did need new tires, to be sure. But that was only the physical message. What had to be resolved now was the import of the metaphysical one before the issue could be put to rest. I worked at it a bit, but was still caught up too much in the literalization of the issue. Finally, I let go, asking for clarity. As soon as I gave space enough around my intellectual pursuit of it so my INsight could be loosed, up it came. 'Why, you're just spinning your wheels in your current state of perspective about your Life as a writer,' the still small voice spoke. 'Spinning my wheels,' I mused. In a matter of minutes I had clear meaning for what I had been doing. Just a few months before all this wheel-spinning began, I had the distinct feeling within that I was to begin a new offering in the writing world. Instead, I had put that off and engaged my time in editing, over-editing actually, all of the manuscripts that I have been privileged to have come through these same fingers. Edit, edit, edit, edit. *Ad nauseam.* As I came to understand the full meaning of the wheel-spinning, I laughed uproariously at how smart my automobile was, this supposedly inanimate object that has informed me so frequently about my current state of affairs. In the wake of this understanding came the initiation of a new manuscript, followed by some speaking engagements—which subsequently led to manuscript I'm currently working on. Which, it now seems, will undoubtedly lead to more speaking engagements and opportunities to teach, perhaps not even in the more traditional sense. Even the development of my current website, with opportunities galore for teaching and learning from the participants, has come from that single notice to stop spinning my wheels. Now that I have moved ahead, those front wheels on my automobile also have stopped spinning.

"Not convinced yet? Okay, here's another story about my friend the automobile. This time I was heading down Route 21 between Berryville and US 40, east to Little Rock. As I got into the car that day, I knew without question that my Life had become way too complex. I had taken on responsibilities that took

me away from my primary purpose of teaching—teaching in a broader definition than I have formerly understood—but teaching, nevertheless. It wasn't
this new way of looking at teaching that was troubling me, however. It was the
complexity of my Life that had become troublesome. So, herein lies the real
point of this story.

"As I headed down route 21, along the magnificently beautiful journey it is,
I began to notice that every time I applied the brakes a light would correspond-
ingly flash on my dashboard. 'Oh, oh,' I recall muttering, 'I hope my electrical
system isn't awry.' As I said these words, I could metaphorically relate that I
was feeling burned out, as though my own electronics were malfunctioning.
But I dismissed this out of hand as being too silly to take seriously. Then, as we
often do, I began to try figuring it all out intellectually but only further frus-
trated clarity by doing so. So, yet again, I let go of it, turning it over to the gods
of INspiration and INsight. Just as I let go of it, and turned it over to my Muse,
sure enough here came INspiration and INsight. As always is the case, all I had
to do was show up. The door to INsight and eventual Enlightenment had
always been open. But I had given myself to, placed my faith in, the intellectual
pursuit, instead. Now having arrived at the proper threshold, however, here
Truth showed its face yet again.

"This time the still small voice of Truth spoke thus: (I'd be willing to bet you
could utter the sentence for me.) 'When you take time to slow down, you will
be enlightened.' I laughed so uproariously that I must have awakened the cows
along the roadside from their midmorning naps. Giving full credence to this
admonition I indeed did slow down, both the speed of my automobile and the
pace at which my mind had been running. For the next two and a half hours I
let Enlightenment inform me in abundance. The depth and breadth of clarity
was extraordinary, and clear as the ringing of the Liberty Bell.

"The long and short of this story is that once I had seen the erroneous perspective I had placed my Life in, I made what had heretofore seemed like
immovable mountains vanish before my very eyes. I released all the self-
imposed ties that had held me hostage to everything but my main purpose.
Then I was free to act out of the single-mindedness of divinity once again. And
here I am, just to prove it.

"As a quick aside, to reinforce the beauty of affirmations that show up to
provide evidence of the rightness of decisions made, I'll confess a brief conversation with one of my sons that took place right after this incident with my car
had transpired. He had been smitten with a woman friend who lived hours
away from him, so their relationship between visits consisted mainly of e-mails

and phone calls. Every time I spoke with him he was absolutely high on her. Then, one day, I was speaking with him and out of nowhere he blurts out, 'Did I tell you about breaking up with my friend?' I allowed that he had not told me and asked what had happened. It appeared sudden.

"He went on to explain that their contact initially had been once or twice a week and that this level had been just about right. Then it began to become more frequent, and then even more frequent, until he just couldn't get any of his own Life's work done at all. 'That's why I shaved my head, Dad,' he concluded his explanation. 'Wait a minute,' I rejoined, 'did you shave your head because you broke up with her, or because she called too often? Which one?' 'Neither,' he said, 'I shaved my head because my hair was getting too much attention.' In that moment the decision I had made earlier that very same week took on the nature of absolute Truth for me. As an aftermath, my son and I not only have an interesting story to share, but also have a code phrase for: 'simplify, simplify, and simplify even more.'

"I said earlier, while speaking about the marvelously simple process Jesus outlined for us, that once you give yourself to the process, ways in which we thought as a child would begin to simply melt away—as long, that is, as we stay in our divinity and operate from that. Let me show you what this means with an even simpler story about a gift that simply showed up one day. Not too long ago I was giving myself over to the writing that must be allowed to come through me, and I found myself in a space of great appreciation for the character that was developing as the story was progressing. His personality was tickling my fancy, so outrageously was he behaving at a particular moment. In fact, I was so enjoying him that I began to laugh out loud at his last move. The more I thought about how this hilarious event showed up through my fingers, the more I laughed—and laughed—and laughed even more.

"Tears were streaming down my cheeks, I was enjoying it so. Right smack in the middle of all that hilarity I began to feel immense joy from a different place, and of a different kind. Not laughter, but joy aligned with the celebration of a past relationship. To cut to the quick here, when I was around nine-years old, I seem to recall, my father's business partner died after a prolonged battle with cancer. I had not seen him since he went into the Veteran's Hospital in Buffalo. One night my parents announced that Dan had died. Period. That's it. In a few days, they suggested that I go to the wake and funeral services. Even then, as a youngster, I wanted only to remember him as I last saw him: with a smile—albeit a weak one—adorning his face; and prominently displaying the generosity of Spirit that intentioned his behavior, despite his pain.

"What I'm sharing with you now is not what came up at this particular moment as hilarity. No. What emerged from behind the curtain was my grief over not having had the opportunity of saying my good-byes with Dan. At that very instant, I was given the extraordinary opportunity of telling Dan how much I Loved him. And how much I appreciated him always for his display of respect for my dignity, and for his simple, but profound, ways of teaching me about the greater good. He was much like my father in this regard. That is the European way. At least it is the way I have come to know, learned from my immigrant father and his European immigrant friend and partner, Dan, who were like brothers.

"Yes, in the moment of extraordinary joy, all the tension that had held that childhood thought of unresolved grief and expression of gratitude and appreciation in place dissolved, setting it free. It happened in but a nanosecond, and with little effort from me at all. All I had to do was to not be afraid to acknowledge it, which is the key to setting it free. In the wake of its release, I sobbed and sobbed and sobbed. Tears are such a marvelous way of celebration, of washing away the tension and related emotions that bind us to the past. The veil, by something akin to a counterpoint, had been parted and I returned to the divinity of my relationship with Dan. The hard nutlike surface that had formed around his death—and my unresolved grief—had been cracked open. A new, beautiful, sturdy oak tree was growing instantly in its place. You see, if we would only allow divinity to be what it is—in all its power to enlighten—transcendence is sure to follow. If this has not yet happened with you, be assured that with adherence to your gift of virgin birth, your divinity will carry you there from time to time.

"I'd like to shift gears now and ask you to consider yet another application of the metaphorical/metaphysical configuration. You will recall from out last major session together that I dealt somewhat with the relationship between our divinity and our personal health. Just to reinforce this understanding, I'll now share just one story about the process of using one's ailments as metaphors for one's spiritual placement in everyday Life. During a conversation with a friend, he divulged what appeared to him and his doctor to be a somewhat serious stomach ailment. Apparently he had been troubled by it for several years but just couldn't shake it loose. As a result he had some allergies, one of which was to milk products, which, to my INtuitive voice sounded like some kind of childhood perspective gone awry. 'It's more about missing the sweetness of the milk of human kindness,' I could hear it said within.

"As I listened to him talk about it, I began to discern considerable emotion-ality within his claim of stomach troubles. I'm not speaking here of simply being emotional about his claim of sickness. Rather, I'm speaking here of an underlying emotionality that was speaking volumes on another level. I wasn't made privy to its contents, I felt, because this was his to come to understand. Several times, however, I heard the small quiet voice speak within, and I asked my friend: 'What is it emotionally that you cannot stomach?' I felt foolish say-ing this out of the blue, but I also have come to know that it is up to me only to deliver the information and then let it go, so as to not take responsibility for what one does with that information. Handling it this way allows me to con-tinue seeing the one receiving it only as the divine perfection he or she is. Thus I need not accept the appearance of the claim as the truth of the matter at all.

"My friend paused for a bit. So long was his pause on the phone that I thought for a moment that he'd hung up. 'Are you still there?' I asked. 'Yes,' he responded. 'I'm just thinking about your comment. I'm not coming up with anything right now, but I have a session with my holographic repatterning practitioner this week. Maybe something will show its face then.' We changed the conversation to another topic and then moved on with our respective lives.

"A week or so later my friend called and said, 'Well, you were right. There was something I wasn't able to stomach. I learned in my session this week that I had taken responsibility for my mother's death when I was but a youngster, and that is something I can't stomach any longer. Wow,' he said, 'is that a big one or not?' 'I'll say that's a big one,' I responded, 'and you'll probably feel a lot better soon.' 'I do already,' he said. "But something told me that he was wasn't completely through it yet. Let's do a fast forward now," Christo says to the gathering.

"Sorry to belabor this, but there is a discerning point here, several in fact. One is that I can do only so much with my ears, only so much can I do by sim-ply listening and reporting. The other person must do the real work, the work we are called to do when we recall the expression: 'God helps those who help themselves—by going within for help.' We do this work, going within to God for help. My INtuition had come forth in this case to suggest some other take, some other perspective on his 'dis-ease' within himself, the feeling of dishar-mony within him. My INtuition also was telling me in the last conversation with him that he wasn't quite finished with it yet. This prompt had come merely through my listening to the energy he was letting off beneath the words.

"Anyhow, later my friend called back to let me know he was much better now. He was still being very careful with what he was putting into his stomach and had decided to finish his medication. His doctor had told him to take it for two more weeks, and then he'd start to feel better. Here it came. My INtuition, reared its head again, full-brunt this time. Of course you all know that if the label on a bottle of medication says to take it for three weeks, that means to the one who believes it that they are guaranteed to feel lousy for up to three more weeks. It's a sure bet.

'Well,' I say, 'if you're already healed on the most important level, the cure is sure to follow almost immediately. I'm to tell you that there's some reason you're still holding on to this, or you wouldn't still be taking your medicine and being overly cautious with your eating pattern.' He started to protest my suggestion, but then remembered to check within for information from his guides, as he calls them. He's really good at that. Calling his INtuition by the name 'guides' doesn't change the validity of the information any, so why not use the guides for the Truth they bring? 'Yes, they say I should check further in my next session with the practitioner, so I'll follow that,' he concluded.

"A couple weeks more went by. Then he calls back, starting the conversation not with a hello, but instead with, 'Well, I'm done with it! Have time for the story?' he asked. 'Sure, shoot,' I said. 'What I found out last week is that I had taken on the responsibility not only for my mother's death, but my father's, too. I was not only despondent over that, but feeling mighty lonely without them. I just couldn't stomach this loneliness any longer, so I had to get help with it. And did I ever get help. I sobbed and sobbed and sobbed and sobbed, until all that came out of me. I feel so free from all the tension I had held around all that now! What a miracle this is!' he exclaimed. 'I still would have been sick if I hadn't followed up on the suggestion that this was something else other than a medical problem. I wouldn't have accepted the suggestion that the outward manifestation contained the symbolic meaning of what was going on within me before this but I sure do now!' he proclaimed with conviction.

"There's no reason to continue this story, except to say that he has safely returned to his divinity now, and has discontinued giving it any more thought. For him, the rest is now nothing but a detail. Can you just imagine, parting the over-50-year veil of self-deceit so he could once again see his divinity?

"Now, to a short version of another. A few weeks ago I had lunch with a friend who was having major difficulty making a decision about something in his Life. During lunch he was struck by the drastic action I had taken so I could concentrate on my Life's work instead of being distracted by unnecessary details. He confessed that he needed to do the same kind of thing, but wasn't quite sure yet of what his real purpose was. After a fashion it occurred to him that his purpose would show up if he just cleared out the major distractions in his Life. The drive for creation needs space in order to both show its face and to flourish, and he had finally seen this in a flash of insight. Let's fast forward again.

"The other day I saw him at an art opening and he was complaining bitterly to a mutual friend about his hip hurting badly. There was some slightly off-color kidding about it, as men are likely to do, and then my mouth opened and out came this: 'You don't suppose that it's just too painful for you to move ahead, do you?' I asked. He looked at me utterly astonished. 'That's exactly it,' he confessed, without a moment's hesitation.' I'm terribly afraid to make the decision that will free me. It's just so painful to think about it,' he reflected.

"'Ah,' I said, 'so it's the thought and not the act itself that's so painful to you.' I let that just hang there. After a bit he said, 'What do you mean by that?' 'Well,' I continued, 'you just said that it was just too painful to think about freeing yourself from the burden that has kept you from moving forward. That's quite an admission. If this is indeed true, then all you have to do is change the thought. Can you think of some way to reframe how you're thinking about this that will make it less painful? Like that this decision will free you up for being yourself once again, so you can do your Life's work and be engaged with what really nourishes your Soul? Need I say more?' 'No,' he responded hesitatingly, 'I can see the Truth of such perspectives. I'll just have to sit with it for awhile. This has been extremely helpful. I can feel my Spirit lifting some already. Thanks.'

"Well, we parted company, and I have yet to hear from him. I did send him a brief note of encouragement following our brief chat. And I included a quote from *Catch 22*: 'There is no established procedure for evasive action. All you need is fear.' Like all of us, my friend just needs a reminder from time to time that fear is what holds us back. I have a strong sense that he's well on his way now.

"In each of these cases, INtuition led to parting the veil of illusion so the Truth of divinity could return. In each case, metaphor was the representative of the real culprit: an inappropriate—no, the false—cause of the matter. But what a gift that metaphor was in each instance. In each instance metaphor had waived the flag of discontent so its owner could go within and clear away its effects. In each instance, the one troubled was returned to his or her own divinity once again. The cured had returned home—or should I say that the cure *was* home?

"Well, now you have several simple examples of the deeper meaning of metaphor coming to rest on the concerns that trouble. And of how the troublesome concerns can be cleared up with the gifts of INsight and Enlightenment. The final result, as always, of course, is transcending the old with the new, and we are returned to our Life of divinity in the process. How wonderful this gift of Life is to us! When we use it for this Loving intention then this is so.

"Just remember that whatever we take in as Truth for us has a significant impact on our body's health. Healthy thought manifests as a healthy body. Beginning rightly ends rightly. As Deepak Chopra so wisely reminds us: 'Every cell in your body is eavesdropping on your thoughts.' What a piercing reminder of simple Truth this is.

"With this as the foundation for our deliberations, I would like to turn you loose on ferreting out any stories similar to the ones I have just shared with you. I am convinced that each of you has used your considerable intuition to steer yourself to INspiration, INsight and Enlightenment, but perhaps without even knowing it, so unconsciously do most of us pass through Life. Or perhaps it's because you simply have lacked this convenient vocabulary to speak about it, either to yourself or with another whom you can trust.

"We're going to take about half an hour now, during which time I'd like you to scan Life in order to find even one example of when you were awakened to some Truth about your Life that led you to make considerable change for the better. Just one will do. Then turn to either side of you and exchange this story with your neighbor. Be not afraid to do so. We're all family now, are we not, so what's not to share? I'll stroll hither, thither, and yon during this time in order to make myself available to you for any purpose whatsoever. My assistants will also be readily available to you during this time.

"My main purpose in this brief exercise is to let you know that you have already been using this process, but mostly unconsciously. Now I want you to develop your confidence to the point where you'll use it more and more consciously. Another purpose, of course, is to provide you opportunity after opportunity to hone your skills of discernment. Now let's get to it.

Christo watches from the podium as people go inward to seek clarification. In just a few minutes people are already sharing stories, so Christo gives a sign to his assistants to make themselves available. He then joins them among the gathering. He is fully confident that the participants are growing immeasurably in their ability to discern such things consciously. This pleases him beyond words.

What transpires is deeply inspiring to all. Christo and his aides are amazed by the high degree of trust and confidence people are placing in one another. Sharing is occurring at deep and profound levels. It is obvious to everyone that the participants are grasping with aplomb the metaphorical ties to inharmonious coping. The enthusiasm that exudes from them as they share their stories rings out loud and clear. As they disperse throughout the gathering, Christo and his aides are hearing marvelous connections being made. Calls for clarity and the use of wonderment as a key to unlock the door of awe-inspiring Truth abound. The participants have learned their lessons well.

From one couple Christo and his aides hear phrases declaring the pain in hips and legs related to the fear of moving forward. From another, the pain in one's buttocks related to her attitude toward her spouse. From still another, that diabetes relates to the view that one has lost the meaning of natural sweetness in Life. From another couple comes the link cast between failing eyesight and the failure, or the fear, of seeing the real meaning of certain portions of Life clearly. They go even so far as to link farsightedness with being a visionary and nearsightedness to being more introspective and practical. One speaks of arteriosclerosis, hardening of the arteries, as stemming from being hard headed or narrow-minded. Another attributes the meaning of a stiff neck to one who is being stiff-necked about one's view in juxtaposition with that of another close to them. Still another speaks about multiple sclerosis as referring to the hardening of views about many aspects of a loved one's Life. Some are daring to go even beyond this phase and are discussing the bodily posture which emanates from various thought forms, as when, for example, the one with stooped shoulders seems to be carrying the weight of the world on his back. The range and scope of variation is fascinating, to say the least.

From some there are stories of people coming to the realization that their own physical ailments are really not that at all, but rather symbolic representations of mental outlook. The gathering is beginning to resemble what those who sat at Jesus's feet must have looked and felt like as they opened to their own divinity on the other side of pain expressed from some kind of fear. It is a marvel to behold. On it goes. Christo lets the activity continue for the full thirty minutes he had allowed, and he then returns to the podium to call their attention to what he has seen transpire.

"Ladies and gentlemen let me ask that you complete your immediate statement for now. You can finish whatever else needs completion during our refreshment break. What you have just demonstrated is quite miraculous. I say miraculous simply because of the fact that you certainly would not have allowed yourselves to do this at the beginning of our time together a few short months ago, perhaps not even when we began today. But miracles like this can be everyday experiences if you will just give yourselves over to being present to one another for such explorations. Of course, making ourselves fully present to one another while at the same time removing prior restrictions on our perspectives on various aspects of Life releases us from the bonds of the past or future—neither of which are real, as we have learned.

"When we are in the present for one another, we really are fully open to our Muse's guidance, are we not? When devoted to focused presence, we are placing ourselves in the lap of INsight and Enlightenment and at the parting of the veils that lead us back to our divinity. I have just witnessed you doing that with great delight! I applaud your willingness to do so with aplomb. The pace at which you are growing in confidence of your divinity is indeed amazing.

"All of this could not be more affirmed than by a message from a friend on his holiday card a few years ago. It went something like this: 'Why wallow in the past? I am not the God of I WAS. Why be concerned with the future? I am not the God of I WILL BE. Be with me in the present, for I am the God of only THE PRESENT. I am THAT, I AM.' And so are all of us the very same: THAT. And we come to *really know* 'that' in the Oneness we find ourselves in when committed to Loving presence.

"You heard me say earlier today that I can heal only so much with my ears. We have come to understand, have we not, that merely by providing a safe haven where others can open to themselves is a saintly act? That it is when we additionally serve as a mirror to reflect one's own understanding back to them that INspiration, INsight and Enlightenment can be engaged? That the cycle is complete when one has learned to be with that same still small voice within without someone else around? Yes, of course. We have learned that.

"Before we move on to the next levels of competence, I want to take just a moment to drink in the deeper meaning of being there for someone—a meaning I'm convinced even those who feel it would have a difficult time putting into words. You have heard this particular poem before, but not at the level of understanding at which you now reside. The piece has a simple title, *LIFE*, and it goes like this." Christo proceeds to read the poetic verse very much as one would speak to another with whom he has the most intimate relationship. While doing so he connects in this same intimate manner with each of those present. His tone is reverent, respectful, and sensitively compassionate, in a word: elegant.

Life

come, sit with me
let yourself simply be
plunge, if you will, to the depths of your grief
loosen the slipknot
on your weary body and ravaged soul
freeing your burdens
your anger and your pain
whatever it is that discomforts you
whatever it is that you feel

come, sit with me
open to the joy that is you
letting laughter's release unfold your Truth
allowing yourself to bask in my Love for you
caressing your mind, your body, and your soul.
bathe in the Light of transformation
knowing that all you have to be
is you
and that I'm always here for you

come, sit with me
travel with me through the universe
be open in your silence
be mindless in your solitude
resting your thoughts and feelings here beside me
fully present in this art of relationship
and you will come to know
yet again
that we are One

come, sit with me
no matter what the condition or circumstance
no matter what our past
it is safe now.
in Eternal Friendship
this presence is all that matters.
all we must do is be what we both are

and these precious moments become our Truth
and authentic Love our bond.

Christo pauses just long enough to allow the fullness of bliss that savoring such a relationship provides. The connection between the gathering and Christo is indeed this precious and ever so meaningful. Ever so gently, he begins once again: "What is it that brings us to this seat of dignity, this place of trust, so fully? Is it the simple invitation that disarms us from the fear of disclosure? Is it the fullness of hope brought to the nature of pain and need? Is it the depth of compassionate commitment that beckons one to the seat of one's own meaning?

"I certainly cannot speak for anyone other than myself, and even this takes some doing, so deep is the relationship within, so profound its impact, so filled with the meaning of Life is its character. The true character of meaning can only come, it seems to me, as we come to know another as we know ourselves. The paradox is that we come to know ourselves only to the degree that we open to another.

"True interdependence is thus born. Not codependence, but the Truth of interdependence that makes the sharing of our individual completeness as divine beings possible. This, my friends, is divinity personified in all. It is what makes Oneness what it so delightfully and sacredly just is: Life. Thus, the First cause of divinity allows transcendence beyond the old ways of separation—and the inevitable pain that separation perpetrates and perpetuates onto our society. Now we are able to land and reside in the blissful state of authentic Love lavished on all of Life.

"Well, seeing where you have allowed yourselves to go in such a short time has taken me to a very special place: to the place where bliss infills. I am grateful for this brief display that is but a single example of what Life can be on an increasingly regular basis. For me, this came about primarily because I was so inspired by the depths to which you have made in a very real and profound way the ultimate connection between the spiritual and the material worlds.

"Let me ask this: How many of you feel that you have a grasp on the link between the metaphor and the meaning of Life? Raise your hand if you do." Just as Christo thought, the show of hands indicates their relative comfort with it. "Good," he continues, "this will be a solid foundation for our work together in the next session after the break. At that time we'll take a brief look at some of the parables, just to reinforce what by now must be clear to you: that the metaphysical tool of metaphor is indeed that which informs at the deeper levels of meaning for us. This link between the metaphorical meaning of scripture and our daily living can now lead us to some very helpful understandings beyond the literal. Let's take a twenty-minute break for some refreshment. Addio."

CHAPTER 8

Untying the Knots That Bind Us

Christo feels well rested, despite the fact that he has been continuously committed to service of the entire gathering before him for several hours already. From his teaching forums he has learned well that being totally present in any setting is refreshing on the most important level: spiritually. In addition, having learned that taking more frequent breaks for physical nourishment and for couching within for spiritual replenishing—even if only for twenty minutes or so—he is ready to go again at the drop of a hat. Upon "waking" from his brief meditation, Christo can sense the collective energy of the crowd compelling him to return. The hat has indeed dropped, so it seems. Christo warms at the thought. The warmth works its way up to his face in the form of a generous smile as he poetically parts the curtains once again and heads back to the podium.

"Namaste," Christo faces the participants, bowing in every direction with folded hands punctuating the sacred greeting he knows to be the Truth. Again, before he can utter a word, the crowd returns his greeting, this time with even more warmth, if that were possible. "Namaste, Christo. Namaste," flows this treasured greeting, now ever-so-freely given, so deep in its authenticity. Christo feels the subtle change in its power coming from the gathering. "Thank you, my dear ones," Christo begins. "I hope you can feel what I am feeling. I am feeling the extraordinary power of authenticity and the deep intention of Love unabashedly expressed. Do you feel its power surging throughout this entire space we're occupying?" Although his question was initiated only as a rhetorical one, the answer is as clear as though he had asked for a show of hands. The gestures of hands on hearts, smiles on nodding faces, and affirming glances from one to another render the thought of floating a survey query seem redundant.

"Ahhh," Christo breathes, "such a marvelous place you have allowed yourselves to progress to in such a short time. Now you are seeing what intention and conviction placed in a particular direction can do in the spiritual world. Just know that you can do and feel this on your very own every moment of every day, simply by giving yourself to it. Yes, Mecca is found by making sure every step is in that direction. You are doing precisely that now. Congratulations to one and all!

"By now, are you beginning to feel the difference between force and power in bringing your divinity into play with Life?" A puzzled look collects on their faces in response. "The difference between force and power?" they seem to be asking. "Yes, I asked about the difference between using force and power in parting the veils of illusion so we can return most naturally to our divinity once again. This is a most important distinction to make," Christo continues. "David Hawkins, in his stunning piece called *Power Vs. Force*, says it much better than I can, so I'll quote him at some length here." Christo begins the distinction made between force and power with great reverence for the Truth therein. He reads his reference to Hawkins' work slowly, punctuating with emphasis where necessary, even repeating for special affect when he feels it's appropriate.

> 'On examination, we'll see that power arises from *meaning*. It has to do with motive, and it has to do with principle. Power is always associated with that which supports the significance of Life itself. It appeals to that part of human nature that we call *noble*—in contrast to force, which appeals to that which we call *crass*. Power appeals to what uplifts, dignifies, and ennobles.

> Force must always be justified, whereas power requires no justification. Force is associated with the partial, power with the whole. Force always moves against something, whereas power doesn't move against anything at all. Force is incomplete and therefore has to be fed energy constantly. Power is total and complete in and of itself and requires nothing from outside. It makes no demands; it has no needs. Because force has an insatiable appetite, it constantly consumes. Power, in contrast, energizes, gives forth, supplies, and supports. Power gives Life and energy—force takes these away. We notice that power is associated with compassion and makes us feel positively about ourselves. Force is associated with judgment and makes us feel poorly about ourselves. Force always creates counter force; its effect is to polarize rather than unify.

Polarization always implies conflict; its cost, therefore, is always high. Because force incites polarization, it inevitably produces a win/lose dichotomy; and because somebody always loses, enemies are created. Constantly faced with enemies, force requires constant defense. Defensiveness is invariably costly, whether in the marketplace, politics or international affairs.

In looking for the source of power, we've noted that it's associated with meaning, and this meaning has to do with the significance itself. Force is concrete, literal, and arguable. It requires proof and support. The sources of power, however, are inarguable and aren't subject to proof. The self-evident isn't arguable. That health is more important than disease, that Life is more important than death, that honor is preferable to dishonor, that faith and trust are preferable to doubt and cynicism, that the constructive is preferable to the destructive—all are self-evident statements not subject to proof. Ultimately, the only thing we can say about a source of power is that it just "is." (Pp. 132-133)

Christo pauses at the end of this citation and lets the implications of the juxtaposition set in. Finally, he speaks the Truth so many are already thinking: "How many of you began to substitute the word ego or unconsciousness, or even literalism, for the word force before too long?" As he suspects, most raise their hands. "And how many," he continues to pursue the obvious, "how many of you rather automatically substituted the word consciousness, Truth, or divinity—or even metaphor—for the word power?" This time almost all acknowledge their act in this regard. "Well, there you have it. In just a few minutes we have a summary of what we've been speaking to for our entire two sessions together.

"Force, or our old perspective on ego, if you prefer, appeals to something we call crass. It is incomplete and feeds off our energy constantly. Ego regularly consumes, draining our Life force just as constantly. Force is associated with judgment and makes us feel poorly about ourselves. And power, Truth, or divinity—what about these sources? Divinity has to do with meaning, motive, and principle. It ennobles, appeals to what uplifts, dignifies. Divinity is total and complete in itself, and requires nothing outside of itself. What a marvelous affirmation of the two paths we have to choose from for the eternity of Life's journey.

"It is clear as a bell, is it not, that if we go the way of force, the external authority we have been worshipping all this time, that destruction is on the way? Isn't it equally clear that if we choose the way of power, we are headed for an effortless affirmation of our divinity at every turn? In the final analysis, is there really any choice at all once we see these two options placed so clearly before us? I see none. One is illusion, and thus unavailable for choice to strike its pose. The other is the only spiritual reality, and thus renders the illusion nonexistent. What's the answer then? Make sure every step you take is in that direction.

Christo pauses for an internal reality check and resonates with what flows next from him: "We can call divinity, or Truth, or power 'the conscious principle that guides our action towards dignity and the noble.' Principle is tantamount to beginning rightly so we can end rightly. What we're talking about here is the underlying invisible principle within by which we manifest Life visibly without. If we commit to living this way, we are exercising the power that emanates within to ennoble our world without. What could be more True—and rewarding—than this? What more need our purpose be? I can tell by your energy that you have ingested this lesson very well. All you need do with it at this point is to let it assimilate completely. We'll give it some space so it can do exactly that.

"I'd now like to shift things a little so you can—rather effortlessly, I might add—come to see this principle of Life impersonally. This will provide the space for the fullness of Insight and Enlightenment to take hold. This is tantamount, in essence, to letting go and letting God. When we give something no more thought, we give it space to do what it must. It must either leave us completely, which is not our intention, or it must find its way to transcendence, which is our spiritual intention. For spiritual intention to be fulfilled, it needs room to percolate. Just like hot water poured into our coffee pot, it needs space, room—and in the case of the coffee, time—in order for it to seep deeper and deeper into our world of meaning. In the case of good, rich coffee, eventually, with just perfect timing, the full-bodied flavor reaches its peak. Metaphorically speaking, we are no different. Having been etched indelibly on heart's lining so it can serve as our guiding principle, the spiritual intention eventually—with perfect timing—reaches the depths within our heart, so we can etch this same rich meaning as the texture for all of Life. So we can live from that same sacred meaning no matter what strikes us, no matter what comes into our journey.

"As a means of expanding our understanding of this principle, let's focus, then, on some holy writ, so to speak. So many of us get our underwear all tied up in knots over the real meaning of scripture and the parables Jesus used so well. However, the only real problem is that virtually no one has taught us to read scripture as Jesus admonished us to do. 'God is about spiritual Life,' Jesus said, 'and it is therefore in the eye of spirit that we must learn of God.'

"The Gospel according to John begins with the Truth for all to embrace:

> In the beginning was the Word:
> the Word was with God
> and the Word was God.
> He was with God in the beginning.
> Through him all things came into being,
> not one thing came into being except through him.
> What has come into being in him was Life,
> Life that was the light of men;
> and light shines in darkness,
> and darkness could not overpower it.

"Using the tongue of metaphor to mediate this glorious initiation into the Truth of metaphysics, let me restate John's marvelous depiction of Life as we actually live it. The beginning of anything new is the Word: a symbol that depicts meaning, a divine idea that is a metaphor expressed. This Word is with and of God: the Word of Truth. This is what makes it divine. It therefore is Godly or divinely right from the beginning. It is only through the First cause of divine idea that all things come into being. This is beginning rightly. Divine idea is the newborn Christ child who continually is reborn from within. Without divine idea nothing is demonstrable. Divine idea, the Truth that emanates from us, is, therefore, omniscience expressed. The 'Him' of whom John speaks is 'Truth' that sits at the seat of our divinity. It is Truth that occupies the throne in the kingdom of Heaven.

"Demonstration comes about only by beginning with divine idea and committing to the Truth of it for us until it comes to fruition. Without divine idea there is nothing present with which to begin anything, let alone with which to accomplish something. This is the spiritual Law of Creation. What has come into being through the manifestation of idea is the fullness of expression of how we see Life, and therefore, how we live it on every plane of our existence. It is this Life that comes forth out of the way we continually see Life: out of INsight that gives way to the light called Enlightenment. Enlightenment is that to which darkness gives way—always. This is omni-action personified. Nothing can stop Enlightenment from showing its way into the universe as transcendence. Nothing is more powerful than Enlightenment. It has the power to move mountains of illusion. This entire process associated with the Creation Spirit is the omnipotence that conquers all.

"Here in the marvelous initial stanza of John's 'Prologue' is the design for Life as we have been speaking about it all along. If people would begin with a translation of John's explanation akin to the metaphorical explanation I just expressed, what might our lives look like from now on? In a word—yes, you have it—Life would be *divine*! In fact, according even to John, it would be divine, God. Wouldn't Life be so much simpler if we lived it this way—if we lived this meaning consciously all throughout our existence? You bet it would be!

"At this stage of our development we have come to understand that the world of the Christ Spirit is the metaphorical or symbolic Word that gives the deeper meaning of Truth." Christo departs from the world of spoken words momentarily, ever so briefly—but deeply nonetheless, and the gathering makes the instant connection that another seemingly 'unseemly something' is about to come from his mouth, his body language being that readable to them by now. It so amusing that a tittering of laughter is released from one corner of the arena, and then from another—and yet another—until the entire crowd is in a state of dramatic laughter.

"Okay, you caught me again!" Christo awakens to the comedic proportions of enlightened INsight's portrayal on the stage of human Life. "Yes, you caught me, so I might as well fess up to it. Ready for another shoe?" he laughs. "GO FOR IT!" the crowd rings out in response. An extraordinary sense of camaraderie has developed in this very special setting, which is a tribute to one and all. Christo laughingly begins in response: "As crazy as this may sound to you—well, not really—or at least not now, anyhow. As I was saying, what I want to pose to you is that most of us have divided our world out of our natural human configuration of dichotomy, of duality. As you understand so well by now, we have divided our world into the haves and the have-nots. Into the larger and the smaller. The greater and the less than. The taller and the shorter. The darker and the lighter. The gay and the straight. Finally, we are divided into the self-righteous and the simply righteous—on and on and on, yet again. Such diversionary tactics never cease as long as we live in a literal, linear, forceful world of duality that separates one from the other. It is the world of duality that separates everyone from every other, as well as every thing from every other thing. This is a world that forever guarantees the pain that separation engenders. It is a world that also forever guarantees the behavior exemplified by the phrase 'the ends justify the means.'

"Instead, we can have a world where the means validate the ends, the ends of Loving lavishly. Living in such a world, as you now understand, means that we must begin with a different premise, a new principle. When we begin rightly, from a perspective of Oneness—rather than one of separation or duality—we must end rightly. When we begin rightly, with Oneness, it follows that every image must contain fidelity to Oneness, and nothing contrary to Oneness. We are learning in our work together that Oneness can be a marvelous journey in the spiritual world, in the world of ideas and thought. We are also learning that as we think, so shall our lives be. We are learning yet again that Life regularly brings us symbolic meaning which informs us of spiritual Truth. Yes, Life is abundantly rich with such treasures that inform and enlighten, and transform our lives. All of which leads to transcendence beyond the past into the Truth of our present Life as divine spiritual beings.

"We also know that in order to grow from such information we must learn to read the symbols correctly—at least as they apply to our own spiritual lives. It would be entirely inappropriate and erroneous to think that meaning unique to one is so easily generalizable to another. The nature of certain feelings felt deeply can be, I think, widely and commonly understood. On the other hand, while a Truth may in general apply to all of Life, it may not apply particularly from one to another. Meaning must come from that which resonates uniquely in each of us. Anyhow, the shoe I want to allow to drop now is this. It took me long enough to get there, didn't it?" Christo catches himself, jokingly. "Well, I just wanted to add some spice to it. A little drama never hurts to punctuate meaning," he continues.

"Ready? Here it comes," he playfully stretches out the delivery. "Okay, let's see how smart you've become by now. What do we call those images we are learning to read from our Life of sleep? Well, what do we call them?" he teases from them. 'DREAMS!' the gathering returns equally as playfully.

"Yes, DREAMS!" Christo reinforces with a glint in his eye. "DREAMS! Dreams are what we call those images we recall from Life behind the closed shades of our eyelids. Now, smarty pants, let's see if you can get the next answer right. What do we call those images we see when our eyelids are open?" There is a pause, which informs Christo that uniform understanding is lacking. "Okay," he says coaching, "here's a hint. When we are awake and things happen to us, or we happily or not so happily go on our way, what do we call this part of our lives? We call this Life outside of our dream state what exactly?"

Christo sees the lights begin to come on behind their eyes, and gives the assembly time to gather collective consciousness around this simple term. "All right, then, we call those images…" Christo says leaning out toward the crowd with hand cupped behind his ear mimicking one who can't quite hear another. "We call this Life when we are awake what?" Seemingly like an avalanche of snow appearing out of nowhere, the crowd bellows in unison: 'REALITY!'

"Exactly!" Christo returns. "REALITY! Exactly, REALITY…EXACTLY INCORRECT!" he follows with an oral punch. The participants are momentarily stunned by his forceful declaration. 'What? Have you gone mad?' they seem to be saying. "No, I haven't gone mad, no matter what the appearance may be," Christo jokes. "What is mad is that we dichotomize. We dualize, if I may turn that noun 'duality' into a verb. We dualize even this aspect of our lives. Let's back up and reframe how we look at such images, these wonderful symbolic gifts.

"Let me complicate, or at the very least, confuse, things a bit further so clarity can scream out at us for the Truth of the matter. Here you sit before me, clearly awake, with your eyes wide open. Now, close your eyes for a moment. Bring into view a loved one you'd like to have very close to you right now. Bring that person clearly into your mind's eye. *Feel* your feelings of abiding Love for this person. Got it locked in?" Christo guides them. He reads the comfort of the crowd as having settled in with these Loving images. "Now," he continues, "look at your loved one directly in the eyes, and tell them you Love them. You always have and always will. Feel their response, even without them saying anything. Hold these feelings right there. Now answer this question for me. Actually, answer it just for yourself. You are awake, are you not? So this vision you have been enjoying must be reality. Is that, too, correct? Or is what you're feeling nothing more than the conscious creation of imagery that you are bringing to Life? Just a few moments ago, before we began this exercise, you may have felt bewildered, or weary, or enthusiastic. Yet all that changed into other feelings as you took yourself to another place—and you changed your perspective, even if for only a few moments. This what is meant by each of us having the responsibility for creating our Life. In this case, we did it consciously. Most of the time we go through Life unconsciously and blame others for what Life brings us.

"All of what comes to us simply comes as imagery, whether we are asleep or awake, whether we are conscious or unconscious about it. The one thing we know for sure about it is that all of it is nothing more, or less, than symbols awaiting our mediation, our translation. So dream state or not, it's all the very same: food for thought. It is manna from heaven, the meat this world knows not of. Unfortunately most of us have been asleep to this vast Kingdom of

Heaven—this Kingdom of thought—that is here to serve us in our spiritual presence.

"But we're smarter than that now. Let's see how big we can make our Life of Oneness. If we are learning to use Life—this so-called reality—to inform us metaphorically about our spiritual state of being, how is it we want to make reading it different from the way we would read our so-called dream Life? Symbols are symbols, no matter where we find them. Is that not correct?" Christo waits for affirming nods, which come instantaneously, informing him that the gathering is still with him on this adventure to *real* reality. "All right, then. If all of Life, *no matter where we find Life—inside or outside of our eyelids*—affords us the symbolic presence of Truth within, how is it we should make the sources of Truth appear to be different? Isn't the *real* source that still small voice within each of us—no matter what we're dealing with?

"So, to complete this scenario, then, what will we call *all* of this—all the sleeping dreams and all of our waking dreams—that feed us this sacred Word that heals, that enlightens, so we can be born again as a child? As I see it we can either make up a new term for it, or we can choose one of those two we normally use. If we set aside the opportunity to create a new term for this, we can choose to call it all—within the spirit of Oneness, remember—either 'dreams,' or 'reality.' This is a tough leap to make over the chasm of duality isn't it? So well trained are we to maintain duality. But that is not our Life's principle any longer. Not since we have come to understand Life as spiritual. We have crossed that precarious swinging bridge to the other side: to Oneness. Yet, until now, we have not felt its precarious nature. So domesticated have we been rendered in the unconscious way of coping with Life, instead of living it. Yes, now we have severed the ties to the swinging bridge that has been so precarious. We have let the bridge drop into the chasm that has separated us. To our delight, just like magic, the chasm closes behind us, leaving us treading solidly on the groundedness of spiritual Life throughout eternity.

"Ahah! You thought I forgot to hold you responsible for properly labeling the *common* space from which *the Word* comes, didn't you? No way, folks! Let's get the task clearly before us. No matter whether our eyelids are open or whether they are closed and masking the openness from us in the form of sleep, what is the space called from which symbols are afforded us? Regularly, in either our waking *or* sleeping Life what is that space called? I'll give you a hint: where does all of it come from? What's the common denominator? Think 'large' now. How big can you make it? This exercise in perspective is exactly identical to the one we used when determining how large we could make God.

Let go of it now. Don't intellectualize it. Intellectualizing is the process we use to grasp onto control over Life. Grasping has a choking quality to it. Open your intellectual grasp on Life's imagery—let go of it—and see what appears out of nowhere in its place. Let INsight reign now. Let INsight reign instead of intellectual grasping. Set yourself free once and for all," Christo chides.

He waits patiently, and he can feel the reins—and reigns—of control loosen.

At just the right moment, in perfect timing, he asks: "My dear divine ones, when I asked the question, I referred to waking and sleeping—what?" Instant Enlightenment strikes simultaneously throughout the gathering. Seizing on this acknowledgment, Christo shouts: "*WHAT*?" and shakes them to the right side of reality. "*WHAT*?" 'LIFE! LIFE! LIFE!' chants the crowd in stunning unison. "YES! LIFE! LIFE! LIFE! LIFE is the correct answer. We call this place 'Life.' Life. Life is the place from which we obtain meaning. The symbols we are fed, the Word for us, comes from Life itself. Each symbol is a gift of grace that informs. Which leads us to INsight. From which darkness gives way to Enlightenment. And Enlightenment takes us to Transcendence, where our Resurrection into a new world, a new body of thought, is complete. This is the new bed we have created. And sleep in it we must.

"*All* of it, whether we are awake or asleep behind those veils of illusion, the veils of duality constructed out of domesticated illusion, *all* of it is *Life*! It is *Life* that informs us—symbolically, metaphorically—of Truth for us. All of Life, no matter where we find it, either when asleep or awake, has but one purpose: to inform us, so we can live—consciously—from our Truth. All we need to do is to pay attention to, stay aware of, our role in translating, mediating if you will, the language of deeper meaning. By doing so we come to really live Life instead of barely even coping *with* Life as a task we have come to despair. Living, *really living*, then, becomes a continual celebration of meaning, by which we come to peace of mind and joy of heart. Bliss infills. We are home once again in our divinity.

"Let us put our fear of death behind us now that we understand that the spiritual world is about nothing but thought. Spirituality is not about physical Life, at all. Spirituality is about our Life of ideas, the First cause in creating what we have formerly called Life. What we really are creating is our state of mind. The condition of our thoughts, our state of mind—this and this alone—accounts for how we experience Life. Beginning rightly ends rightly. In this sense we are learning how to take responsibility for our lives: for how we experience Life and thus for all Life brings us.

"So, as conscious thinkers now, let us put the physical idea of death aside once and for all. Listen to yourself declare these Truths as I declare them. I can only take you to the threshold of meaning. I can describe and deliver. But only you can decipher for yourselves. Now, together, let's step across the threshold from mortality to immortality. Repeat after me, within the privacy of your own meaning: There is birth—of ideas. There is death—of ideas. But *LIFE*, my dear ones, goes on. Life is infinite in its domain. Life is infinite in its exposure to us. Life is infinite in its ability to deliver Truth to us. And Truth, being always the undeniable power

It is, is immortal in its character. It is Life that is omniscient; Life that is omnipotent; and Life that is omnipresent and omni-active. It is the Life of ideas; of thought and belief; the seat of Loving Creation, and the First cause. Life is the beginning rightly which always ends rightly—always.

"Finally—yes, *finally* you say—we have arrived at this place where we can just sit back and watch, like in a good movie, the marvelous drama Jesus created for us to enjoy. This master teacher called Jesus of Nazareth brought to us *the Way, the Truth and Life* to be thoroughly enjoyed through the eternity of it all. He did so through stories so beautifully, so simply, told. All this time all anyone really needed was just the proper decoder, much like those childhood rings with the secret decoder in them that we used to find out what was going to happen in the next episode of Superman on the radio. Or was it some other fictional character? It matters not. All that does matter is that we now hone our skills in the use of our sacred decoder: metaphorical unveiling. We search for symbolic meaning that takes us to INsight and Enlightenment, and on through Transcendence to our Resurrection.

"Sit back now and think not. Simply let meaning come to you, without force. Let power reign instead—the natural power within that brings significance to Life. Let what you see and hear in these stories, in all of Life, be the symbols that inspire powerful meaning for you. In so doing, your Loving intention is realigned with the principle that guides you faithfully through Life. Beginning rightly in the Loving principle guides you always to Loving. Let us use this sacred filter of Loving to give dignity to all of Life, so it can all be rendered brilliant in its elegance.

"Let's turn the lights down in our theater. Everyone has a drink and a bag of popcorn or a box of candy, so all the creature comforts are taken care of. Just sit back and enjoy this now. You will recall the parable about the man at Bethesda, so I won't repeat that one. Nor will I refer to those mediations we dealt with during our first session together—unless, of course—we have new

INsights to share. What I'd like to begin with is the story that tells of Jesus with his apostles in the boat on the lake. My bet is that you're already mediating the metaphors, just from this one sentence description. Am I right? I am right, aren't I?" Christo jokes pleadingly, as the gathering breaks out in laughter that affirms the Truth of his proclamation. "Of course I'm right. Aren't you good, though!

"All right, here's the setting provided for us in the gospel of Matthew (8:23-28).

> 'Then he got into the boat followed by his disciples. Suddenly a storm broke over the lake, so violent the boat was being swamped by the waves. But he was asleep. So they went to him and awoke him saying, 'Save us, Lord, we are lost!' And then he said to them, 'Why are you so frightened, you who have so little faith?' And then he stood up and rebuked the winds and sea; and there was a great calm. They were astounded and said, "Whatever kind of man is this, that even the winds and seas obey him?"

"Let's see if I'm on the right track as far as you are concerned. Give your-selves a few moments to collect your views about this story. Remember, we have come to understand that such stories are marvelous settings from which to discern symbolic meaning in a spiritual sense, not the physical." Christo pauses long enough to gauge that they are ready to begin with their own trans-lation in tow. "Okay," Christo begins, "how many of you think that this story is about the emotional instability we sometimes feel as we sail across Life's waters?" Most of the hands go up immediately. "Good. Now, let's say that some emotional storms come up amidst the journey the disciples are taking with Jesus.

"How does Jesus treat these storms? When it is said that he is asleep, how many immediately equated that to Jesus's giving the emotional turmoil no thought?" Again, a sea of hands affirms this translation. "And then, when awakened, that is, when some of the disciples asked Jesus to quell the emo-tional upset, what did he do? If you agree that he said to them something like this raise your hand: 'For goodness' sake, do you want to put your conviction, or place your faith, in fear? Or in peace?'" Again, affirmation reigns. "Good, you're right on track.

"Now, how did Jesus quell the stormy thoughts? By rebuking them, by put-ting them in the proper perspective, did he not?" Heads nod in unison, much like the bobbing-head dolls we see sold in toy stores. "Ah…you are seeing with such spiritual clarity now!" Christo rewards them. "And the treasure of a last line in the parable, 'Whatever kind of man is this, that even the winds and the sea obey him?' What a marvelous piece of storytelling, worthy of a Shakespearian tale!

As a way of cementing this translation, visualize with me, if you will, a time when you might have been in your car taking a trip with your children. If you have never done so, just imagine this anyhow. You've been riding along for a few hours and suddenly one of your children wakes up from a frightening dream, a nightmare. She's crying, filled with fear, and unable to really talk about it. She's only two-years old, after all. What happens in this story from this point forward? By crying, she announces her fear. In her own way, she is asking for you to quell her fear for her. We know the truth of such messages if we've raised children consciously. So we stop the car and take the child in our arms, telling her that it's only a dream; that there's nothing to be afraid of. 'Don't worry, sweetheart,' we say, 'Mommy will take care of the boogie man for you.' In the vernacular, of course, 'I'll take care of the bogey man,' means 'we'll make it safe for you by taking away the fear.' Can't you just hear the child's inner response? 'What kind of person is this that can make me feel safe again? What kind of person is this that can actually take my fear away from me and leave me in peace?' And the child is thus comforted, until she is taught to do so for herself at a later age.

"Folks, isn't this exactly what Jesus did? In this story we have the tale of spiritual immaturity in relation to one's emotional perspective. See how simple this is becoming? And easy, too. Before we proceed to another story I just want to nail down one important point about the way you have handled similar cases, a point that reflects on you as a spiritual being. Your response to such a situation puts you in precisely the same class as Jesus—and you didn't even have to go to a special mystery school to get you there. You merely exercised your spiritual powers of Loving perspective to teach your youngster that she need not worry about such things. You let her know that you would be a bridge for her until she became mature enough to exercise emotional discernment on her own. From where I stand, this Truth about your spiritual maturity makes you just as divine as Jesus said you are. So get over any remaining remnants of belief that you're not, already!

"Here's one couched in language that should intrigue the women present. In the largely pristine and sexually unenlightened society in which we live, it would, at the very least, be uncomfortable to speak about this publicly. This is the story of the cure of the woman with a hemorrhage. Again, I quote from

Matthew (9:20-22), the gospel in which so many of these stories about Jesus are found.

> 'Then suddenly from behind him came a woman, who had been suffering from a haemorrhage for twelve years, and she touched the fringe of his cloak, for she was thinking, 'If only I can touch his cloak I will be saved.' Jesus turned round and saw her; and he said to her, 'Courage, my daughter, your faith has saved you.' And from that moment the woman was saved.'

"What a delicious story this is!" Christo proclaims. "Once again, collect your thoughts around this story and let's see where it goes," he instructs them. "I see that now you are needing less and less time for this assessment process to unfold. What a marvelous affirmation that you have given yourselves permission to see Life's examples as wonderful clues for spiritual meaning. Once permission is given, the new perspectives just flow to you," Christo confirms as the bobbing dolls nod in unison yet again. It's obvious that every member of this choir is indeed singing from the same page of the hymnal now.

"Now let's test the spiritual waters. How many of you would declare that the woman's hemorrhaging is symbolic language for having been profusely exercising an ill-formed thought process for a long time?" At this point, Christo doesn't need to ask for a show of hands. He is reading the answer to his rhetorical questions as he goes along, so in touch is he and the participants with one another. "Good start. Isn't it just possible that the ill-formed thought process was founded on 'bad blood' between her and someone else? Could that bad blood have been between her and her parents whom she may have thought led her astray with what they had taught her? With what emotional foundation they had provided? Was it her parents' limited ways of thinking which held her in captivity? Or, perhaps, their compulsion to arrange her marriage at a young age rather than let her sort that out by herself? We don't know for sure, do we? 'Bad blood' may be taken to mean simply any form of thought that has been slowly discharging, or fuming in someone, until it finally has reached its end.

"It's akin to having reached the point in any relationship, either with a way of thinking—which is what spirituality deals with—or a human relationship. When we finally reach our 'ouch point' or find ourselves at the end of our rope, or hit bottom—no matter how you want to say it—we give it up for something better. We move on. There is no point in wreaking revenge on either that past way of thinking or that past relationship. The best revenge, it is said, is living well. Affirming 'I can get along without you,' or even better yet, 'I can flourish without you,' is the best message you can give Life in any form. It conveys the conviction of—faith in—one's own goodness, without bad feelings of any kind attached to the past. It is about repenting—about changing how we deal with that part of our Life—and then moving on. Is this not really what this story is about?

"For the sake of this story, we don't really need to know exactly what the bad blood was about. We only need to know that she had come to the realization that she had to change how she saw Life or it would kill her. She simply had to get out of that erroneous thought process through which she viewed Life. So along comes Jesus, just in time to clear all this up for her."

"Oh, and let me not forget this. We haven't dealt much with the symbolism of numbers, except for a little the first time we met. In order to reopen the door to your curiosity in this regard, let me lead you to the threshold in this way. The number three exemplifies a complete cycle. The number nine would be a higher level of completion. The number twelve, composed of four cycles, is an indicator that this woman is on her way to more mature thinking, is well on her way to spiritual discernment. Get the process?" Christo pauses, giving the meaning time to settle in. "Perhaps we'll get into more regarding numerology later, but for now, you get the idea of how the number twelve speaks to us. Or at least how it is intended to speak to us.

"Let's jump to near the end of the story for a moment, where Jesus calls the woman his daughter. This is a clear declaration that her previous thinking was immature, is it not? As he speaks with her—although we never are given the benefit of the entire conversation Jesus has with those he heals—Jesus finds that she is still thinking as a child. Again, to her credit, she wants to rid herself of the bad blood and start Life anew. She wants to be born again.

"All right, then, let's continue the story as it is presented. The story indicates that when she reaches out to touch his cloak she is thinking, 'If only I can touch his cloak, I shall be saved.' The cloak? We have spoken about the meaning of cloak before. The cloak, you will recall, is that form of thought with which we clothe ourselves. Mixing our metaphors some would say that our frame of mind forms the lenses through which we view Life's endless gifts to us. Said yet another way, the cloak is the warp we have used to weave our Life's imagery. No matter how you think about it, the woman is finally coming to the stage in Life when she recognizes that if she can just begin, just touch the hem, this way of thinking—Jesus's spiritual perspective on Life—that she will be saved. The seamless garment represents the completely spiritual approach from which Jesus so eloquently speaks.

"Remember what I said early this morning about my Christian foundation? That while I hadn't seen anywhere in holy scripture that Jesus proclaimed himself to be anyone's savior, quite to the contrary he did give us that which saves. Remember me saying that I had come to know that it was Jesus's teachings that saved me from myself? You now understand, I am sure, that what I meant was that his teachings regularly save me from the ways I formerly thought about Life. So, this is the way in which I am saved. You will recall that I dealt with Jesus saving us from our sins through his crucifixion the last time around. So I won't dwell on the value of the teaching around the crucifixion here and now. Besides, I'll bet that by now you can do that one very nicely by yourselves, thank you.

"To continue, then, it is said that Jesus turned around and saw her." Christo sees that they are right with him, so much is their anticipation openly displayed. "Yes, you are absolutely correct. Jesus stepped back from his perspective and saw Life from her perspective. When he told her she had courage, he meant, of course, that it takes courage to acknowledge that you need to change your perspective on Life. 'From then on,' Jesus says, 'it takes obedience expressed as conviction to the Truth, faith placed in the new, the spiritual, way that saves you from yourself.' And from that moment on, she was saved—from herself. She was saved from her self-willed erroneous form of thought.

"What do you think took place within the woman as Jesus taught her the Truth? Yes, exactly what takes place in all of us. When, by INtuition, we find ourselves at the threshold of Truth, and we step across the barrier *to* Truth, we arrive at the home of our Muse—of our divinity that INspires toward INsight. That which renders INsight as Enlightenment. Yes, and then on to Transcendence. And, by golly, darkness then gives way to light. We are indeed saved. Not by the man, Jesus, but by his teachings. The process through which the Truth makes us free saves us. The *process* that is the way—that leads us to Truth—that comes out of the infinity of immortal Life.

"Would you formerly have thought that such profundity could have come out of such a simple story? Not with the means we had been given up to this time. But now you are born anew. Spiritually, your means are more mature. They have matured from the material to the spiritual. You have indeed arrived at the kingdom of Heaven. And you have had yet another virgin birth. What marvelous midwives you are becoming! I marvel at the rapidity with which you have come to Life, have come to see Life as the magnificent gift it is.

Christo pauses long enough to discern the next step in this marvelous process of Enlightenment. "All right," he begins anew, "I think one more brief exposition is in order, just to cement your understanding about spirituality and the way we utilize it to the benefit of all. By now you have come to the same conclusion that I have, I am sure. And that is this: the Bible is rife with examples that say pretty much the same thing. Jesus was a master of reinforcement. He used slightly different stories in order to reach those who needed to hear the meaning in a way that made a difference to them. As the expression goes, 'When we are ready, the teacher shows his or her face.' For example, we can tell our children the right thing to do in any particular situation. However, if they're not yet ready to hear it they just won't. But when they *are* ready, watch out! If you tell them one more time just when they are ready—although you may have told them many times already—they finally not only get it, but they usually follow quickly with something like: 'Why didn't you tell me this before!'" The gathering laughingly responds out of familiarity.

"Sure, you've all had this happen to you in one way or another. Well, here's another brief example from scripture. Again, this is from Matthew (9:27-32.)

> As Jesus went on his way two blind men followed him shouting, "Take pity on us, son of David." And when Jesus reached the house the blind men came up with him and he said to them, "Do you believe I can do this?" They said, "Lord, we do." Then he touched their eyes saying, "According to your faith, let it be done to you." And their sight returned. Then Jesus sternly warned them. "Take care that no one learns about this." But when they had gone away, they talked about him all over the countryside.

"So, folks, what do we have here? Yet another manifestation of the story about Bartimaeus, the blind man along the roadside who asked Jesus to make him see. You will well recall the rather lengthy translation of that story from our last time together. I belabored the story at that time so you could be shown that Jesus's work was really no different from what we do regularly. During seemingly chance conversations with friends and whomever, INsight and Enlightenment occur. The veil of ignorance is parted to the transcendent value of being born again. Yet again we are shown to be midwives to virgin births all throughout our lives. What a lovely profession to express all we are worth: midwifery.

"Okay, let's do our parallel journeying through this parable. This one begins with the men shouting to Jesus, the son of David, to take pity on them. What shouts out at Jesus, really? Is it the men who are shouting, or their less than mature spirituality of thought that shouts out to Jesus? Yes, the latter, of course. Such perspective is so clear once we open ourselves to it. Its display has such a focused warp to it that it shouts out to us loud and clear. This is exactly what the story is saying to us. 'Their cry to take pity on them?' 'And calling Jesus the son of David, a royal, yet human lineage implied?' Both of these declarations speak to spiritual immaturity, don't they? Sure, because it is they who must take pity on themselves, in order to give up their old ways. Then, also, who must understand that it is not another who must give them pity, or heal them. It is not the authority without from which we get our healing. It is the authority of INspiration and INsight that enlightens.

"When the men reached the house, it is said, Jesus spoke to them. The real meaning here, the metaphor that informs? What is it? You could just jump out of your seat to yell it to me, couldn't you?" Christo says, acknowledging their growing enthusiasm for the Truth that now courses through them. The light stemming from INsight is burning that brightly now, from one and all. The train is indeed on the right track!

"The house that is reached is the house of thought Jesus portrays. When Jesus asks if they believe he can heal their blindness, what he really is saying is: 'Do you believe that I can show you a different perspective on Life; a different way to live your Life; a pathway to your inner Authority?' Indeed, by their belief in his teaching ability, he is able to open their eyes—'touch their eyes' it is said. Hasn't someone or some thing that changed our perspective on something or about someone touched us all? Of course it has. This is not too difficult to figure out, is it? Not with this language of metaphor we are now using, this tongue we are now speaking. Yes, I see this awakening in you: this speaking in tongues that you just acknowledged within yourselves. Speaking metaphorically is definitely the speaking in tongues that is spoken of in the Bible. Speaking in tongues means the translation of Truth that is spiritual in nature, which is the process Jesus told us we must be used in order to understand God—the God of Spirit that God is. We are One in that, One in Spirit with God. Thus we must speak the same language if we are to understand our Oneness—and *be* Oneness always. We must be single-minded in our Oneness of Spirit, extracting meaning spiritually through the metaphorical tongue that is the foundation of the kingdom of Heaven.

"Well, of course, these two men are healed. From your understanding of numerology—even as limited as you may think it is—if three is a symbol for completeness, what would you suspect the number two means? Yes, you are correct. The numeral two is a sign of incompleteness. Close, but no cigar. Approaching completeness, yes. Indicated by the two approaching Jesus in order to arrive at a more complete—that is, correct or right—perspective on Life.

"Hah! Isn't Jesus the clever one, though? He tells the men not to tell anyone about what happened. We can take this literally to mean that he knew that they were not yet fully spiritual in their understanding. After all, they came to him in their immature state. So by telling them not to tell everyone, he knew that by using reverse psychology that they would surely go and tell *everyone* they came upon exactly what had happened.

"However, spiritually speaking, what meaning does Jesus's admonition have? Once again you have it. You are *so* good! What he is saying is that they shouldn't tell anyone that *he, Jesus,* had healed them. Rather they should tell the Truth, that Jesus had shown them the way: he had only taken them to the threshold of their own meaning, their own divinity, so that they could become Inspired, could gain the INsight necessary to become enlightened. He was giving them the opportunity to become disciples of the new way of finding the Truth within—which was to be their new way of Life. Indeed, they took him up on his admonition and spread the word across the countryside," Christo finishes with a sigh.

"Had enough?" Christo inquires. "Have you had enough so that you can now move forward translating scripture, mediating between heaven and earth, if you will—both for yourselves and others, until they can do it for themselves? I have full confidence that you can—and will." Christo tests the waters once again, and senses that although most know that they can now speak and translate in this marvelous new tongue, that they are still a bit reluctant to do so. He looks within for guidance in the face of this perception and receives exactly what he needs in a flash of a moment.

"Okay," he begins, "I sense you have a bit of reluctance to move forward without just the right prompt. So prompt I will. This is no different from fully acknowledging your divinity so you can live from the Truth of your divinity without fail. Something tells me that although you are convinced of your divinity on deeper and deeper levels, that you need something to bump it in the night so you can operate from its Truth completely. We shall deal with that after the break.

"But for now, let's deal with this 'tongues thing.' It's sort of like expressing the greeting 'Namaste' in your heart, if not on your lips, every time you meet someone. Whether you say it out loud or not, those you greet with a loving smile in your heart that paints your face, inherently they *know* that you are coming from that very space which honors their divinity. Which embraces their dignity above all, without fail. It's the very same with the metaphorical way. All you need is a little reinforcement to take it to a deeper level. So here it is, hidden in scripture. Now your inherent ability and your charge—your calling to do so—will become clear to you. Once you have the 'permission from on high,' it will be easier for you to accept and to live," Christo assures them.

"So here it is," he continues. "This could get really heavy if taken literally. As we have learned by now, however, these stories are to be taken spiritually, metaphorically, symbolically, if we are to arrive at Truth instead of intellectual pride. I'll quote from various portions of Acts, Chapter 2, beginning with 2:1 and finishing at 2:13. It is in the Book of Acts that we first deal with the concept of tongues. Later, it appears again in the first letter of Paul to the Corinthians. Let us begin rightly first with this from Acts. The story starts with a meeting of the Apostles.

> When the Pentecost day came round, they had all met together, when suddenly there came from heaven a sound as of a violent wind which filled the entire house in which they were sitting; and there appeared to them tongues as of fire; these separated and came to rest on the head of each of them. They were filled with the Holy Spirit and began to speak different languages as the Spirit gave them power to express themselves.
>
> Now there were devout men living in Jerusalem from every nation under the heaven, and at this sound, they all assembled, and each one was bewildered to hear these men speaking his own language. They were amazed and astonished. "Surely," they said, "all these men speaking are Galileans? How does it happen that each of us hears them in his own native language?

"Then the men in the gathering begin to name the places from which the others have come," Christo explains. What is important is that they name a wide range of locations from which they came, implying that they all spoke different languages reflecting their different origins. However, the text says all could understand the words being preached and remark to each other:

> [we] hear them preaching in our own language about the marvels of God. Everyone is amazed and perplexed; they asked one another what it all meant. Some, however, laughed it off. 'They have been drinking too much wine,' they said.

"Don't you just *love* this?" exclaims Christo. Because you have received the gift of tongues itself, this will seem much clearer to you now than otherwise might have been the case. Once again, let's take it bit by bit. First of all, literally, Pentecost is the name given to the festival celebrating the descent of the Holy Spirit, fifty days after Easter. It is part of the Jewish tradition; it is the harvest festival on the fiftieth day after the second day of Passover. Aren't both of these mediations liberating? The descent of the Holy Spirit refers to what? That we have a way of understanding meaning that is different from the norm: different from that which we normally have used, particularly in this case, to knowing about Godliness. The Holy Spirit refers to the ability to gain meaning from the metaphorical understanding rather than from the literal meaning of Life's offerings. We know now, don't we, that such meaning is symbolic in nature, and leads us beyond the intellect to INspiration, to INsight, and on to Enlightenment? Indeed this new kind of meaning, Truth, is to be celebrated. According to the Jewish tradition, such meaning is to be harvested in a festive manner.

"Notice how both traditions referred to use the numeral fifty," instructs Christo. "What meaning do we give to this?" he prods. "Yes," I hear you saying that five is the number meaning change of some magnitude. What might the numeral fifty mean then? Right again," he confirms, "the numeral fifty connotes change of great magnitude, as signified by ten times five. Metaphor is such a treat!" Christo laughs. "Indeed, those gathered are in for a change of huge proportions.

"'Suddenly,' they say, 'a sound comes from heaven.' Heaven represents what? By now we know that the kingdom represents the infinite number of ideas that come from divine inspiration. The sound is expressed as a violent wind that fills the entire house in which they were sitting. Yes, the winds of change sometimes seem violent. Particularly when they bring us something so drastically different from what we had before they came to us. What did this enormous change deal with? It dealt with the entire house in which they were sitting. It changed for good the house of thought, the literalism, in which they were sitting. If changed that which they had erroneously used to translate Life until this dramatic change in perspective blew through them. It gave them their new breath of Life.

"This new perspective appeared to them as tongues of fire that separated and came to rest on the head of each of them. Of course this new manner of garnering meaning took hold of each of them. It burned an indelible meaning in them that would stand the tests of fire from one and all. From this point on, it would be the manner, the tongue that would bring only Truth to meaning. Indeed, they were all filled with the Holy Spirit. The symbolic meaning of language could then be used to treat Life's purpose. *Indeed*, it gave them power to express themselves! The power of *Truth*! Not the force of intellectual argument.

"As John Krakauer says: 'All religious belief is a function of non-rational faith, and faith, by its very definition tends to be impervious to intellectual argument or academic criticism.' Speaking in tongues, then—speaking metaphorically—eradicated the literalization of interpretation represented by the attitude and practice of the Pharisees. Therefore, speaking in the tongue of symbolism, of metaphorical meaning, becomes the new covenant: the new testament to Truth.

"The rest of this parable is testament to the discernment that it is the common tongue of metaphorical meaning, the power of metaphysical treatment, that enables all, no matter which their home, to see the same Truth in Life. Otherwise, knowledge is left to the literal approach, which, by its very nature, is open to the elements of rationality, objectivity, self-righteousness, intellectual argument and academic criticism. Each of these is simply academic. Or should I have said simplistically academic? In any event, each is but a detail in a sea of details. This is not to demean them, but rather to reinforce that such means only lead to Truth, point to it, but they are not Truth itself.

"To conclude this reference, the text says that everyone is 'amazed and perplexed.' Surely such a dramatic change in the way to treat Life would be, at the very least, amazing and perplexing. Until, that is, one makes the conversion to tongues of a different nature. The text also states that some laughed it off, saying the others had been drinking too much wine. Such a dramatic way of speaking could well make some think that those who spoke metaphorically would at the very least be nut cases. The Truth is that those who now can take meaning metaphorically, metaphysically, are indeed drunk, drunk on the spirits of sacred meaning.

"Now," queries Christo, "do you feel at least somewhat reinforced in your ability and charge to speak in your new tongue? Let me tell you, for a while others who are unfamiliar with the metaphorical tongue, or meaning, will think you've lost it. That has been so with me. I once dated a woman who told me she dreamt that she was going to meet someone—who just happened to be me—who spoke in this 'funny' language that almost everyone didn't understand. I like Albert Einstein's comment about such reactions to Truth: 'Great spirits have always encountered violent opposition from mediocre minds.' Great meaning, we might say, has always encountered opposition from those who don't understand. That would be those who must use the mediocre, that is, the ordinary meaning gained from literally discerning understanding rather than going directly within for the Truth that divinity freely provides us.

"Let's go just one baby step further, this time with a couple of brief references from the first letter of Paul to the Corinthians (12:11). When listing the gifts that are bestowed on each of us, Paul makes this note: '…to one, the gift of different tongues and to another, the interpretation of tongues.' Let me be absolutely clear about this declaration so you don't use this against yourself. It is often said that each of us has only one gift. From what I have seen of others, this is not true at all. What *is* the Truth is that no matter what gifts have been bestowed upon us, they are to be used for the highest good. The highest good is inherent in the expression of our divinity. Everyone, as I see them, has many gifts. All that these gifts require is that we be open to them: acknowledge, accept and use them for the greater good.

"Here you sit, as more than ample testimony to this proclamation. The very first time we met I suspect that no one here would have suggested that he or she spoke in tongues. You may have if you come from an evangelical tradition but those are tongues of a different nature. Yet, simply because you have opened yourselves up to a new way of shaping perspective, I would say that there's nary a one here who now cannot both speak and interpret tongues. Especially after the little exercise we'll use to gain a little more confidence in doing so. It's all about allowing and acknowledging, isn't it? Beginning rightly ends rightly yet again!

"Paul affirms the predicament, and power, of speaking in tongues once again in the same letter to the Corinthians (14:2). Listen carefully to this: 'Those who speak in a tongue speak to God, but not to other people, because nobody understands them; they are speaking in the Spirit and the meaning is hidden.' Now perhaps you will recall Jesus's admonition to the Pharisees, that is, that they spoke only in the literal meaning of the law, instead of in the Spirit of the law, that is, metaphorically. Have you not found it to be true, for example, that when I first spoke to you in metaphorical terms that it had no meaning for you? Believe me, from the expressions on your faces, and the confused energy I felt from you, this certainly was true. But now, how do you feel? No problem, right? Right!" Christo adds, emphasizing the Truth of the matter.

"Yes, Paul was correct, but not so if you take his letter literally. He was correct in that those who take meaning from the symbolic language of Truth are having God's intention, God's word, spoken through them. Each of you is that midwife through which God speaks when you translate meaning metaphorically. Paul was also correct to the point that nobody understands those who speak metaphorical meaning. Why not? Well, who has taught them to do so? Those who cannot need not feel guilty about not understanding this vastly different language. It's only a matter of ignorance, a product of domestication based in the rational, literal view of Life. But a new teaching is at hand, a rather simple way of learning and using it for daily living. Truly, without it, there *is* no Life. There is only coping with the sterile vagaries of details that flood us in the approach that has in it no heart, only the head.

"Paul goes on in this same chapter to teach that prophecy is the better gift to express because if no one can understand the meaning, what good is it? Further on he says that he'd rather say five words with his mind to instruct others than ten thousand words in a tongue. How confusing this is to one who would read it literally. Let us look for just a moment at its Truth, however. First of all, here's the number five again. Paul is dealing with the power to change, in this case, to change meaning. Literally, the expression 'words in tongues' means the spoken word, the literal meaning of something, no matter whether it is spoken in Latin, Greek, or Aramaic. Saying five words with his mind, however, would be taken to mean that he would create meaning by giving thought to it. By creating symbolic meaning of and for it.

"Metaphorically speaking, words of the mind are thought pictures, symbolic meaning. So what Paul is saying that he'd prefer to inculcate people with the symbolic meaning of Life's offerings, instead of only teaching literally about meaning. Literal debate doesn't produce much of lasting value, except distortions of Truth. Metaphorical meaning, on the other hand, emanates from the Holy Spirit, which is the seat of our divinity that informs as Truth for us. Each of us has the tools, although we don't always use them consciously. When we don't use the tools of INspiration, INsight and Enlightenment consciously the value-related discernment that is needed to head us in the direction of Mecca, or not, is often lacking. Perhaps what we need is schools of metaphorical meaning to teach us the pathway to Truth. As with passing through the eye of the needle, one must commit single-mindedly to learning the metaphorical perspective. Otherwise, Life's investments will fall on fallow ground. The contrary path of rational literalism is wide and easily tread. Unfortunately, however, it goes nowhere. Spiritually speaking, it's just a dead-end.

Christo hears a prompt once again and displays his pleasure at the INtuitive strike with a broad smile. "Okay, I'll bet you've picked up that I have another shoe to drop, or perhaps a story to tell. Well, you'd be wrong on the first count—but absolutely correct on the second count," he says with glee. "I'd forgotten all about this. It's a fun story to sit with, so I'll go ahead and share it with you. If you'll indulge me, that is." Christo pauses with a laugh emerging from his heart and continues: "Actually, even if you don't want to indulge me, I think I will share it, anyhow." he tells the amused gathering.

"Here's the setting. Long ago and far away I attended a month-long retreat, hoping to become learned in the ways of being a competent spiritual director. I didn't much care for that term, but that's a story for another day. One evening about midway through the program the participants were scheduled to have a healing by the Holy Spirit. As an aside, the month was laced with the marvelous mix of scripture, practical teaching, sharing with others, tasting the divine in meals, both physical and spiritual, song and dance, liturgy and healing services of all kinds.

"To continue, on this particular evening, there were only a half-dozen of us who had not yet been anointed by the Holy Spirit, as it were. All the rest had been, but were to receive a second anointing only after we fledglings had been initiated. Our sponsor in the local assembly of Benedictines, both men and women, along with some who served as devoted staff, was to be a special guide in this process. Mine was a man of extraordinary spiritual discernment and one of powerful entreaty in prayer.

"To make a long story short, when the priest who was guiding the ceremony asked me what gift I wanted in the name of the Holy Spirit, I was dumbfounded. 'What gift do I want?' I asked myself privately. 'God has already bestowed gifts on me,' I thought, 'and has done a good job of it, too.' Out of my ignorance, or perhaps naiveté, I responded to his query with: 'Whatever God wants to bestow on me is good enough for me.' He rejoined with, 'Surely you want the gift of tongues, don't you?' said in utter disbelief at my answer. Well, I wasn't to be challenged there or anywhere. My heart was showing me how to respond, and here was an outside authority suggesting something contrary to that. So I reinforced my earlier response by reiterating the very same sentiment. As I recall, his rejoinder was, 'Well, you just sit for a while and think about it. I'll be back.'

"Wanting not to raise a stink, I took his question seriously. I prayed, asking for discernment. What came up was that if he wanted me to have the gift of tongues and I was willing to let God decide, what's the issue? Either is okay. Plus who's to say that they couldn't be one and the same? A few minutes later my questioner returned. He inquired again, 'You want the gift of tongues now, right?' 'Sure, father, that'll be just fine,' I responded. I'm shortening this a bit to save some time. Actually, this exchange went on for a few more turns of games-manship. So adamant was he. And I.

The long and short of it is that he then anointed me with the gift of the Holy Spirit. After the service I went straight to my room and prayerfully retired for the night, thinking absolutely nothing about the gift-in-waiting. In the middle of the night I awakened to go to the bathroom. I turned on the light so as not to trip over anything. As I returned to bed I glanced up at the large painting of Jesus on the wall and spoke to it, to him, as though he was the man in charge. 'Look,' I said, 'if you want this to happen, have at it. But you're the one who's going to have to do it, not me. I'm going back to bed,' I said in a huff.

"With that I turned the light off, hopped into bed and pulled the covers over my head. As soon as my head hit that pillow I broke open like an egg in the hands of a skilled chef. Out of my mouth spewed an array of noises and sounds so unusual I thought for sure that I'd lost it. What was coming out of my mouth, not running through my mind, mind you, was an array of guttural sounds and singsong utterances of a very different nature than I'd ever been exposed to, neither before nor since. The sounds were nothing like I had heard in the services when the religious community spoke in tongues—theirs were liltingly beautiful. What was coming out of me was more like something I could only imagine indigents in some other part of the world would have spo-ken.

"Folks, this went on for better than three hours straight, with no let up in sight! I finally just had to shut it off in order to prepare for morning prayer ser-vices followed by breakfast. I mean to tell you, I was mighty tuckered out, to say the least. Yet I had the inner feeling that something not only unusual, but certainly sacred, had coursed through me. The entire episode was highly uplifting, yet unenlightening in its literal content. As I was shaving that morn-ing, I came to the realization that it didn't matter that I didn't know what had been communicated in the usual sense, only that I had felt the uplift from such a supposed holy visitation. In the shower I opened myself to it once again, just to see if it was something I could initiate, just upon request. Believe me when I say that this was affirmed—in spades.

"Apparently the priest who wanted tongues as a gift for me must have told anyone who'd listen about our fencing match the evening before. Almost everyone of these caring, curious people asked me if I had received 'the gift.' All I had to do in response was to smilingly point to the bags under my eyes and they knew the answer straight out. My friend, the grand inquisitor—a dear, sweet, highly learned, holy man, by the way—asked me after morning prayers if I had received the gift. I responded in the same way I had earlier, to his absolute delight. 'Wonderful!' he exclaimed as he turned to head up the stairs with a smile of satisfaction on his face, 'I'm so glad you got what you wanted!' In response to his wit I laughed myself up the stairs to breakfast.

"In retrospect, I realized that the trigger for the release was my declaration that I was willing to let go of control over the situation. Once I had proclaimed that it wasn't my job, God seemed to take over. And did God ever take over! Later, within the context of the writing that has come through me about Life as metaphor, I have realized that it was at about that time that I began to speak in *that* tongue: in metaphor. The other had served as a sign that I was willing to let go and to move on to another way of viewing Life. What a mighty, powerful symbol it was!

"So, my dear friends, let this be a lesson to you. Be willing to let go and let God. Be willing to let go of the control you have exercised by thinking in a particular way all your Life. Be willing to be shown another way, a way that could just take you deeper into the meaning Life holds for you. Believe me, if you do let go—and let the Universe of ideas flow naturally, and listen to them for the good they do for you—Life will never again be the same. I am living testimony to that Truth.

"Well, then, let's close this topic with a brief practice session, and then we'll take a break for dinner before continuing. In my letter of invitation to you I asked that each of you bring a Bible with you, even if you were not Christian. The idea is to use a common source for our study of meaning, not to inculcate you with Christianity. Not that Christianity is bad, mind you. I like Gandhi's response to Christianity. When asked what he thought about it, he is said to have responded something like this: 'I think it is a brilliant idea. But I haven't seen it practiced anywhere.' Now is the hour. This is your time in the sun.

"At this time pair up with someone on either side of you. Don't fret if the seat next to you is empty or the rows are uneven in numbers of seats. You'll work it out, or you can just do this brief exercise by yourselves. Once we begin in earnest, my aides and I will circulate to assist in any way we can. This is not a test, only practice, practice you can repeat either alone or with another. For now, you and your partner will choose a particular parable from the Gospels. All of the books are rife with examples. Choose just one, and both of you read it silently. Then turn to one another and have a metaphorical discussion about what you have chosen to understand. I strongly suspect that this will come very quickly for all of you. If it doesn't, don't be at all concerned about it. Merely raise your hand, and one of us will come to you directly to assist. Remember, this is not for some kind of grade, so leave your intellect and competitive nature behind. Coming from the seat of your divinity now, collaborate on discerning Truth from scripture. You've already done it with a personal happening, so more than likely this will be easier. Ready? Go for it!"

Christo stands back for a minute or two to give everyone a chance to get on track. Just as he had predicted to himself, the larger portion of the group begins almost immediately, with the rest fast in pursuit. Christo gives the sign for his aides to fan out. He discerns who needs help within his proximity and casually moves in that direction. In no way does he want to convey the idea that there is any hurry to arrive at Truth. Learning the process is the treasure here. Not winning some fictional prize.

After about thirty minutes, it appears that nearly all of the participants have completed their practice episode, so Christo and his aides initiate their return. This being the easily recognizable sign to bring things to a close, the participants do so with some reluctance. It is obvious by the enthusiasm they have been exhibiting for the task that they have been enjoying practicing what they had learned. The same enthusiasm continues, only now to casual comparisons with other neighbors about their own adventures in this regard. Christo glows in the acknowledgment of the growing competence among the gathering. Although he had been enormously pleased over how far the previous group had come in such a short time, this gathering was building solidly on that foundation and was taking off into the wild blue yonder beyond his fondest dreams for them. And he says so.

"My dear friends, it is time to call this brief activity to a halt. From my observation, as well as from reports from my aids, this has been a mighty powerful experience. By a show of hands, how many of you now feel competent enough to continue on your own? Perhaps even competent enough to share the process with someone else?" Without fail, the entire assembly affirms the depth of confidence in their ability to move on. Christo is enormously pleased for them. "I am so pleased for you and those you'll soon be reaching. And so proud of you for exercising your reach beyond the past," he adds refreshingly.

"At this time I think it's best if we take an early break for dinner. This will provide you some time to share freely with one another, as well to assimilate everything we've dealt with today. This is an intense way to learn, and you are handling it so very well. So, as a little reward, let's take two hours for dinner. I suggest you walk to dinner in order to get a bit grounded, as well as to provide the necessary opportunity to get your blood circulating again. The mind can discern only what the seat can endure it is said, so give yourselves every opportunity to stretch yourselves and nourish your body properly. The Soul is about full for the day, I'd say. So let's now feed its counterpart.

"When we return, we'll have a short session tonight, followed by light refreshments and some time for socializing. Tomorrow morning, after any church services you choose to attend, we'll begin with a light brunch and set about tying up some loose ends before heading for the finale. That one promises to be a humdinger, from what I'm hearing within. I can't wait to see what it looks like, myself," he closes, laughing. "See you promptly at 7:30."

His aides approach Christo and suggest that they would like to have a brief feedback session; just to be sure they're all on the same page. Christo readily agrees, and they huddle for fifteen minutes or so backstage. From the ensuing discussion, it is apparent that all is going well. Everyone seems to be on top of things but, of course, only time and practice will tell. Christo suggests that the group fan out across the dining section in that part of town so the participants can have the benefit of counsel if needed. Then off they go, merrily on their way. It is obvious that all have been well-fed up to this point. Now there's only grounding to be accomplished naturally.

CHAPTER 9

Sending in the Troops

As the gathering begins to assemble after dinner, they are mellow from all the commiserating and dining pleasure. From his meanderings through a number of the restaurants, Christo and his aides have come to understand that although the participants have gained significant confidence in reading Life metaphorically, as well as reaching an even deeper understanding of divinity, they still aren't quite comfortable with their own divinity. It was almost as though they needed to give themselves permission not only to see their divinity from yet another perspective, but also to *feel* their divinity from within. This convinces Christo that his inner Authority was indeed correct in guiding him to the next steps along their journey together.

As the bewitching hour arrives, precisely at 7:30 PM, Christo enters the arena from the front this time, exuding his Loving energy in every direction. His light casts across the entire arena as he approaches the podium. "Namaste, well-fed ones," he opens half-jokingly. "Namaste, Christo," the participants return his greeting with tenderness. "Thank you, dear ones. Thank you," he honors their greeting. "It looks like we're all pretty mellow by now. So I think I'd better take advantage of your mellowness by leading you to falling in Love all over again," he teases.

His invitation to fall in Love catches them unawares, just as he wants. "I know that most of you are already married. I also know that depending on your current disposition on this matter, most, if not all, now understand that you are wedded to God, or Godliness. The falling in Love I want you to witness now, as our closing topic for the day, is the falling in Love with your own divinity and the divinity of all. It is the foundation for Life itself: for living fully in the Kingdom of Heaven, for living as inheritors of all the gifts of the Kingdom as our treasures.

"Where do we begin?" Christo asks himself out loud. "Ahhh," he continues, "it occurs to me that in the concentrated activity dealing with translating the Word you might well have not come to a full understanding of the connection between your ability to do so and your divinity. Let's see what we can do about that. If we begin with the premise that Jesus was divine, we have a good chance of beating the self-defeating denial that we are not. Sound confusing? Just remember that we're dealing with this spiritually, using metaphors as our basis of understanding. Considering Jesus as a master metaphysician, one who used meaning symbolically-derived to 'heal' someone of his or her misconceptions, places him in a category most would call 'divine.' He was divining others. That is, Jesus was using INtuition to guide another to INsight and Enlightenment. Where does one obtain INtuition? By behaving as or like God: letting the potential for Truth emit as the still small voice within. We say that God creates. That God emits divine ideas. That God envisions imagery that, when placed in the lap of conviction or faith over time, manifests the image from which it came. Is this all not divine, from divinity? Most who give any power to something larger than they are would probably affirm this as divine. How about you? Do you?

"If we use the stories of the healings Jesus did as gospel, even if only in a metaphorical sense, Jesus is thus divine. Now that each of you has metaphorically-replicated these very same kinds of healings, why is it, then, that you would refrain from accepting your own divine nature? In sharing your stories with one another, has each of you not employed INtuition as a guiding principle? Has each of you not found INspiration waiting at the doorstep of INsight and Enlightenment? Are these not the still small voices heard within?

"Well, if you doubt this, then point to that place outside of yourselves where all this INspiriation, INtuition, INsight and Enlightenment comes from. Anyone. Please point to the place outside of yourself where they are found.

"Now that we have discussed some of the parables and other scriptural references from the Bible, we also have seen these same elements described in more volatile phraseology. The result is the same. Describing INsight or Enlightenment in the context of having it strike like a bolt of lightening out of the blue, or like a clap of thunder that awakens you in the night, are nothing but different metaphors for the same act. Is this correct or not?" Christo rhetorically inquires of the gathering.

"Of course it is. Is this not what Jesus found? Is this not what he did? And just what was it you did? Has what you've done produced the same results as Jesus? Absolutely! Well, if we called Jesus 'divine'—in part at least for exercising his divinity—why not acknowledge yourselves in precisely the same way? Indeed, even without Jesus as our exemplar, if you were simply following your INtuition in dealing with a particular issue of your own making—and you were led to a place within where you became INspired to follow a particular course of thought which then led to INsight and Enlightenment—could you not still accept this as an act of divinity? I would hope so, for this *is* an act of divination, pure and simple. If you don't believe me, look up the definition of 'divination' in the dictuary, and see what you end up with," suggests Christo, with tongue on cheek. "There you'll have your altitude changed, I'm sure," he continues, purposely distorting language with that same mischievous look in his eye, just to point out the distortion of one who believes not in her or his own divinity, nor in the divinity of all.

"Does it not follow that one who engages in divination is divine? Or at the very least is divine in character? Still doubtful?" he asks, and then pauses. "One step at a time, Christo," he says to himself, and then turns back to his listeners. "Well, if, for example, one engages in painting as one's Life's purpose, does he or she not call him or herself a painter? Is not the one who cares for those in a hospice called a caregiver? Is one who teaches others by leading them to the threshold of their own Truth not called a teacher? Yet the very same people who would agree with these labels are reluctant to see themselves in the over-arching purpose they themselves are: *divine*. Is the same not true for all of us who—either consciously, or even unconsciously—engage Life's purpose from the seat of our divinity? Can we not be seen for what we truly are—divine—rather from the standpoint of what we do with what we are? Divinity is our vocation. Our avocation is that through which we express our divinity.

"Let's not make the mistake of thinking this is merely about a label. This is about owning what we really *are*. I think it's safe to reach this conclusion. Even though there will be some who will want to argue the point on academic grounds. The only real difference between the analogies I use and this consideration of our divinity is that we all are regularly actuating our divinity, yet reluctantly calling ourselves by the name of our trade rather than of our profession: the dispensation of Loving care which emanates endlessly from the All or One we see as divine. As a yogi is to have said: If you can't see God in *all*, you can't see God *at* all. If we just adjust our vocabulary to accommodate the synonym 'divine,' the same is True. In God-speak, a name is just a label put on others, that, when peeled away, lets us see God in all. By all means, then, let us not let Life be about labels. Let's make it about owning what we are and acting only out of that.

"Has it not dawned on someone yet that what we have been doing here—using the marvelous process of spiritual creation—means living in the image and likeness of God? Is this not the containment spoken of by John in his Prologue?" As Christo heads to the completion of that query he sees that indeed some have reached this same conclusion. Not wanting to leave it to doubt, he asks the question out loud: "How many of you have given yourselves enough room to reach this same conclusion? Have you made your God and yourself large enough to contain this Truth?" To his surprise, and delight, the vast majority has come to the same place in their formulation of divinity as Christo has. "Oh, this is a marvelous achievement," Christo affirms to himself, so as not to humiliate anyone who has not yet reached this understanding. He smiles to himself in deliberate celebration, nevertheless.

"So now, at least, you see how it is possible to be divine, whether Jesus was divine or not. Let's see if we can't find a way to strike while the iron is hot, so you can accept your divinity on some other levels. You will recall in our very first meeting I invested a good deal of time in explaining how you and I were exemplifying at least two of the characteristics attributed to God: namely, Loving and Creator. Under other circumstances I'd probably review those quickly now, just so we could further validate divinity as our very nature. Apparently, even though we can accept that Jesus said we are divine as God is divine—and have also come to our divinity by expressing divination—we still need to clear away some of those old images that cloud the completeness of this Truth from ourselves. So let's do it, but not by a public display of intellectual pursuit.

"Instead, I'd like to begin my approach by quoting once again from two of my favorite poets. The first is the Persian poet Hafiz, who leads us to a particular understanding about knowing God. It comes from his poem entitled, "Someone Should Start Laughing."

> I have a thousand brilliant lies
> For the question
> How are you?
>
> I have a thousand brilliant lies
> For the question
> What is God?

> If you think that the Truth can be known
> From words,
> If you think that the Sun and the Ocean
> Can pass through that tiny opening
> Called the mouth,
> O someone should start laughing!
> Someone should start wildly laughing—
> Now!

"Isn't this a wonderful commentary about God: that we cannot describe God with words? In the absence of words, what do we have? Meaning garnered from another source. From within. A friend once asked me about my belief in God. My response to him was that I didn't *believe* in God. I simply *knew* he existed. His rejoinder to me was that he wished he could know that. His mind just couldn't get wrapped around some intellectual understanding of God. 'There were just too many counter-arguments to the contrary,' he would often say. My counter to his counter was simply that knowing there is some power higher, or greater, than us is not an intellectual matter. Thus, it cannot be described in words. It can be known only by feeling the resonance with what the Truth of God's existence means. And this resonance could only be received by a sense of greatness felt within.

"How does one describe the feeling or resonance one feels when touched by an act of kindness gifted upon us, for example? Words do not contain what has transpired within. Oh, we can call it a feeling. We can label it ecstasy, or bliss, even. We can describe the tears that sealed the sentiment within our heart, even the power of the feeling that etches it indelibly on the lining thereof. But can we really find the words to describe the essence of having been touched by an act of spiritual generosity? Hardly. Poets come as close as anyone, but even their vocabulary and poetic skill cannot match the resonance with the Truth we feel, the Truth of Love resonating with the very same that resides within. We can try to intellectualize it, but it cannot be done. Not with any real accuracy.

"So, dear ones, how do I begin to help you understand the features of God that correlate with your very own, so you can finally accept your divinity without doubt? I'll take you one step closer to the lip on the threshold of Truth by sharing another of my favorite poems. This one comes to us from yet another Persian, the Sufi poet, Rumi. Here's what Rumi says to us, spiking clarity:

> You think of yourself
> as a citizen of the universe.

You think you belong
to this world of dust and matter.
Out of this dust
you have created a personal image,
and have forgotten
about the essence of your true origin.

"Here we are again, back in earth, yet reflecting on the spiritual. Rumi defines for us so clearly the earthly presence we have defined for ourselves. Why is this so? Even a few days ago you might have answered that it is so because we are earthly humans. Not so now I suspect, at least not so in the context of this spiritual translation of Life in which we are engaging. As we now know so well, Life is a metaphor, and little else but. That being so, God also is a metaphor—and so are we. God and we are metaphors, but symbols of creative energy expressed.

"Metaphorically speaking, it is from the idea of mankind that we are spawned. It is from the creative spirit of our mother and father that we were conceived. It is the creative energy emanating from the merging of sperm and egg that excites the extraordinary intelligence in all substance, in the only substance there is. All is formed and perpetuated in the Essence of God. Scientists are telling us now that this is so, whether or not they call substance 'God.' If calling the Essence scientists speak of 'God' offends you, merely refer to it as Essence. But by all means, whether you call it 'God' or 'Essence,' do treat it with the reverence it deserves.

"Scientists also now say that all of Life is constructed of this Essence. My, oh, my, what is the world coming to?" Christ teases, with a wink. "Pretty soon there will be 'groupies for God' dressed in scientific garb!" he mocks.

"Interestingly, all of this clarification is good and fine but it still only deals with it intellectually, more or less objectively, they say—even though the more recent annotations of like kind are showing a lessening in the hardness of literal rationality. To me, it has been entertaining that those who believe only in what they can see, what can be objectified, think that such observations actually are objective. Hardly. As long as a human intellect is attempting some kind of discernment intellectually, from his or her perspective about that topic, it will be subjective. The childhood loom we carry within guarantees that this will be so. Objectivity is impossible in such circumstances. At best, so-called objectivity is relative.

"So what are we left with? Subjectivity. Once one permits him or her self to enter the world of subjectivity, intellectual argument loses its power to interfere. From there on, INtuition, INsight and Enlightenment must prevail. As these come from within each person, in the ways only they can feel them—*know* them, *take meaning* from them—they are subjective. I dare anyone to question that what I *know* is resonating within me or anyone else. Rational, linear, literal approaches cannot work in the world of Spirit. And Spirit is the entire fabric of which Jesus's teachings are woven. The warp of metaphor, while using the metaphysical approach to living, determines the final outlook.

"Well, so what, Christo?" you say to me. Right you are! So *what*? Once again, what is *the* answer? Life is *about* what, not about whom. It is not about *who* we are and *who* is right. It's only about living *what we are*, each moment of every day. Life is about living the Essence of God, our divinity—always, no matter what. It is the condition of our divinity within that defines our outlook. As long as we reside in our heavenly outlook, seeing all of Life as divine, Earth will indeed be exactly as it is in Heaven. If we do not live from our divine Essence, Earth will be exactly as it is in Hell. Either way, we will have chosen exactly where we have landed.

"Of course, all this language and discussion comes from varying levels of approach from humans. Those on either side of the spiritual fence will call one or the other either enlightened or unenlightened. How, then, do we arrive at a clearer understanding of all this? It can't be done intellectually, objectively. Not when we are about discerning spirituality. Intellectuality and objectivity leave us only on the surface of deeper meaning. This takes us back to the Life of the metaphor, the Life of First cause effecting what it must. This we have labeled Creativity. If we add the adjective that modifies, it might look and feel like divine or Loving Creativity. We all know how either comes about now, no matter what we call it.

"Tell me, dear ones," Christo focuses the point sharply, "how can divinity come from that which is not? How can Loving acts or responses—or even just Loving thought—come from that which is not a Loving intention? It cannot. On the other hand even though someone might appear as non-loving, or lacking divinity, appearances, as we well know, are not Truth. All of us—indeed, all Life forms—are divine in Essence, divine as our natural meaning. It is only that we don't always act out of that Essence. Or out of our most natural state.

"The state I'm referring to here is our state of mind: our perspective, our outlook about what Life brings us. Although our natural state is Loving

Essence, and is divine in its makeup, we maintain the rights of choice. With the right comes the responsibility for using choice for highest good. Here again, we all know what this is. It's not a matter of gradations in good. Any choice is either for highest good—or it is not. There's no in between. If it's not for the highest good, we'll know it soon enough. If it's not for the highest good, all it takes to make it good is to reinstate oneself on the road to Mecca. And make sure every step we take goes in that direction.

"Interestingly, all of what has been, and can be, said about divinity, Godliness, and Essence comes out of the mouth of humankind. Is all of it, on either side, divinely inspired, or not? Either way, one must make a choice regarding the ideas one entertains. Again, it is how the choice is exercised that guides what comes of the choice. This is "God's Law" of First Cause once again.

"During our first meeting together, I invested considerable energy explaining some of the character traits attributed to God by mankind. I can repeat all those things to you once again, even though you know yourselves as Loving. Even though you know that when we are fully conscious we all operate from some inner guidance system that never fails us. Some call this 'the Truth that makes us free.' We all know that there is a kind of guiding principle that steers us called 'the highest good.' We know, too, that there is a Spirit that animates us; that there is something we have come to call 'Soul' that expresses as depth of character. We know that we have a Life abundant with divine ideas, with no limits placed on our ability to express all of them through our own unique ways, with all the innate talent and ability we have within us.

"As long as you know all this, and I can tell by your expressions and body posture that you do—so very well, by now—I'm not going to take you through that again. What I am going to suggest, however, comes out of my understanding that rarely does one obtain full meaning without meaning resonating within. Such resonance most often comes when one allows the still small voice to speak within. This is the voice that shows its way as the magnificent resonance we call INspiration, INsight and Enlightenment: that inner knowing that bumps us in the night, in our seat of darkness, so the darkness can give way to light. Here's what I suggest for anyone who has yet to feel one's divinity to the core of his or her being. More than likely, if you are not feeling this, and/or not yet trusting this as Truth for you, it is likely because you are still hung up in an old paradigm, stuck in the old ways of looking at yourself, at God, and at Life in general.

"One good way I have found for jarring one out of the mental imagery which binds us is to take out your *Webster's Unabridged Dictionary* and whatever form of holy writ you use. Begin in a space in which you will not be interrupted. Write down the word 'God' and see how many synonyms you can locate for 'God.' You don't need to be exhaustive in your study. Give yourself just enough opportunity to stretch your understanding, but not so much that it will send you on a yearlong anal-ysis," Christo emphasizes for effect. The emphasis he places on the ending of his last sentence has meaning clear to all. "You may come up with terms like 'goodness,' 'spirit,' 'soul,' 'principle,' 'truth,' and 'love.' The terms matter not. Really, they don't.

"Once you have a reasonably expansive list of synonyms for God—those man-made terms used to define God—then look up the meaning for each. Again, don't be so expansive as to exhaust your interest. However, don't dismiss any of the meanings out of hand, either. Give each meaning full consideration. As you study the various meanings, place each in a column on one side of your paper. As you note them, take them within, one by one, for the meaning that resonates for you. Then ask for Enlightenment as to how you manifest or demonstrate the meaning in the same ways as those attributed to God. Believe me, before long you will find that you regularly reflect God's gaze in daily Life. These marvelous creations of imagery—we call them words, or *the* Word if we want to be Truthful—describe in remarkably accurate ways how we behave when acting out of our divinity. It all depends, of course, on the frame of mind in which we place these words and what characteristics are attributed to them.

Christo pauses ever so slightly to let his explanation sink in. He follows with: "Now let me warn you about something very important to keep in mind. If you are moving along through this exercise without seeing and feeling any connection whatsoever between Godliness and your own Life, I want you to understand that you are greatly undervaluing yourself as a spiritual being.

"Each of the terms you will be fathoming symbolizes some manner of understanding not only about God, but also about how God shows itself to the world. Also, because of their symbolism, they are showing you some meaning about yourself, and how you show yourself to the world. Remember, all of Life is a metaphor that informs us of inner meaning for us. If you're not making the connection, however, don't despair.

"Rather, sit back and exhibit the courage to let your world be big enough—indeed, to let your idea of *God* be big enough—to contain you in it. Have the guts to change your perspective. Get back on the road to Mecca, your personal salvation that only you can provide for yourself. See if the choices you're making in this regard are coming from the high road or the low road.

Then be not afraid to choose again if need be. That's all it takes in any instance where one's feeling of resonance with highest good is lacking: make another choice that puts you back in step on that road to Mecca.

"This is getting a bit heavy, so let me break the heaviness up a bit by sharing with you a story I recently received from Olga, a friend in Greece. The author is unknown, I am told, but whoever wrote it, I am grateful nonetheless. I'd like to read it to you—it goes like this:

> Jerry is the manager of a restaurant. He is always in a good mood. When someone would ask him how he was doing, he would always reply, 'If I were any better, I would be twins!'
>
> Many of the waiters at his restaurant quit their job when he changed jobs so they could follow him around from restaurant to restaurant. Why? Because Jerry was a natural motivator. If an employee was having a bad day, Jerry was always there, telling the employee how to look on he positive side of the situation.
>
> Seeing his style made me curious, so one day I went up to Jerry and asked him: 'I don't get it! No one can be a positive person all of the time. How do you do it?'
>
> Jerry replied, 'Each morning I wake up and say to myself, I have two choices today: I can choose to be in a good mood or I can choose to be in a bad mood. I always choose to be in a good mood. Each time something bad happens, I can choose to be a victim or I can choose to learn from it. I always choose to learn from it. Every time someone comes to me complaining, I can choose to accept their complaining or I can point out the positive side of Life. I always choose to the positive side of Life.'
>
> 'But that's not always easy,' I protested.
>
> 'Yes it is,' Jerry said. 'Life is all about choices. When you cut away all the junk, every situation is a choice. You choose how you react to situations. You choose how people will affect your mood. You choose to be in a good mood or bad mood. It's your choices you live your Life with.'
>
> Several years later, I heard that Jerry accidentally did something you are never supposed to do in the restaurant business: he left the back door of his restaurant open. And then? In the morning he was robbed by three armed men. While Jerry was trying to open the safe, his hand was shaking from nervousness and it slipped off the combination cylinder. The robbers panicked and shot him. Luckily, Jerry was soon found and rushed to the hospi-

tal. After 18 hours of surgery and weeks of intensive care, Jerry was released from the hospital with some of the fragments from the bullets still in his body.

I saw Jerry after the accident. When I asked him how he was, he replied, 'I were any better, I'd be twins. Want to see my scars?'

I declined to see his wounds but did ask him what had gone through his mind as the robbery took place.

'The first thing that went through my mind is that I should have locked the back door,' he replied. 'Then, after they shot me, as I lay on the floor, I remembered that I had two choices: I could choose to live or I could choose to die. I chose to live.'

'Weren't you scared?' I asked.

Jerry continued, 'The paramedics were great. They kept telling me that I was going to be fine. But when they wheeled me into the ER and I saw the expressions on the faces of the doctors and nurses, I got really scared. In their faces, I read, 'He's a dead man.' I knew I had to take action.'

'What did you do?' I asked.

'Well, there was a big nurse shouting questions at me,' said Jerry. 'She asked if I was allergic to anything.'

'Yes,' I replied.

'The doctors and nurses stopped working and waited for my reply. I took a deep breath and yelled, 'Bullets!' Over their laughter, I told them, 'I am choosing to live. Please operate on me as if I am alive, not dead.'

Jerry lived, thanks to the skill of the doctors, but also because of his amazing attitude. I learned from him that every day you have the choice either to enjoy your Life or hate it. The thing that is truly yours—that no one can take from you—is your attitude. So, if you take care of that, everything else in Life becomes much easier.

"What a sweet story!" Christo declares. "Not only does it deal with the dualistic ways in which we can make choices, but, even more important—and the very point I want to stress—is that it speaks to the attitude with which we make them—what drives our choices. Thus we come full-tilt back to the expressing the attitude of the intellect or that of the heart. As we have come to understand, Truth comes from only one: the heart. Therefore, if we are sincere about our commitment to Truth, it is only from the heart that our attitude can reflect that Truth. End of story. Well, now, back to the Truth we left before this charming story appeared on our doorstep.

"Once you come to recognize as your very own the same traits and behavior God witnesses, ascertain your *feelings* as you resonate with that meaning for you. Know that you could not—most assuredly, could *not*—resonate with them unless they occupied you. What a wonderful affirmation of our divinity, is it not? We cannot *feel* something within if we don't *have IT* within. Resonance is what renders something as True for us, and is found only within us.

"In any event, at some point, if you will just allow this of yourself, you will come to know, to discern, your divinity, without fail and without qualification—without the veil that formerly clouded your True self from view, *your* view. More often than not our friends and family, despite being able to point out our seeds of vulnerability, can easily point out our spacious divinity at the same time. Of this you can be sure: when one is coming from one's own seat of divinity, all you *can* be is divine to them. Just as they are divine. It is only when they forget their own divinity that we are not divine to them. This same shoe fits on our feet. When we cannot see another as divine, it is *only* because we are forgetting our own divinity. When we find ourselves failing to define ourselves correctly as divine, it is only because we have dislocated Truth in a moment of self-constructed demise. This dislocation of our divinity is that place where we find ourselves ill at ease, feeling inharmonious with the world. It is the place from which we must find our way back on the trail to salvation if we are to avoid a sense of permanence in our dis-ease or disharmony.

"What does this shift take? All it takes is a re-membering with a clear sense of our divinity once again, a rejoining with our understanding that the uneasiness we feel or sense or otherwise come to know is but a gift of symbolism that says that we have gone astray from our divinity. Each one is a gift that says to us: 'Stop. Look. Listen to what's happening within.' And then return your steps in the direction of your most natural state of divinity. All it takes is that one first step in another direction to get you on your way. The rest is down hill from there, down hill towards Heaven, where one and all is divine. God is that. You are that, as am I. And they—all the theys—also are that. All *is* that.

"Just the other day a dear friend handed me the lyrics to a marvelous piece of music called, 'In His Eyes.' The music is by Mindy Jostyn, with lyrics by Mindy Jostyn and Jacob Brackman. I'll change it only slightly to 'degenderize'

God. Listen carefully, now, to one inspired view of how God sees us: of how we are seen from the seat of these artists' hearts, from the seats of their divinity. In this marvelous melody they are depicting what we are when we allow ourselves to see our divinity and act from it. Actually, whether we do or not, this is such a lovely description of the Truth in which we are seen." Christo pauses, takes a deep breath, and proceeds to exude the Soul of Life in his delivery.

IN HIS EYES

"In God's eyes you're a fire that never goes out, a light on the top of a hill.
In God's eyes you're a poet, a painter, a prophet, with a mission of love to fulfill.

Outside there's a world so enchantingly strange, a maze of illusion and lies.
But there's never a story that ever could change the glory of you in God's eyes.

In God's eyes you're a radiant vision of beauty, a gemstone cut one of a kind.
You're fine as a diamond, deep as a ruby, rare as jade in God's mind.

No need to believe all you may have been told, no need to live in disguise.You're brighter than silver, purer than gold, a pearl beyond price in God's eyes.

God sees only goodness. God's vision is true. And nothing can change the perfection of you in God's eyes.

In God's eyes you're a fire that never goes out, a light on top of the hill.
You're a rose in the forest, a prelude from Bach, a triumph of heavenly skill.

Outside there's a world that keeps breaking your heart, and tearing your dreams down to size.

But guiding you homeward, piercing the dark—is the love light that shines in God's eyes.

Now and forever that light never dies. You're dearly beloved in God's eyes."

The air is pregnant with pause. Moist eyes are everywhere found. Wisely, Christo lets everyone bathe in the warmth of Spirit that blankets every corner of the arena. He waits. And waits. And waits some more. Finally, he takes a deep, appreciative breath and wades, ever so delicately, into this sea of emotion. "I can see," Christo begins, "that you have been deeply moved by this extraordinary gift of song. Where did it touch you? I suspect it resonated with that song within you that awaits expression. Resonated with your very own music that awaits fulfillment: your own particular brand of divinity expressed through you.

"You know what else?" Christo asks, beckoning further meaning from within. "Hear this carefully, now. The *only* reason such lovely infilling touches us is because we have the Truth of it within us. We cannot see beauty, for example, if we have none within. We cannot appreciate the Word if we don't have appreciation for the Word we are within. In exactly the same way, the counter forces of fear or anger cannot trigger us if they are not within. We have all of it, all Life offers within. All of Life is contained within, as the perfection of our completeness. So you see, we lack nothing. We need another not to fulfill or complete us. We need another only to reflect to us our completeness—so we can share our completeness with another who also is complete. Completeness shared is blissful, to be sure.

"This is the perfection of which Jesus spoke when he said: 'Be ye perfect even as God is perfect,' perfect meaning 'complete:' having all the treasures, all the imagery, all that is possibly contained in the kingdom of Heaven—the kingdom of divine thoughts, divine ideas that we use in creation. If we didn't have all these symbols within, in this vast store house of Truth called Life, we couldn't recognize any of it in the mirrors Life presents to us. In a word, without the completeness of symbolic meaning, we would be at a loss to resonate with much of Life at all. Yet, there isn't one of us here, or anywhere for that matter, who could not resonate with Love, beauty, sexuality, poetic justice, anger, danger, fear—we could go on endlessly but need not. I can tell you've gotten the message.

"The message that has been hidden from us, however—because we have been led to dwell in the house of literal rationality and judgment—is that we have it all, because we *are* all of it. This is the All in all we attribute to God. Created in the same image and likeness of God, it is we, too, then, who have it all. Which, when we follow our course of beginning rightly in this virginal meaning of Life, comes to mean that we, of the same Essence as is God, also are All in all. All we are. All we see. All Life brings to us. Such is the definition of Oneness.

"Are we any closer now to *really* knowing our inherent divinity—and to knowing divinity in all? To *being only the divinity we are,* and to expressing ourselves faithfully to, obediently to, divinity? I don't need any affirmation of hands raised. I can see in your eyes and hearts that you are right there. If any of you do feel the need for more, you can gain reinforcement by going back to the material from our last time together. It's available now for your edification.

"But you don't need more words now. You need the quietude, the stillness of body and soul, to let all this meaning assimilate into the fiber of what you are. The size of this virgin birth—this newly realized self-concept that is now unadulterated by external view, uncontaminated by any self-deceit, fresh and unadorned with anything but the Truth of that knowing resonance—is huge. It is so huge as to be represented as the birth of healthy septuplets. You are the extraordinary midwives who deliver this glorious birth of Truth to the world. Be assured that sometime soon, very soon now, you will be living it fully, and blessing the rest of the world with your own unique brand of divinity that brightens all. No longer is your light hidden under a bushel, dear divine ones.

"We are adjourned for the evening. We'll reconvene during brunch promptly at 11:00 in the morning. Rest well. I acknowledge and celebrate all you are, and the magnificence of your divinity all the more. Namaste, and good night," Christo concludes with obvious testimony to the light he sees shining so brightly from all.

"Namaste, Christo," returns ever so softly, so genuinely, so very apprecia- tively from the gathering. The deliberate filing out that connotes the Transcen- dent space in which all now find themselves reinforces this sweet return.

Christo is overwhelmed by the magnitude of the Spirit's presence at this moment. The arena is filled with a sense of promise and an air of inescapable Truth rendered in one and all. He smiles warmly as he greets his aides, who are similarly affected by this reality. Putting his arms around the shoulders of sev- eral at once he leads them out towards a sound night's rest. The deeply Loving presence accompanies all, on through to their awakening.

CHAPTER 10

Coming Home to the Seat of Immaculate Conception

During the brunch scene everyone appears to be well rested, but not particularly because they had a good deal of sleep. If anything, it is because the sleep they had was a deep sleep. The kind of deep sleep that comes from a mind at peace and a soul filled with joy. It is the kind of sleep one has when one feels completely at home with him or herself, contented with the heart's content and the Soul's embrace.

The fact of the matter is that after the session last evening had closed, the call to simply unwind before going to bed struck many of the participants. A good number of them decided to follow the inner calling and just hung out with one another for awhile. They shared deep feelings. Scenes painted themselves with Enlightenment. Inner landscapes were brushed by their comfort with the place in which they now found themselves. Across the board there was a depth of meaning that permeated them beyond previous reckoning.

This truism is confirmed time after time as Christo and his aides circulate through the various gatherings during the brunch hour. Such confirmation is not really needed for Christo to know the Truth about such claims, for he feels the Truth in the depths of his bone marrow. He knows both within and without that the showdown is on its way.

True to his word, promptly at 11:00 AM Christo strides happily across the stage to the podium. The gathering in all its fullness is ready for whatever this resting in Truth shall bring. Beaming love throughout the arena with a broad, deep smile across his face and a twinkle in his eye, Christo greets them with the usual—yet at an even deeper level that ever before: "Namaste, dear divine ones." Before he can utter another word, the mass speaks out in the form of a generously spirited: "Namaste, Christo." Within these words there is a warmth that informs Christo that they are indeed home, but just don't know it fully yet.

"Thank you, one and all. Your energy tells me that I should extend my greeting just a little. I do so by saying to you with absolute authority: 'Welcome home, one and all.' On the most important levels you *are* home. For the rest of the matrix that inhabits your being, this is but at the very threshold of total Truth for you. So you look like a True believer who has one foot outside the door where it seems more familiar to you even yet. But the other foot—the one that is now comfortable in your transcendent world of spirituality—it is successfully, and blissfully I might add, planted firmly and safely inside—beyond reluctance and doubt.

"The goal, as you know, is to become single-minded about Life. Right now the situation looks akin to the schizophrenic who splits his personality between one world and the other. What some of you are witnessing is like a spiritual schizophrenia. Not to worry. This is easily curable, and you will be solidly all the way through the door of the spiritual realm quickly now. Just keep walking with me in the direction of personal salvation and we'll soon be there.

"Our time together before you depart will be invested in getting you all the way across the gap that separates you from yourself. You don't need a great big push, only a gentle nudge from a familiar space. So that's where we'll begin this morning, at a place that is now familiar to you. That which you will soon call your real home is in sight. It's just around the corner. We'll round the corner ever so carefully, so you won't be delayed any longer in your journey to home. So you'll be sure to arrive safe and sound. And whole.

Christo pauses to let the feelings of safety and trust sink in. He takes a deep breath and heads them around the curve this way: "Let's begin, then, with a brief sorting out of how we've gotten to where we are right now. We've seen how those largely unconscious images we took on as a child have loaded our warp upon which we weave Life. We've seen both the warm and fuzzy and the bold and brittle threads as they found their way onto the warp. We've felt both kinds of feelings deeply enough to be able to acknowledge any kindred feelings whenever they appear.

"We've also envisioned from our field of memories what happens when someone or something from the weft we call Life crosses similar threads on our warp. In a word, the juncture of familiarity perpetrates a resonance within. It exaggerates that same feeling because it is layered in our fabric. This exaggeration forms the *resonance* that has become our devoted friend by now. It is the ego put to work on our behalf; the flag-waver that invites us to look within rather than without for what's happening at a given moment.

"So, armed with all we need to return to that place of peace and harmony, we go within. We go within not to plow some fear-filled field of yesteryear. Rather, we go within to allow the light to pierce and clear the clouds that have kept us in the dark all this time. We have practiced—both through sitting meditation and active meditation—letting Truth come through to us with the clarity only it can bring to the surface. We no longer question whether the Truth is that which comes out of the spiritual approach of INtuition, INsight, Enlightenment, and leads on to Transcendence. We no longer question that each of the latter is the natural response to the issuance of innocently-placed wonder.

"Finally, we no longer doubt that the awe we witness on the other side of innocence is the affirmation of Truth personified through us. Awe thus becomes commonplace. Instead of seeing what seem like miracles appear before us, we come instead to know the meaning of such shifts—these so-called miracles—as our inalienable right. They show up regularly as the gifts of our most natural process of Loving Creation. Now miracles are simply a fact of Life. Real Life: the commonplace, the Life that permeates our spirituality. This is the Life we now call 'our divinity,' 'Godliness.'

"Do not think for a moment, folks, even though they are commonplace, that their special nature is lost. Oh, no, quite the contrary. Because we are now conscious of their presence, we are ever-aware of their special nature and of the Godliness they represent. Before, when we were mostly asleep, these same occurrences seemed different than they really are because they abruptly awakened us from our slumber, from the land of the dead. So they looked bigger than Life to us. Now that we're awakened from the dead, however, we know that they *are* Life. And we are to celebrate Life for all Life is.

"We now know, as well, that when we consciously apply only threads of harmony—those threads we have come to identify as our divinity—that our warp looks and feels very different to us. In Truth, it *is* very different. From now on the threads of divinity glow in their Truth as the foundation for weaving Life as divine. Each thread is now golden, fully alchemized in its ability to transform that that comes to it.

"There can be no doubt that what comes to us will come to us just as it is. Just as it did when it earlier crossed the threads of our warp. But now—because we have understood the meaning of those feelings deeply felt—when Life brings their familiarity to us, we read Life in a very different manner. We read all of Life from the seat of our divinity. Using *only* those lenses, we read each intersection of what could appear to be a potentially disturbing characterization with equanimity instead. We recognize them for their inharmonious coloration, but we treat them *beyond* appearance. We treat them with divinity. We respond *only* from our perspective *of* divinity.

"Therefore, rather than point fingers, or respond in kind when something now mild in appearance—mild because it is no longer exaggerated by the contents of our old warp—we now embrace the person's divinity. In the process, we cast away the appearance of the imagery that would have formerly disturbed us. If we have some remnants of that old warp still within us, we now simply look at each of them from the very same perspective: our divinity. Likewise, we embrace the gift for what it is and cast away its memory in favor of the Truth it has brought us. This is transcendence.

"For example, this is not to say that we should tolerate someone who is physically or emotionally abusing us. It's not about allowing the abuse. It's about the attitude or frame of reference we use to deal with it. We separate the act from the actor. We love the actor in all her or his divinity. And we treat the act only in a way that holds the perpetrator accountable. In this way, that someone retains his or her dignity while they fulfill their responsibility for accountability. We hold ourselves responsible for Loving no matter what. They must be held responsible for their actions. Thus both are held accountable. And in the long run, both win.

"What we have also come to understand is that by allowing this powerful change of transcendence to come about, we have essentially become alchemists. We have learned to use our divinity to shift the meaning of Life from that which we *see* without, to that which we *know* within. Our vision is shifted completely, as is that which we will have seen. Talk about alchemy! Indeed, when we change how we see, what we see changes before our very eyes. But don't fool yourselves any longer. It's our perspective that changes how we see. All we see from our seat of divinity suddenly becomes exactly that: divine. This is the ultimate personification of the win-win scenario. Just as Jesus did, I call it 'grace,' the grace that is our sufficiency in all matters Life brings us.

"How are you enjoying this movie called, 'This is Your Life?'" Christo asks. The gathering is so 'with it,' that he doesn't need any confirmation from them at all. "Good, then. My aides will soon be along with popcorn and drinks," he teases. "Where else have we been? We know that all along this journey to fully acknowledging your divinity there has been some discomfort. It's difficult to shift the meaning that has formed our lives so dramatically to date. Yet, step by careful step, we have traversed through the eye of the needle.

"Just like the Master Jesus taught us, in order to reach divinity we have to give up all our treasures of old. Not our material treasures, but rather those ideas and beliefs that have gotten us this far on our journey. Once we have cast these aside, the new can appear and be shaped to need. When a door to the past closes, a window open to newfound opportunity awaits us. Believe me, every one of you here has closed the door to the past perspectives you have used to translate Life. Every one of you now speaks in a very different tongue: the tongue of metaphorical meaning that leads to metaphysical presence. From the perspective of perspective, every one of you is in a vastly different place than you were when you arrived yesterday.

"In each shift that has taken place divinity is now embedded. Divinity is that which makes Enlightenment and transcendence—your resurrection—possible. Through our conversation last evening, you have come to the understanding on yet another plane that you and all are indeed divine. In each instance along the way—wherever Enlightenment has displaced ignorance—you have had a virgin birth. The only difference between the presence presently felt and that, which was previously ignored, is your conscious awareness of it. So now you consciously know that you can regularly gift yourself with the virgin births represented by new perspectives appearing in their swaddling clothes.

"Oh, oh," gasps Christo, "I've inadvertently let the cat out of the bag. That declaration isn't quite the Truth, is it? As a matter of fact, it's not even close to the Truth. The Truth is that I wasn't keenly aware of the inner prompting that was telling me to move to the main point of this morning's session. So the Truth simply by-passed me and burped it out in its own way.

"If you were paying attention, and I know you were, the last phrase to come out of my mouth—before I confessed, that is—was 'swaddling clothes.' Where does this phrase take you?" Christo tosses out the bait. Knowing smiles cross the faces of the entire gathering, lighting up the arena in an aura of anticipation. "You, of all people, I'm sure, will remember that I promised no more shoe-dropping. I guess I'll just have to shift your perspective a bit so you won't hold me accountable for that crazy declaration. Rather than drop a shoe, I'll drop a bomb instead. There," Christo jokes, "I'm cleared from any accusation of duplicity or deceit.

"Believe me, to many the perspective I am about to take you through would be seen as a bomb, larger even that the atomic bomb. Not so much by you, but by those who have invested in a belief founded so strongly in rational literalism. Pretty strong language I'm using here. The strong language I'm referring to, of course, is that of metaphor, in juxtaposition with the literal, objective, rational language used so frequently in religious circles.

"So as not to drag on this drama, I'll get right into it. What I want to share with you now is the story about the birth of Jesus. With this story must come some consideration of the immaculate conception. If not, our discovery would be incomplete. While we're at it, we might shed some metaphorical light on Jesus's being the son of David. Because the story of Jesus's birth is so often treated literally, the symbolic nature of the virgin birth is simply lost to most. Let's see what we can do about that.

"The stories about immaculate conception and Jesus's birth are as follows. I take them first from the Gospel of Matthew (1:18-26) and then from Luke (2:1-20). First, let us hear the word according to Matthew:

'This is how Jesus Christ came to be born. His mother Mary was betrothed to Joseph; but before they came together she was found to be with child through the Holy Spirit. Her husband Joseph, being an upright man and wanting to spare her disgrace, decided to divorce her informally. He had made up his mind to do this when suddenly the angel of the Lord appeared to him in a dream and said, "Joseph, son of David, do not be afraid to take Mary home as your wife, because she has conceived what is in her by the Holy Spirit. She will give birth to a son and you must name him Jesus, because he is the one who is to save his people for their sins."

Now all this took place to fulfill what the Lord has spoken through the prophet:

Look! the virgin is with child and will give birth to a son whom they will call Immanuel, a name which means 'God-is-with-us.' When Joseph woke up he did what the angel of the Lord had told him to do: he took his wife to his home; he had not had intercourse with her when she gave birth to a son; and he named him Jesus.'

Christo continues reading carefully: "And now this from Luke. Then we'll deal with this information metaphorically to see where we come out.

'Now it happened that at this time Caesar Augustus issued a decree that a census should be made of the whole inhabited world. This census—the first—took place while Quirinius was governor of Syria, and everyone went to be registered, each to his own town. So Joseph sent out from the town of Nazareth in Galilee for Judea, to David's town called Bethlehem, since he was of David's House and line, in order to be registered together with Mary, his betrothed, who was with child. Now it happened that, while they were there, the time came for her to have her child, and she gave birth to a son, her first-born. She wrapped him is swaddling clothes and laid him in a manger because there was no room for them in the living space. In the countryside close by there were shepherds out in the fields keeping guard over their sheep during the watches of the night. An angel of the Lord stood over them and the glory of the Lord shone around them. They were terrified, but the angel said, "Do not be afraid. Look, I bring you news of great joy, a joy to be shared by the whole people. Today in the town of David a Savior has been born to you; he is Christ the Lord. And here is a sign for you: you will find a baby wrapped in swaddling clothes and lying in a manger. And all at once with the angel there was a great throng of hosts of heaven, praising God with the words:

Glory to God in the highest heaven, and on earth peace to those he favors.

Now it happened that when the angels had gone from them into heaven, the shepherds said to one another, "Let us go to Bethlehem and see this even which the Lord has made known to us.' So they hurried away and found Mary and Joseph, and the baby lying in the manger. When they saw the child they repeated what they had been told about him, and everyone who heard it was astonished at what the shepherds said to them. As for Mary, she treasured all these things and pondered them in her heart. And the shepherds went back glorifying and praising God for all they had heard and seen, just as they had been told.'

"There we are," concludes Christo with a deep breath, so he can begin now by placing what they have just heard in juxtaposition to some metaphorical mediation. "It is tempting," Christo resumes, "for me to speak about how some of what is in these texts might not be true at all. Or, at the very least, that it could be highly distorted by those who have altered scripture to give it the meaning they desired. That is not my purpose today, however. My only purpose is to read these wonderful stories now in metaphorical terms, just as we were admonished by Jesus to do. If we are to deal *with* God in spiritual terms, why should we not then also deal with stories *about* God in spiritual terms?

"You will recall Jesus teaching us that if we are to learn of God, we must do so spiritually: treat God spiritually. We must look at God in Spirit, with our thoughts, and not in material Life. We do so by using the meaning that comes from the Word, by using those symbols that provide meaning from within. Jesus also taught largely by the example of his Life—and by stories *about* Life. If we spiritualize them as Jesus admonished us to, we come to the understanding of the real use of stories. They are fictional propositions that tell us Truth. This is the path of the Holy Spirit: the avenue of divine ideas upon which we walk. It is this path that enlightens, through which darkness gives way to light. Let us, then, look for the metaphors in these two representations of Mary's immaculate conception and thus of Jesus's virgin birth.

"First off, we see Joseph spoken of as the son of David. Yet David was his father, far removed. It's biological lineage that's being spoken of here. Later on, Jesus is also spoken of as the son of David and Abraham. In the material world, such designations speak to Joseph's, and thus Jesus's, rich heritage. He is the son of the first born—the first cause—lifted right out of Genesis in the Old Testament. And 'David' refers to King David, thus once again giving both Joseph and his proclaimed son, Jesus, special stature. Indeed, even in the old way, literal rationalism, Jesus was special. So special was he that they wanted Jesus to demonstrate his heritage as the son of a king, so he would be their leader on earth, just as King David had been.

"But Jesus was special not for these reasons. Jesus was rendered special by his teachings, which in and of themselves made him the metaphorical king of kings. His ideas, his ways of seeing spiritual Life, of reframing God, were kingly in nature. It is *his ideas* that were to rule, and not Jesus himself. Metaphorically speaking, Jesus represented a heritage that sprang from the idea of the First born, the First cause, giving way to all that follows it when the First cause is expressed faithfully, with conviction—with all our body, mind, spirit and strength—and with a single-mindedness that is guaranteed to bring First cause successfully to fruition.

"Metaphorically, we also know that Jesus favored not the lineage attributable to man, but only to God. Hence, metaphorically, we are all children of God, and not of our so-called biological parents. We begin at First cause and flow through our parents; it is through our midwives that we are given to Life. Spiritually, then, we are all brothers and sisters, no matter what biologists may render us."

Christo pauses between each of the distinctions made between the literal and metaphorical perspectives so the participants can absorb each layer before going on to the next. "Now," he continues, "we have another means used to elevate Jesus's importance. Here Mary is depicted as being impregnated directly by God instead of by her husband. Again, if we look at Jesus's teachings, these are enough to elevate his importance to the world. And in addition, the virgin birth is not unique to Jesus, for it is used in other parallel stories for the same purpose. So, for our purposes we shall discard the literal treatment of Mary's immaculate conception and Jesus's birth for the moment.

"What other metaphorical clues do we have in these stories? Well, first off, Mary is found to be with child through the Holy Spirit, directly from God, it is posed. Metaphorically speaking Mary represents the feminine aspect of God, depicting receptivity and acceptance. She represents that within us that comes as immaculately conceived, that with which both she—and thus we—are impregnated. 'Immaculate' speaks to the idea of purity, of being faultless, perfect, innocent, spotless, stainless, untarnished, and unsoiled. 'Conception' speaks to the origination of an idea. If we marry these, much as Mary did, we come up with an idea whose time has come: an idea that heretofore has not been taken seriously. Perhaps it has never been seriously considered. But as part of a metaphorical story, it makes perfect sense.

"What the story of Mary's immaculate conception tells us is that we have a new perspective being delivered to us, impregnating us, actually. It is a perspective that can save us from all our ill-found ways of perceiving—from all our sins, from all those ways that have missed the mark in guiding us to the means of living our natural lives as divine entities. It is this new perspective with which God impregnated Mary. And it is this very perspective that was embodied in the figure of the baby Jesus.

"On the other hand," Christo continues with great zeal, "we have Joseph, who is depicted as wanting to send Mary on her way. His way of thinking is the counter to Mary's. Having made up his mind to separate from this potential, he represents the old way of thinking, the Old Testament to which he was married. Metaphorically, Joseph is tied to that view by the linkage with his physical lineage, which represents 'for all time,' all the way from the founding father, Abraham, on through others, including King David.

"Ah," Christo delights, "but Joseph's views change when he, too, is struck with a new perspective about all this. In the form of an angel, this messenger from God brings a new perspective that allows Joseph the grace to accept the appropriateness of this new revelation. This new way is now considered proper because the angel of God has given it credence. In the language of metaphor, it is right simply because God's gifts of INsight and Enlightenment—which have come out of Joseph's dream or vision as legitimate ideas—have now also declared it so. Thus INsight and Enlightenment are rendered sacred, divine in origin. Truth now reigns for Joseph, in the form of the Word that has come from within, not outside of him any longer. As a miracle for all time, Joseph has thus also been impregnated, but by God, not man. Indeed, yet another immaculate conception is witnessed. And the only child Joseph will midwife is the same one all of us will give birth to, regularly. Indeed, unto us a child is born: God's gift of new birth we are to fulfill.

"We should be careful here to understand that a dream is a dream is a dream, no matter when or in what form it comes to inform us symbolically. The same is true for every vision. Whatever comes to us from within is that, no matter when it chooses to inform us with INsight and Enlightenment. Just as in dreams, their purpose is to offer us symbolic meaning about Life's Truths. Their purpose is to deliver. And as for us, our purpose is to decipher. But unless we work through the framework of symbolism rather than of literalism, the gifts will have been wasted, just like Life itself. If we don't use all the symbols Life provides for us as a means for discovering inner Truth, Life itself will be a waste in our view.

"So the visions or dreams, these visitations of informers or angels from God, are rendered holy. They are holy or sacred because they lead us to transcendence, our resurrection beyond the old perspective. In this case, as in all cases, the new perspective is seen to be the First cause. By its very implantation into Mary's mind, and then Joseph's, who finally relents to its validity, it is that which heads them in the direction to which it points.

"Here again we have every step towards our salvation, the ideal, begun and taken in exactly the right direction. This is the model we are to follow: to be obedient to the divine gifts we receive moment by moment from within. It is to these we are to be most faithful if we are to reap the harvest they intend. As in the story of First cause, this rendering also represents the birth of metaphysics: the idea that everything that manifests in earth is born out of a First cause, or initial dream—the newborn idea or divination that points us to the higher road upon which we are now to travel. Until now, this has been the road less taken.

"By the way, as a quick aside, all this relates perfectly to the dream Life referred to by the Australian Aborigines. Looking at their take on dreams is another fascinating study of metaphorical meaning.

"More to the point here, however, when we add to this Mary's abiding devotion to the clarity she receives in her dream, yet another new perspective comes to Life. Joseph and Mary are wed, but he is willing to give her up, essentially by annulling the marriage. Mary, who initially differs with Joseph about birthing the new brain-child, is witnessing to the vow she has taken to hold her marriage to God most high. Her choice is not to demean or diminish her relationship with Joseph, but only to establish the Truth that we are wedded first and foremost to Godliness—to that which comes out of us and points to highest good. The divine. This takes precedence over the earthly considerations, represented here by Joseph's concern over how others will think about Mary bearing a child while being virgin.

"In a very real sense—metaphorically, that is—we have depicted in this story the symbolic description of the new era replacing the old. It is the New Testament to Truth replacing the old means, the Old Testament that was bonded with earthly considerations rather than with the spiritual, thus rendering it replete with illusion.

"Mary's testimony is about staying faithful to the gift of divine idea. It is that which is special to us about this story. It is that which represents the riches that come to us in the night. The testimony is that which is represented by the star that guides us out of darkness to the newfound perspective or idea, that which comes to us as the kingly babe. It is the Enlightenment that represents the magical gifts of wisdom, the Magi that visit upon the Life of the newborn INsight. That is the story of the virgin birth—and, yes—the story of our spiritual Life.

"I just adore the presentation of the bright star in the night that guides the 'wise men' to the stable. The storyteller could just have easily portrayed this scene using a sunrise out of the east to depict the birth of a new perspective about Life. But isn't the contrast between the old and new more dramatic when envisioned as a single bright light guiding us out of darkness? As a light by which those who are wise are guided to the scene of its birth—the birth given of the First cause? Is this not a story of darkness giving way to light? A story about ignorance giving way to Enlightenment, and about transcendence leading us to resurrection portrayed as being born again: being as a child? Don't you just *love* it?" provokes Christo.

"An added wrinkle appears here when it comes time to name the baby Jesus. You will recall that Joseph is told to name the newborn Immanuel, which means 'God is with us.' Later, Mary and Joseph name him Jesus, which means 'God saves.' Truth is all in a name it is said, provided that we understand that a name is merely a metaphor for the Truth of God in all. Understanding that all *is* God, by *whatever* name, is the key. All we need do is go within in order to hear its still small voice. It is Truth that reigns, after all—and that which makes us free—from all outside distractions of illusion.

"Through the benefit of metaphor once again, we gain understanding of the meaning of Jesus's name as a correlative for what Jesus came to teach us: that a change in perspective sheds new light on Life as it comes to us. Indeed, this teaching alone saves us from the error of a warped perspective. It enables us to clear out the perspectives that hold us in darkness in favor of those that shed light on the Truth that lies within. From this perspective it is not about Jesus himself who saved us from our sins by dying on the cross for us. It is what Jesus's *teachings* save us from, that is, our erroneous ways of shaping Life through a mostly unconsciously developed perspective.

"Isn't this fun?" Christo exclaims joyously. Again, he needs no response to his rhetorical request. People are on the edge of their seats, so enthralled are they with Christo's explanation. He pulls them in a good bit more by asking: "Had enough or do you want more? How many want to continue this glorious walk through the eye of the needle? Raise a hand." The unanimous affirmation of his intention speaks louder than words. Indeed, the gathering is enjoying this to the hilt. "Well...all right, then," he drags his words out in feigned deliverance, "I'm not sure I can go much further but I'll give it a try." They mutually hold the space in amusement.

"Now let's look at what it is that Mary sees in her vision. You will recall that an angel who told her that she was giving birth to a son had visited Mary. In the parlance of the metaphor, she would be giving birth to a brainchild. As a midwife, she was to see to it that this sacred new idea, in all its divinity, was born into Life. Again, the baby Jesus represents this new concept. As we later learn from the transcripts depicting him, the example of Jesus's Life and all the teachings that come from it are rife with divinity.

"His teaching reverses the old way of thinking about Life. The old way has us believing that all is to come from outside authority, that we are separate from God and from his elevated son, Jesus. That only God and Jesus are divine, when we are filled instead with original sin, and thus need healing from an outside source. That we need to work hard to overcome our natural affinity for sin so we can one day reach the heavenly state.

'On the other hand, Jesus's teaching is about all of us being divine. It's about all of us being perfect, just as God who infills us with glorious creations of thought is perfect. It is about all being One. It's about being in Heaven every moment of our lives simply by devoting ourselves to the Truth of our divinity and the divinity of all. It's about being a society of healers. It is in these very enlightening perspectives, founded in the purity of Love, that our perfection is personified.

"It is these teachings of Jesus that change our world from darkness to light. It is these that enable us to acknowledge and accept and live our divinity, to live Truth as it comes to us. So *abundantly* does the Truth of enlightened perspective come to us. This is the grace of God that is our sufficiency in all matters. Please—*please*—" Christo pleads, "don't ever again allow yourselves to come at Life out of fear of lacking something. There is nothing we lack when we address that which comes from within in all abundance, infinitely so. All we need to do is to become aware of our perspective on all that comes to us and discern whether or not it falls under the rubric of 'divinity.' If the answer is affirming, then by all means we just need to stay with it, stay on track with our voyage to Mecca. If, on the other hand, our perspective is found to be contrary to divinity, all it takes is one more decision to change it. All it takes is one decision to begin our walk straight towards Mecca once again: a simple decision to pick up our bed and walk, and to sin no more. How simple can it get?

"Let's look for a little lighter side of all this, lighter in the sense of how clever the authors of this story are. Even the seemingly smallest detail sometimes affords us a present if we just look at it that way. Let's take the idea of Jesus's being born in a stable and placed in manger. There was no room at the inn, the place where the norm resides. What a dramatic depiction this is! Can you imagine a better way to describe the distance between what this new birth represents than to seat it in a place beneath the dignity of the imagery common to the day—in a stable? Placed in a manger, a trough from which animals are fed?

"Metaphorically speaking, of course, there is no room given in common everyday thought to such a simple, yet profound, INsight. When most everyone holds the thought of material Life being the be-all, and end-all—instead of using the material to inform the spiritual—how many would even be able to understand such a shift in perspective, let alone house it in their mind's eye? It is so far out of their realm, they—the representatives of this new spiritual configuration—are sent where others wouldn't even think of going, where others wouldn't even think of laying their head. Or think of exposing themselves to. Indeed, there's no room in the inn or house of literal thought for such profundity. It is seen as so obscene by those unfamiliar with it that it must be cast aside, and thus demeaned as much as possible.

"But Jesus and Mary are not at all uncomfortable with their quarters. They are right at home where they belong, in a place quite different from the norm. Indeed, that which saves is about to be born.

"And how about Jesus's being wrapped in swaddling clothes? You will remember with me, I am sure, that clothes are the ideas and thoughts in which we wrap our lives. Those perspectives we use to clothe our outlook on Life. Swaddling clothes are tight wrappings used on an infant. For most of us, our clothes are so loose as to accommodate most any perspective, except that one found in the seat of our divinity. The authors wanted to keep the clues for understanding all this so mysterious that they placed them within, where most of us would never look!

"Anyhow, our clothes symbolically represent those perspectives gained from without. In the case of Jesus—this wonderful gift whose Life is about the perspective gained from Inner Authority—in contrast with our clothing, we find that his is tightly wrapped. Said another way, being tightly wrapped represents the idea that we must exercise single-mindedness toward the necessity of going within for the Enlightenment only divinity can grace us with. Again, what a marvelously simple message this is. It's perfectly akin to the story about going through the eye of the needle, and the one about walking the straight and narrow path. Indeed, the new birth needs to be tightly wrapped.

"Yes, my dear ones, Life is indeed simple. At least if we just follow the simple process Jesus came to teach us. Yes. Jesus's teachings are the way to Truth. And Truth defines Life from the perspective that comes from within: from the seat of INspiration, INsight, and Enlightenment.

"I know very well that all this would be considered heretical by many in organized religion. This troubles me not, for I know that I am responsible only for letting it out into the world so that others can do with it what they feel led to do. Mine is only to deliver. Theirs is to decipher for themselves. No matter what they do with what moves them, it is of no consequence to me. All of what they do only speaks to where they are in the seat of divine perspective.

"If you just sit with all this for a time—or, better yet, give your own INsight to it—you'll be utterly amazed at what a magnificently rich and enlightening story the immaculate conception and virgin birth make. I could go on ad nauseum, but will save you from that. I think we've gone about as far with this as we need to here. I do suggest, however, that you do wrap yourselves in these swaddling clothes for awhile—at least until you feel comfortable in them. What a difference it will make in your outlook.

"Of course, you're welcome to investigate this marvelous story further on your own. Over a snack when we break, on the way home today, or with a neighbor—if you dare," Christo teases. "I'd love to hear about your travels in this direction if you'd care to share them with me. Who knows? We might even be able to rewrite the gospels," Christo delivers with tongue in cheek.

Christo's use of humor contrasts with his sudden shift to solemnity. Slowly, with a serious tone in his voice and look on his face, he punctuates the last half hour or so: "I have something to tell you. If you remember nothing else, remember this: The entire story of Life is about nothing but the Creation Spirit. What we think is that which we use to create our world around us. When each divine spiritual gift as idea is born unto earth—comes to us who inhabit the earth—the prophet Isaiah is affirmed in his praise: 'Unto us a child is born…and (its) name shall be called Wonderful.' Our only purpose, then, is to honor the gifted child of an idea thus by keeping and demonstrating the divine idea divinely. When the name is stripped away, it shall be known for what it is: God personified—as is All the very same.

"In a moment we'll take a short break before closing out our day. However, before we do, I want to be absolutely sure you understand the purpose of deal-ing with these stories right here and right now. Has anyone figured it out yet? What is the correlation between the stories of the immaculate conception and the virgin birth and our work together? Let's have a little survey to test the waters. As with all other questions I ask in a series, feel free to change your mind if you resonate with a different one than you originally chose. Come purely from resonance now. Okay, first question: How many of you think the correlation is simply to let you know another way to think about Christmas? Raise your hand," Christo directs with a smile on his face. Not a single hand is raised in the midst of the silliness that frames the query. "No?" Christo mocks, "really? Okay, then, does it correlate with the predisposition to demean those who believe in the literal meaning of these stories? How many think this is so?" Again, there is no affirmative response.

"My goodness," Christo chides, "what could all this gibberish be about? Hmm," he feigns ignorance. "I wonder…could it have anything—every-thing—to do with a portrayal of Jesus's teachings themselves: as a model for us? As a model to erase any doubt about their power to heal? To erase any doubt about our divinity and the heritage the infinite divinity of ideas holds for us all? Could all this be true? Well, just for fun, how many agree with this far-fetched perspective?" By now the sea of smiles and titters of laughter have elim-inated the need for a show of hands, but the entire assembly acknowledges with affirmation bathed in glee. "Wow," Christo returns to them, "you got it! Of course you got it!" Christo emphasizes. "You were right there with me all the way. What a magnificent testament to Truth each of you is! Thank you one and all for hanging in there with me. And to think no one threw any rotten tomatoes at me during this explanation! Wow!"

Christo is quick to add, "You've been so good, as a reward I want to give you just a little more condiment to place on this delectable meal. Let's traverse just a little bit further along the metaphysical stream, and apply this new perspective to how Mary must have raised Jesus, how she carried the metaphorical Truth to the end in fulfillment of her responsibility. Surely Mary recognized that her newborn son was not only a physical being but also a metaphor for what he represents. Surely she knew that the new perspective had not only to be birthed but also to be imbedded in Jesus so he could teach it widely. It would have been next to impossible for a woman to be respected in the same way as a man in that generation and in that foundation of religion. Mary, as the symbol for immaculate conception, would have to see this new perspective transmitted through the metaphorical virgin birth of her son, Jesus.

"You will remember that Jesus told the crowds that he had not come to *change* the laws, but rather to enlighten others *about* the laws. What he came for was to enlighten others on the change in perspective they must have in order to be free from the shackles that bound them to the old way: the letter of the law. Indeed, he came to teach the Spirit of the law. This would take a complete change in perspective if Jesus's charge were to be fulfilled. It had to be a change that could only come from within, from the irrational, the subjective: our divinity.

"The Pharisees represented the contrary view, argued by rational linearity: the use of intellectual objectivity alone to meet the challenge of the sacred. They just never got what Jesus was talking about, just as most of us haven't. We'd rather stay in our limited understanding and argue from outside rather than go within and trust the Truth that can be found only in there. It's just too uncomfortable to change, to even think of, for most. But that *is* the challenge, is it not: to face the new as a distinct possibility for changing our lives into something much better?

"Now, tell me this. At whose knee are most of us raised? In most cultures, who has the most influence over those who are born and raised in a family?" Christo pauses just long enough for the obvious answer to surface. "Of course," he continues, "it is the mother. Who, then, do you think had the most influence on Mary's son? Was it Joseph? Could it have been the religious leaders of the day? Or was it Mary, who on some level—some very deep level I might suggest—who knew of Jesus's purpose, and the way he must travel?

"Be careful here. Don't leap way ahead in Jesus' Life to the crucifixion and retort that it must have been some kind of perverted mother who would lead her son to that eventuality. If you like, I'll be happy to take you through that story metaphorically when I visit with you in our regional meetings. For now, it will suffice to say that Life isn't always as it seems, rarely is it so. So just let that go for now and follow me to the end of only this story.

"Wasn't it *Mary* who made sure that he followed the path to his Mecca, his salvation, in a most single-minded manner? That's where I'd place my bet. Throughout the story of Jesus we don't find Joseph around much, but Mary is almost always present. Metaphysically this says to us that we can take this to mean that we must have a continual commitment to First cause if it is to fully come to pass. We can't be cavalier about it. We must stick with it to the end. And in the end, there was Mary with Jesus. Just as we will be with the divinity of Truth as we not only acknowledge and accept the Truth for what it is, but also commit to its fulfillment by expressing our unadulterated faith to it throughout our spiritual Life.

"Perhaps this says something to us about where the changes must come from if we are to refresh our world and all that is impacted by it. It has become more and more difficult for this to happen, at least in our culture, particularly because so many mothers are working mothers now. And there are single mothers, who are worn to a frazzle from all it takes to keep a family together, let alone to see that it flourishes.

"So what does that leave us with? With US, that's what it leaves us with. Many of us in this gathering are grandparents, or getting mighty close to being grandparents. Why not give some thought to using what we're coming to understand to teach our sons and daughters and grandchildren, so they won't continue to repeat the road of insanity so many are on? You know the definition of insanity, don't you? It's going down the same road over and over again, thinking you're going to get a different result. It's time to change that definition! Let's change the word 'insane' to mean 'the sanity we find within.' Hence in-sane takes on a different perspective altogether. It is the sanity we find only within that must be manifested from now on.

"I'd like you to give further thought to this, so we can discuss it more fully when I visit the smaller regional gatherings in the not-too-distant future. I will also want to discuss with you the relationship between spirituality and the world of work. But that's a topic that can wait for another day entirely.

"Okay, you've sat long enough. And you have done a marvelous piece of spiritual work. So let's take a thirty-minute break before we come to the finish line. I'll bet you already know what that looks like. We'll see how right you are when we return. See you after this break for light refreshments. Promptly at 1:30."

Christo is thoroughly pleased at the responsiveness from all levels of the gathering. Even Christo's aides are aglow with the depth and breadth of what has transpired. Christo retreats to his prayer stool where he takes some food and drink in order to ground himself again. Before starting the last leg of the journey, he knows that what he will need in order to provide the clincher will be there right when, and as, he needs it. "Thank God," he hears himself saying half out loud. "Thank God, indeed!"

CHAPTER 11

Home We Are

The last break provides just enough refurbishing on the physical plane for the participants to make it through to closure. Christo and the gathering are totally refreshed in a spiritual way. So much so that it will be absolutely necessary for folks to walk around and have a mid-afternoon snack before heading home, thereby providing a more mature meaning to the act of 'grounding' that we find necessary in the spiritual world.

Christo and his aides greet people randomly as they file back to their seats. It feels to Christo as if they have arrived at just the right place on all levels. What is needed now, Christo knows, is to reach closure on the idea of all being God. Having introduced this idea just a few months ago, it has had time to be assimilated only part way, at best. After all, he had hung it out on the line to dry with but a brief explanation. As a result, some were afraid to even consider such a notion. Others were willing to think about it from time to time, but other worldly activities took them away from focusing solely on such a concept. Still others looked at it as a "trick" Christo was playing on them. A much smaller cluster took it to heart and worked the idea through the offerings from their first session together. And some simply dismissed it out of hand.

All this makes no difference to Christo. He knows that his only job is to be faithful to the prompt; so, faithful he is now ready to be. Armed with conviction and faith, both in the gathering and the agenda that is waiting to be completed, Christo weaves his way up to the podium one last time. He takes a long, deep breath, which corresponds to what he is feeling from the crowd. Placing his left hand on his heart and reaching out toward the gathering, Christo Lovingly bids them: "Namaste, dear divine ones. I send you my deepest feelings of Love and respect for your dignity. I send you the blessings of divinity so you can feel your very own. Remember, you cannot recognize anything in this world if you do not have it within yourself, if it is not already part of you. This is a never-failing Truism and one of God's laws." He hesitates long enough to let his entreaty fully gather the crowd inside a blanket of Oneness.

As he casts his gentle, soft eyes across the arena the crowd responds much like a "wave" in a football stadium. Mimicking Christo and with left hands caressing hearts, their right hands send out Loving presence with great Authority and power. It's as though someone is flooding a darkened room with stage lights: grace blankets all in a bed of emotional fulfillment. The term "Love-in" can't begin to describe the happening. Christo is deeply moved by this release of all emotional ties to past fears. "Ahhh," he sighs, "how lovely. I do indeed celebrate your divinity, for you are divine, nothing less," he assures them. "Namaste, Christo," the gathering returns his greeting. "Namaste. And thank you." Christo knows that all are ready now.

After a few more minutes, by his demeanor Christo signals that it's time to move on. "All right. It's time now for us to take those last few steps that will lead us through the gates of Mecca. How many of you know what this last portion of our time together is to bring to us?" Better than half raise their hands in affirmation of their view. "You think so, do you? Let's see if you're right, right now. What was the very last thing that I communicated to you after our last meeting—that item of reference that probably knocked you off your kitchen stool at breakfast—the only topic we began with yesterday that we haven't completed yet? Of course, the only answer to all of these silly leads is what? WHAT?" Christo demands. "Our divinity," rejoins the gathering proudly. Christo pauses just long enough to let them know that they haven't quite hit the bull's eye. "WHAT?" he repeats, with a long pause following. "Well, come on. You're warm. Very hot, in fact," Christo says, imitating a childhood game of hide-and-seek. "It's not your divinity, although that could easily be a synonym for it. If not divinity, then, what is it? C'mon, you know! WHAT?" In response, folks look around for affirmation, though none comes in words but only in the signs of the recognition of Truth. Suddenly, in perfect unison, the answer rings out through the arena: "Godliness. Our Godliness!" "Yes. *Yes!* YES!" Christo proudly reinforces the accuracy of their answer. "Our Godliness. Now let's deal with exactly that.

"I'd like to begin by summarizing what I said in my second e-mail to you. To paraphrase George Bernard Shaw: I like to quote from myself. It adds sparkle to my presentations." The crowd joins in a spontaneous chuckle. "Look, that's the best I have left in my quiver, so enjoy it while you can," Christo chuckles. "All kidding aside, I want you to listen with very different ears than you had available before now. I'll shift a few things along the way, but the overall pattern will be familiar to you. I'll be interested to see how you greet your Godliness in your present frame of mind.

"I said back then that no matter where you are on your journey, the time has come to investigate a teaching that takes you beyond where you were placed on your childhood loom. Then we saw God as separate from us, much as our parents were separate from us. Depending on what the threads on our mostly unconsciously-prepared warp looked like, we have come to envision God likewise. But that was then, as a child. Now, however, we get to rethread our warp with a much more mature—spiritually mature, that is—translation of Life.

"I began the treatise I sent along to you by asking you to consider that you are God. You will recall, I am sure, that I didn't say you were *a* god, or even more inflammatory, *THE* God. I only said that you *are* God. The general tack I took was that if you are made of nothing but Godly Essence, you *are* that. Therefore, you might just as well accept that as your fate, so to speak. You might as well accept your Godliness as what you would allow yourself to be. I want to take a slightly different tack now, and see where this one goes.

"I know you fully understand that God, divine Essence, is everywhere present and all powerful, all knowing, and ever active. That being so, then, where is God not found? Of what does everything exist if not of divine intelligence, for lack of a better name? Or perhaps the correct phrase is divine Essence, if that fits your contextual container more comfortably. More and more scientists are now affirming the Truth of such matters. Scientists are now speaking of a special kind of intelligence that resides within—that is at the foundation of—all Life. This all-inclusiveness ought to count for something that is very special. So why not render it within the realm of the sacred? Or in the realm of the holy, or of the divine? Why not make it Godly in character? Are we so stuck in 'less than,' that we cannot bring ourselves to a higher distinction no matter what? Well, here's what I'm sensing these days: the time is close when the hundredth monkey will have come to the conclusion that all of Life is indeed sacred—holy—divine—Godly—and the world of theological mythology will have been tipped on its axis.

"If you can embrace this configuration of God, then why is it that we cannot equate its understanding to the logical extension that we—formed out of the very Essence of which we speak as Godly—*also* are God? You will recall my using a few very practical examples of all of us being God, examples that show us that if something is composed entirely of some base unit, like God, that it might as well take on that name. Why not go even go so far as to use the word 'God' for that of which everything is made? I suggest that you return to that e-mail in order to follow the linear pattern of that presentation if this is what you need to further your understanding. Spiritually, however, you are at a very different place. The point is that it doesn't really matter what we call it. The *only* thing that *does* matter is that you *are* whatever *It is! Isness* is our only business, if you recall.

"We have called such Loving Essence by names both scientific and holy in nature. We have called this magnificent Essence 'energy.' We have called it 'electronic.' We have called it 'atomic.' We have named it 'sacred.' 'Divine Essence.' 'God.' 'That.' 'I Am.' What is it that *God's Pocket Dictionary* says about a name? If I may paraphrase once again: A name is a label put on others and things, that when peeled away let's you see God in all. I just *love* that definition! Let's you see God in all! All we have to do is peel off the name and look at what's really there—at what *It* most assuredly just *is*.

"So the only thing that really matters about what *It* is is that *It* surely *IS that which It IS!* Absolutely *nothing else* about this matters! All that is required is that we express single-mindedness about its validity as the makeup of all that exists. And that we know that it comes seemingly from out of nowhere—except, that is, from the First cause—the initial divine idea that headed it in a particular direction in the first place. And just where is it these ideas, these divine thoughts, come from? We call them divine for a reason, don't we? It's because of their nature, which is our nature, simply enough, and interestingly enough.

"One of the things we have learned together is that if we try to make divine thoughts happen intellectually, hopefully to rise to the occasion, we usually get stumped. If, on the other hand, when, as the expression goes, we simply 'let go and let God,' then divine solutions to all our needs just magically and beautifully *do* rise to the occasion. Again, the words we use to label these angelic beings, these virginal entities, these immaculate conceptions, come from within. We call such angels, these gifts from some holy, sacred place, by the names of 'INspiration,' 'INsight,' 'Enlightenment,' and 'Transcendence.' Again, it matters not what we call things. Just as with us, it's only what they are that counts.

"Well, here we are once again. Everything is made in exactly the same way, only with that sameness distributed somewhat differently. A slightly different composition, but similarly fashioned. The only difference between the oak tree and the persimmon is the seed from which it comes. But both seeds are formed in exactly the same way and contain the identical First cause, that which gives Life to them: 'treeness.' It is the built-in intelligence, makeup, configuration, means of birthing, expanding, and coming to completion that gives them Life, much like that we find in the tiny mustard seed that grows into a magnificent tree. Metaphorically, it's much like the idea that grows and grows and grows, accommodating additional flights of fancy along the way until it is complete in all its glory. Just like the acorn that grows into the mighty oak tree. Much like the egg and sperm that meet to form you and me. And the light from the star that leads us out of darkness.

"Now, all you need to do is decide what you want to call that which is contained in the primal or First cause, that of which all is made. For the large part, here we have come to call it divine. I'm perfectly satisfied if we leave it right there. Or, on the other hand, if we simply substitute the synonym of 'God' for all that is contained in Divine Essence. Or even, 'Hey, you!' for that matter!

"I place naming the divine in the same category as the inner knowing we express when we merely say 'thank you' when someone compliments us for our painting or essay, for example. We know full well, if we really are aware, that we are really only midwives for such lovely renderings—that some higher power urges its way with us as the vehicle of Loving expression. However, we don't need to say all that to the one who compliments us. We know the Truth, and if they have reached the point of similar understanding, so do they. Therefore, it's perfectly proper to use a shorthand form of speech to say the very same thing: 'thank you.'

"Also, it is perfectly proper to greet someone with an inner expression of 'Namaste' rather than having the greeting cross your lips. A smile and a twinkle in your eye say the very same thing as your conveyances of respect for their dignity. It's all in intent, then, isn't it? Communication rests all in intent, the condition of heart from which one communicates. And one *must* communicate—or our body will have nothing to eavesdrop on. Love, it is said, is not Love until it is expressed. The very same is True with our Godliness, for they are all One and the same.

"Just so then, it is proper to call a table which is made out of wood simply a 'table,' even though we know it has emanated from the First cause of divine Essence on many levels: the wood; the idea of the table itself; and its design and function—all of it. We can use the shorthand name for it and be absolutely fine with it, just as long as we don't forget the base line meaning of it all. It's only when we forget divinity, by whatever name we call it, that we begin to take Life for granted. When we forget divinity we are soon to be in that space wherein we lose our conscious expression of it. Instead, we find ourselves wallowing in the egoic effects of unconscious demonstration that drive us mad.

"I have just felt you making the connection from one side of this to the other. Indeed, you have just made the inferential leap across the gap of meaning. All of what we've been talking about here is the way in which Life can be expressed perpetually in Heaven—or Hell. Either way, we will be exactly where we want to be. As adults now, metaphorically, spiritually so—as those of us who have matured in our understanding of how we weave our lives and how we must hold ourselves, and not others, accountable for that act of weaving—we have learned the great, yet simple lesson. Every day we awaken to unlimited opportunities for threading our warp with that which is from—and for—our highest good. Or contrarily, with anything else which is not that.

"Every day we are afforded yet more opportunities to tie back to First cause: Loving Creation. All of Life is all about First cause. The story of Mary's immaculate conception is that. Jesus's birth is that. Each virgin birth that we allow to come through us is that: First cause after First cause after First cause. Beginning rightly so we can end rightly; beginning with Loving Creation so we can demonstrate Loving always. This is the journey that also is the end, all in One. This is the Holy Grail that is ours to have and hold. *This* is the Truth that is timeless—no matter how it comes from within, or when and where. Truth is indeed timeless. Therefore, in infinity and immortality does it reside.

"Is this not the underlying message of the Course in Miracles? Is this not what we have been learning to do with more and more skill during every moment that Life brings us? Certainly here we have been alerted to the loom upon which we demonstrate immaculate conception. Upon which we weave virgin birth after virgin birth. Or not. Here we are again. Right back to that which determines our frame of mind: choice.

"Exercise choice now. It is your mandate because of being an inhabitant of this plane. Call yourselves anything you wish. Only be absolutely sure that you *never forget WHAT* you are. The labels have no meaning whatsoever. Only *what you are* matters. And what you *do with* what you are, how you demonstrate *what* you are *through* all you *do.*

"Well, welcome home! I hope by now that you have come to understand that you *are* home. And no matter where you go, or where you are, you are that: home. Home is wherever your heart is. Wherever you divinity—your Godliness—resides.

"I remind you at this point that it matters a great deal what your intention is beneath the words you speak. So, when I see Life I will continue to intend such phrases as: 'There's God, expressing Itself as that tree. As Donna. As that automobile. As that rose. That leper. The river and the log floating in the river. And I will continue to intend 'Namaste,' whether such greeting comes across my lips or not. Hold this same thought as you traverse down your own pathway each day. Simply decide what kind of Life you desire. Then, with conscious thought, divine ideas—from *your* divinity—just be sure you make every step go in that direction. *Every* step—*all* of them—one by one by one.

"Each of us on the planet, then, is perfectly capable of an immaculate conception. Each of us conceives immaculately on a regular basis. This is our primary function as the image and likeness of God. Each of us is a midwife to virgin birth continually, without reserve. Each of us can use our newborn warp to weave Life exactly in the pattern of the kingdom of Heaven. Yes, Life is a labor of Love. Hold that thought as your mantra.

"So how's the state of your theological mythology by now? Is it any different than it was just forty-eight hours ago? Can you see now that the story of Mary and Joseph and Jesus is a marvelous metaphor for exactly what we've been talking about? Indeed, that story is mighty craftily woven. It affords us the exemplar—as do the rest of Jesus's teachings—for living what we *are* instead of what we're *not*. Only you can tell how it applies to you. Only you can now define your theological mythology. Just remember that you can refashion it any time you wish. As many times as you wish. Your loom is timeless, as is the Truth that now forms its warp. Yes, Truth is Infinite in its power to create—consciously, from within.

"Whatever perspective we have is what Life looks like for us. No matter what that image is, accountability for it rests entirely with us. Accountability does not rest with the other who is only the angel who has been sent to us to point out the purpose for going within next time. When we change how we see, what we see changes. Remember this always."

CHAPTER 12

Tidying Up Before the Parting Gift

Christo breathes deeply, and assesses the scene on every level. "Is everyone resting comfortably with all this now? I suspect, having asked that question, that you have a good deal of assimilating to do before you can truthfully answer it. I'll let you off the hook until we meet again. Besides, I sense that all of you have come a very long distance within, and are ready now to infuse what you have learned into everyday Life. And you don't even have to purchase a loom to do it. For, as you now know, you *are* the loom upon which Life is woven.

"With that in mind, permit me to focus the new warp on something that is of great importance. You will recall during our last session that we invested a good deal of energy learning about the effects of our outlook on our health. I don't want you to leave today without reestablishing that connection. As long as you continue to weave Life from the foundation of your divinity, your body will have nothing to eavesdrop on that will reap anything but your highest good for you. Any ailments you have on any level should drift out of your patterns in a very short time. All I ask is for you to be vigilant in monitoring the condition of your warp. You well know how to do this; so don't wait until some external force jostles you. Check within quickly as you end each day, so that anything untoward that has lodged there over the day can be set free. It's sort of like never going to bed angry. Or without letting go of the stress of the day. Or without saying 'I love you' to God and your other loved ones. Each is a necessary part of good health.

"What I have just reminded you of is very important and not only for daily living. It is especially important now that the craze of a supposed avian flu pandemic has been cast upon us. Remember that only God, that is, goodness, or divinity, is everywhere. All the fear that surrounds this issue is but a detail of mental midgetry. It is a form of fear that serves only to drag us down to its size. Here's the test. What happens when people are ground down with a perpetual feeding of fear? Heaped upon the pain of fear, additional layers begin to appear seemingly out of nowhere. Once an illusion is taken as gospel, the slide is downhill from there. It works exactly like the disturbing threads on our unconsciously constructed warp.

"The same is true with any dis-ease, is it not? The worst thing is a diagnosis believed. Beginning rightly applies here, as well. If we begin with a belief based on the imposition of fear, unless we stop it and change direction, it has only one way to go: to completion. It becomes a self-fulfilling prophecy. It's no different from the exaggerated attack of fear perpetrated upon us after 9/11. The entire country has been thrown into a contagion of fear. Which, of course, has turned into a self-fulfilling prophecy. We are at war. And we will stay at war until our fear is overcome by our more natural state of divinity once again.

"So belief in the pandemic breeds fear. Fear builds through toleration of such thoughts as: 'Can I be safely treated if I get it?' 'What if I can't get an inoculation on time?' 'I'm older. My God, I'm sure to get it!' 'They're expecting how many to get it in our country? I'd better hurry or I'll be one of them.' Panic begins to set it. All of this tension only exacerbates the concern. Tension drives our immune system downward, spiraling until we're sure to catch something—be it avian flu or something else. Therefore the real contagion is the contagion of fear, not the disease itself.

"Ladies and gentlemen, although you'd never know it from public reports, vaccinations are the absolute worst way to deal with the potential for contacting a disease. A vaccination presumes to substitute for the human being's ability to protect itself from disease. Getting the measles, for example, naturally inoculates you from getting it again.

"Permit me to speak about natural inoculation for a moment. 'What the dickens is that?' you ask. Plain and simple language is required here, so that's what you're going to get. This is a test of what we have been learning over these two days. To inoculate means to protect you from within. *HELLO! IS ANYONE HOME?* Isn't protecting ourselves within exactly what we've been dealing with here? First off, because God is omnipotent, omniscient, omnipresent and omni-active, where is there room for anything but God? Perfection? Perfect mind? Perfect Spirit? Perfect Soul? Perfect health? Does the avian flu sound like these to you?

"Second, if anything—any illusion that is not God or divinity, take your choice of words—tries to enter the picture, merely acknowledge it. But don't take it seriously. Rather, then tell it to get behind you, and give it no more thought. You must treat it exactly as you would any part of Life that comes into your warp. Don't spend any energy condemning it, fighting it, running from it, or fearing it. It is just like an errant thought. The minute you let go of it, it is gone into thin air. Pouf! Gone. Period. Give it no more thought.

"What are we then left with? You guessed it: divinity, all there ever was, is, or ever will be. You only have to see it that way for it to be so. NO, that's not true," Christo catches himself. "Divinity is all there is whether you see it that way or not. The wonderful thing about your seeing divinity for all it is, though—and I do mean *all*—is that you are then served by divinity rather than by the flu, fear, or worry, or by any other illusion.

"Remember this: YOU are the one weaving your virgin births on this planet. It is not that someone else who is proclaiming that millions on the planet will die from the avian flu. Of course, if people are overtaken by fear, and haven't treated themselves as one who is divine, then this could well be true. But only for those who choose that route. However, you are now different from those people. You are steeped in the understanding that our divinity out-wits anything that is counter to it, particularly because nothing exists *but* divinity.

"Now, if we are nothing but divinity, does that mean that we can do any crazy thing we want and we will not damage this container we call a body? Let's look at it this way. How do you intend to treat others now that you know that they are nothing but divinity? Are you going to treat them according to whether they exhibit their anger or their fear of abandonment? No—at least I hope not. When we stare divinity in the face, we treat whatever or whoever it is with the dignity divinity commands. Anger and the fear of abandonment stand aside by themselves, despite any appearance to the contrary.

"Well, then, how are you intending to treat your body now that you know *it* is divine? As you begin to respect your own dignity and consciously make only decisions that validate divinity, in a very short time you will be treating your-selves differently all across the board. Getting good rest—mental, physical and emotional—is sure to help. Eating lightly and healthfully also ups the strength levels in proper ways. Lots of greens, fruits and vegetables do wonders. Drinking lots of clean water adds to the health quotient. So does backing off from work schedules that tire beyond reason. Most of all, reducing all forms of stress buttresses the immune system.

"The bottom line is that we want to give as little as possible to our body and soul to deal with. Then, even if you do erroneously contact something, your body will be able to fight it off rather easily. If we load up the tasks for our body by assigning it to deal with continual stress of all kinds—worry, anxiety, fear, abuse, all pushed 'under ground'—then we are placing its ability to handle that which it is geared to do—keep itself healthy—under severe duress. Not very wise for one who is divine, is it?

"What I've been talking about here is eliminating toxicity from our midst. When we consciously stop to declare our divinity in the midst of any toxic moment—personal, physical, emotional, mental, or environmental—we are eliminating the potential for toxicity to touch us. This is exactly the same process as the one we use with our new warp. We can weave our lives with those golden threads, or we can revert to the toxic waste that shows its face in the form of fear, judgment, shame, guilt, and abuse of all kinds. In effect, when we turn our back on toxicity of all kinds, we are saying, 'God is perfect; I am perfect; this isn't. So I'm not going to give that which isn't perfect any thought. I'm going to return to the presence of only that which is: divinity. I'm not going to cast my pearls among the swine.' This, my friends, is inoculation at its best.

"On the other hand, if we have weakened our immune system out of abject fear and increased tension, we are quite likely to be stricken with most anything that comes along. Does it not occur to you that in such a weakened condition that one could even get a bad case of whatever the inoculation is supposed to protect us from? In a phrase, our body has all it needs to fight any disease. Provided, that is, that it has been fortified with good care and the elimination of stress, with care that matches our divinity. All we have to do is listen within in order to obtain all we need to guide us rightly. And when we begin rightly, you know by now that all will follow rightly along the way.

"To top it off, it has been widely said about this so-called worldwide epidemic that there isn't enough of the proper flu vaccine with which to vaccinate. That the pharmaceuticals are producing it as fast as they can, but that still won't be quickly enough. Some are even recommending that we should be vaccinated with some serum that is not even of the same strain of flu virus as that which is supposedly going to strike here. Now just how foolish is this?

"The bottom line for me, and this may not be true for you—you must follow your own conscience, your own inner Authority—is that as long as I entertain the lie of the avian flu, I am fortifying the path upon which it travels. The idea is to inoculate myself against the fear-filled admonitions and the tension that arises from them, and also to nourish my body as a regular routine no matter what. I can do no less for divinity. Then I am prepared for anything, no matter what.

"Let me be very clear here. I'm not telling you what to do regarding the avian flu. I am only telling you how I view it for myself. The choice in this regard, as with all of Life's decisions, is your own to make. It is a choice for which you must hold yourself accountable. All I can suggest is to run Life, all aspects of it—including the claim of avian flu—through your angelic warp and see what it looks like. Be single-minded about keeping the threads purely golden. This way, whatever Life brings you will be far more palatable than otherwise could be the case. Clarity and single-mindedness are two of our most important goals. Say to yourselves, 'from here on I intend to give this illusion no thought. Instead, I am committed to being healthy on all levels. And to giving my body only the bare essentials to deal with.'

"Let's take care of a bit of housekeeping now. I want to take this opportunity to let you know that because you have attended these two sessions, that a record of both the first session and this one is being made available to you at no cost. If you want additional copies to pass along, these, too, can be arranged, at a nominal cost to you. I have listened to the first one myself and am truly amazed at how far we traveled in such a short time. Knowing that gave me great hope and expectation for this session, and you have surpassed both by a great distance.

"Secondly, in a couple of weeks I'll be sending out an e-mail detailing a proposed agenda for regional meetings, smaller in size, so we can get at some of your more intimate questions and concerns. Plus we will undertake some other kinds of exercises that can be used to reinforce what we have been exploring here. I would appreciate your feedback regarding a potential agenda. Even though the one you will be receiving will be based on feedback gained from my aides as well as from my own personal contact with you, we still could have missed the boat entirely. So, because these sessions are for you, be sure that they have maximum potential for speaking to your needs and interests at this point in your development.

"Until we meet for these sessions, please outline the desired course that will keep you on the path to your self-described Mecca. Also, include daily practice, and I do mean daily, with the simple three-step process Jesus has given us for parting the veil of illusion so we can live from our most natural state of divinity more regularly. Practice, too, greeting others, as well as yourself, using 'Namaste,' either privately or publicly. Remember, intention is what drives this greeting to Truth. As these two things—the process and your greeting—become second nature to you, Life will begin to change dramatically.

"As a matter of fact, as these changes begin to surface, take a few minutes to record them in your diary. If your diary is in your computer as mine is, I invite you to print me out a copy, or send one to me via e-mail. If you will permit, I'd like to post those most pertinent to our work together on my website. Believe me, such stories will inspire and encourage beyond belief. Then, in a few months, I will issue a call to all of you; inviting you to submit the one story in this regard you'd like to have represent your Life to this point. We'll have some fun with it, like having some prizes for certain categories and such. The most important thing I'd like to see come of our postings is an ever-evolving inspirational e-book that can be shared with the world.

Christo makes a mental survey of things he wants to be sure to cover, so as to not leave anything of importance out. "I almost forgot. Be sure to practice speaking in tongues. Amongst your companions on this journey hold one another to looking at whatever you are dealing with metaphorically. In your routine communications with one another, don't be too bashful to share a metaphysical understanding of, or metaphorical outlook about, something that was said. In other words, be sensitive to the need for continually honing your skills in this regard. At first you might drive people around you crazy. But once they get the hang of how you're viewing Life, yours will become an example they'll more than likely want to follow. Then let the teacher in you shine, for we all know that example is the only *real* teacher.

"I'd also be grateful for any ideas that come up regarding how this process can be used among the younger generation in order to create a greater sensibility leading towards the spiritual path. The thought also occurs to me that perhaps some of you would delight in spreading the word about things we're learning to other grandparents and similar saging groups. In this way, the sages would be put in touch with meaningful purpose on a deep level, and the younger generation could be lifted to new levels of meaning. This is the working definition of a win-win situation, and should be explored. So, by all means, e-mail me with your thoughts. At this point I've gone only so far as to adapt some of the offerings in Matthew Fox's piece on the reinvention of work. It's exciting, to be sure, and needs only your input to ready it for use.

"Earlier when we were using the steps of Byron Katie's process I had promised you a copy of the process so you can use it to discern Truth out of the frequent malaise in which we find ourselves. I'll e-mail a modified piece in that regard in the next few days. Let me check within to see if there's anything further that needs doing." Tilting his head once again, he listens carefully for just the moment he needs for further clarification.

CHAPTER 13

The Parting Gift

"Well," Christo punctuates, "we're finished here today. The time has come to bid a fond adieu. Personally, I'd like to have you part with a gift that will serve to guide you daily on your journey. Used properly, it will send you immediately within without interference. It will inform you wisely of Truth for you, without even having to ask for it in the first place. All this gift does is place you within; at that place where your divinity can speak in a voice you can now hear. With just three questions—there's that number three again—you will have constructed a marvelous framework for living your day.

"Here it is. Don't worry about remembering it. This, too, I shall e-mail you. By now I know full well that you have a daily spiritual practice that nourishes you. If nothing else, you now have what we have done together to exercise daily. The nature of the practice makes no difference. Only having one does. Bringing yourself to it does.

"After you open your day with whatever spiritual practice you prefer, I suggest you sit quietly, at either your word-processor or simply with paper and your favorite writing instrument. Get yourself in a soft, sweet place of acceptance. Then ask this question: 'What, Lord, are you saying to my heart?' Set yourself free to hear the response to this simple query. Don't intellectualize or work on hearing an answer. Merely allow your hand to write the answer, or your fingers to fly across the keys to record the answer. Once again, this may sound like hocus pocus, but it is not. I hope you can trust me by now. I have recommended this means of going within to many, and it has failed not a single time. This process of noting the answer is called automatic writing. Don't get all caught up in what it's called. Or from where the response is coming. That is none of your business. Your only business is to be faithful to the question and recording the response.

"Okay, then, the first question is: 'What, Lord, are you saying to my heart?' You ask and wait for a response. Let your hand or fingers do what they will. Don't bother to try to understand it as it comes. You can do that when you are completely finished. When the response to your first question begins to wane, this is a sign that it's coming to an end. Don't force it. Just go with it. When no more comes, simply stop and thank God for the response.

"Then ask the second question. 'How, Lord, am I to respond to this?' Repeat the same treatment of what comes from within. Thank God once again for that response.

"Now for the last question: 'What, Lord, do you particularly want me to remember?' Keep in mind the two meanings of 'remember.' It can mean simply 'to recall something.' Or it can mean 'to rejoin, re-member with, something.' Just as before, simply record what your hands will permit and then let go of it. When finished, thank God and sit back for a few moments to reflect on what has transpired. Reflect not on the words, but rather on the simple act of showing up. What a privilege and honor it is to sit in the lap of luxury: God!

"The words? Well, they're something else again! Just sit with what you have been given and read it from the space of metaphor, because that's where it comes from. What comes may be quite startling to you, particularly because you haven't asked for anything except for God to speak to you, so you may listen—and truly hear. Based on my experience, which I have written about, I can only tell you that the more startling what you receive is, the more bizarre it may seem, the more it must be obeyed. I say this because most of us would not dare even think what is best for ourselves, let alone comply with the directive.

"Don't make this tedious. You can do it once a week, once a month, or daily—or just once in a while. It's a process that fits into any day, any time. Just as it was a gift to me, I pass it on now as a gift to you. Happy New Year! Or is it Happy New Day? As long as it's filled with joy—and this will do it—who cares which day it is? We certainly don't need a holiday to celebrate such things. *Every* day is a holiday for celebrating Life itself, the gift Life is to all of us, always.

"Dear ones, this blankets our time together in a wrap of deep devotion to all you are. Sorry to use such poor English, but you ain't even seen the tip of the iceberg yet! With that I bid you a fond adieu. I beckon the depths of your self-respect with the most dignified: Namaste. May you turn to the highways knowing you are Loved and appreciated beyond compare. May each step you take lead you closer and closer to Mecca, the seat of your salvation you so divinely already are. Namaste, dear divine ones," Christo closes with the sweetest of sensations that burgeons within him, and he extends that same fullness of Love's equation to one and all.

In the fullness of appreciation the gathering has for Christo, in unison they return his adieu with: "Namaste, Christo." Then a person from the gathering stands and broadcasts boldly: "Christo, with deepest gratitude, we want to tell you this." Then, as though a bevy of angelic beings has arrived to sing to Christo, the sweet renderings from the precious voices issue forth from a large section of the arena. It is immediately clear to Christo that he's not the only one who can drop a shoe.

About a quarter of them begin:

"In God's eyes, "you're a fire that never goes out, a light on the top of a hill. In God's eyes you're a poet, a painter, a prophet, with a mission of love to fulfill."

Then another quarter of the gathering adds even greater depth and sweetness as they join in:

"Outside there's a world so enchantingly strange, a maze of illusion and lies. But there's never a story that ever could change the glory of you in God's eyes."

And now the next quarter rings out in unison:

"In God's eyes you're a radiant vision of beauty, a gemstone cut one of a kind. You're fine as a diamond, deep as a ruby, rare as jade in God's mind."

Finally, the last of the arena joins in with all the passion they can muster. Everyone continues until the finish, enveloping the scene in a sea of absolute bliss:

"No need to believe all you may have been told, no need to live in disguise. You're brighter than silver, purer than gold, a pearl beyond price in God's eyes.

God sees only goodness. God's vision is true. And nothing can change the perfection of you in God's eyes.

In God's eyes you're a fire that never goes out, a light on top of the hill.
You're a rose in the forest, a prelude from Bach, a triumph of heavenly skill.

Outside there's a world that keeps breaking your heart, and tearing your dreams down to size.

But guiding you homeward, piercing the dark—is the love light that shines in God's eyes.

Now and forever that light never dies. You're dearly beloved in God's eyes."

As would be anyone after hearing one of the great understatements of this or of any other century, Christo is overwhelmed by this show of Loving respect. He stands with his hands crossed over his heart, casting his Lovingly soft—now joyfully tearful—eyes across the arena, making absolutely sure that he makes a last contact with every person in Loving appreciation. As the music comes to an end, Christo folds his hands in prayerful dedication to them. Bowing to one and all, he connotes a parting "Namaste," the silent but profound affirmation of divinity in all.

Slowly, reverently, the gathering winds its way out of the arena. Some are still singing out this tribute. Others hum the tune. Still others, like Christo, sing it silently, in their heart of hearts. All will carry it there forever, never to be forgotten.

Out of respect, Christo waits until the very last person has exited. In a few minutes his aides approach in deference to the extraordinary leadership he has shown yet again over these past two days. As they near him they see that he is blissfully mellow, to say the least. They, too, are in that same frame of mind. It is clear that there will be much for all to process over the next few days, even weeks. It is equally clear that all are up to the task.

"Anyone hungry?" asks Christo of his aides. "Come on," he invites, "you've done a marvelous job, so let's add some steak and potatoes to this fare of bread and wine. I'll even treat," he closes with a wink and a laugh. "No," comes the response of one for all, "you've already treated us to a gourmet banquet the likes of which we have never witnessed. It's our turn now. We'll buy." With a broad grin on his face and that mischievous twinkle in his eye, Christo links his arms with two of his aides and retorts: "I was hoping you'd say that!"

SPIRIT NOODLES

This feature is introduced here to invite the reader's personal investigation (noodling about in spiritual ways rather than material) into her or his own beliefs and perspectives on Life. Such investigation is tantamount to engaging and inquiring about Life metaphysically, symbolically. The reader is encouraged to investigate these beliefs not for purpose of material enhancement, but rather to nourish one's spiritual perspective and insight. As we then come to grips with Truth within for ourselves, thus healing our perspectives on Life, our bodily chemistry and functions also heal as our thinking and beliefs are mended.

Chapter I: The Return of Christo Sahbays

1. What is your current belief about your relationship with God? How are you the same? Different?

2. How do you respond to the challenge that you *are* God? Not *a* god. Or *the* God. Simply God. Period.

3. What is your history of using metaphysics as a Life-giving source?

4. If you have utilized it to help reframe Life for you, what benefits has it shown you?

5. If you have yet to try it, are you open to walking down the path to enlightenment in a different manner than normally used in our society? (Do not be concerned, metaphysics comes out of the highest reverence for God, Jesus and the Christ. In fact it *is* the Christ expressed.)

6. What use have you made of your inner guide, if any? Are you affirmed by external validation or by that which comes from within?

7. Briefly describe your spiritual Life and where you obtain Truth for you.

Chapter II: Cleansing the Unconscious

1. To what degree are you able to communicate "Namaste" to yourself? To others? Do you communicate it orally, or within?

2. Where are your spiritual teachings based? Upon what foundation? What is your current theological mythology of God and Jesus and the Christ?

3. How is it that you and divinity coincide?

4. What veils keep you from discerning your own divinity? From whence did they come? How often do you frequent them? Are the veils helpful or hindering? In what ways?

5. Have you found any ways for profitably dealing with these veils?

6. What is your familiarity with the use of metaphor? Can you identify with Christo's admonition that all of Life is metaphor, the purpose of which is spiritual discernment? Do you have any counters to this perspective?

7. As you think about how the warp of your loom was formed, how would you describe the threads? What kind do you see? Color? Array? Are there any particular patterns that warm the cockles of your heart? Any which disturb, causing disharmony of feelings or thoughts?

8. What does your landscape of theological mythology look like at present? Is it fixed or shifting? How does this feel to you?

9. On which side of the aisle do you sit with respect to the teachings of the church and those of Jesus? Are you happy where you are? Can you tolerate any modification whatsoever?

10. Including the teachings of the church, how has your warp been transformed?

11. As you sit with your warp and visualize a single Life incident forming the weft that is being woven across it, how do you feel? Where are these feelings located? With what are they associated?

12. As you let go of the more debilitating threads of your warp, how does this modify your response to what Life brings you?

13. Are you able to make the link between changing your perspective within and the manner in which Jesus "healed" others? What INsights and Enlightenment does this afford you?

14. Let the idea of awe and wonder penetrate your understanding. Then, whenever you wonder about what to do with your Life, or how to handle a particular situation, simply ask: "I wonder…?" and then become aware of the possibility that the very answer you need is right within you. Just wonder and then let wonder takes its course. It's like pressing the "send" button on your e-mail server. Once you press the button, the message disappears and although you don't see where it goes, soon an answer is upon you. Practice this often and record the results in your journal.

Chapter III: Sowing the Seed for the Virgin Birth

1. From what you now know, what would be your natural response to those threads you want to discard from your warp?

2. Can you see any alternative means of doing so?

3. Are you really open to alternative means? Are you open to rewarping your loom?

4. Get in touch with your feelings about certain portions of your warp once again. Stay with them just long enough to become clearly familiar what they feel like and what they mean. Are you put in touch with feelings of fear, for example? Or abandonment? Or comfort?

5. Identify those threads that particularly elicit resonance within. Can you predict how you will respond to those who demonstrate similar parts of their warp in your presence?

6. What does the bed you have made for yourself look like? Do you have several or just one? What would you like to do with it (or them)? What is your responsibility should you wish to exchange your bed for another?

7. Have you known anyone like the man at Bethesda? How have you interacted with such a person? Do you have any of these same characteristics? If so, how might you modify them for the benefit of all?

8. How does the story about the three divorces strike you? Did your view of the story change any from beginning to end?

9. What kind of healing did the divorced man have? In your view, do you think he can now reshape his Life?

10. How do your psychoses and neuroses show themselves to you? What do you do with them when they show their faces? What do they teach you? How does this help?

11. Describe the framework you use to discern people and their works.

12. How frequently do you go within for discernment of any kind? If you do, do you pay attention to the image you are shown or cast it away and deal with Life as you always do?

13. What is your translation for Jesus's expression that he is "the way, the truth and Life?"

14. In what ways are you and Jesus, as you know him to be, at least similar?

15. How would you describe your state of divinity? Spirituality?

Chapter IV: The Virgin Birth Unveiled

1. Describe the process of divine discernment offered in this chapter. Briefly, speak to each of the three steps and relate them to your use of them in practical terms.

2. What is the strength of step one?

3. Step 2?

4. Step 3?

5. How does this declaration make you feel?

6. In what ways does this process work for you?

7. In what ways does it not work for you? What recommendations would you make for a change in the process? For the way you use the process?

8. Does using the process put you any closer to the purpose and style of Jesus's Life?

9. Does this recognition put you any closer to acknowledging your own divinity?

10. To what degree are you in contact with your innate ability to lovingly create? To demonstrate the creation spirit?

11. Has this process brought you any closer to being able to live "Namaste" as your breathing mantra?

12. Has it placed you any closer to your seat of empathy or compassion? Has your passion for Life itself grown?

13. Let this process sink in. Drop it into your heart. Can you now see how this process can help you love yourself? Love your neighbor as yourself? Love God with all your mind, heart, soul, and strength? If so, you have just met all the criteria for being divine. For being loving. For being God. For being spiritually creative.

14. Can you bring yourself to understand and demonstrate the meaning of loving Godliness—in all—with all your mind, heart, soul, and strength?

15. Distinguish between infatuation and authentic loving. Which are you mostly tied to? How might you shift the balance if need be?

16. Can you identify with your virgin birth?

17. What opportunities are there for exercising your virgin birth on a regular basis?

18. Describe your virgin birth in relation to that which Jesus witnessed.

19. Contrast the meanings of birth and death in this chapter. Do they resonate with current meaning for you? Can you feel a shift at the threshold of your door to spiritual meaning?

Chapter V: Judge Not, Lest Ye Be Judged

1. How does practice of these steps fit in with your ability to use them effectively?

2. Describe a pattern of practice that seems to work for you. Test it out for a few days and modify it to advantage.

3. To what degree can you make the shift from wanting to reduce the effect of your ego to using your ego to good advantage? To making ego a friend who can steer you toward that which will part the veil that clouds you from your divinity?

4. For just a few minutes, visualize a circumstance or incident with another that was disturbing to you. Perhaps it still is. Place yourself in the midst of that situation, recalling each detail, the path it took when, etc. Now, for each step of that process, as you visualize how it materialized, say to yourself: "God is perfect. I am perfect. He or she is perfect." And to the dysfunction you say, "That's not." And drop what's not perfect from view. Continue through the entire scene, repeating the same affirmations. As you do, pay attention to the resonance you have within. What is it before you render the affirmation? During? After? What does it feel like by the time you've finished? Do you experience any change in your feelings since the beginning of the incident? Can you see how this can benefit both parties? Can you see your way clear to sitting with that other person and guiding them through this? If not, worry not. If you have had a very different response now than before, you can be assured that there will be some corresponding shift in the other person as well.

5. Can you sense the difference between your response to what crosses the threads of your new warp and those of the old one? What meaning does this have for you?

6. What has been your understanding of "judge not?" By virtue of Christo's explanation has your perspective changed any? How? Or why not?

7. How does the Law of Three Fingers strike you?

8. Describe the Kingdom of Heaven. How can you tap that for your highest good and the highest good of all?

9. What is your mustard seed? Any examples?

10. What meaning does prosperity have for you?

11. How do prosperity and divine thought and the Kingdom of Heaven relate?

12. What does it mean to be an alchemist? What is alchemy to the spiritual world? What do you see your role to be in the practice of alchemy?

13. Before engaging in Chapter V, what meaning did you give to "forgive and forget?" To "let go and let God?" Any shifts?

14. Look closely at the admonition to "give it no thought." Apply it to your new understanding of the two phrases referred to in the preceding question.

15. How many times are you ready to forgive? To whom and to what is forgiveness necessary? How might you practice forgiveness? Keep a record in your journal, being sure to note the results for all concerned parties. Be willing to share the process and the results with those others.

16. Do you have any fear about giving this process a 40 day trial? Do you have any fear that you might lose your individuality if you did? Do you know yourself well enough to know what you want to express and how? Are you willing to take the risk in order to be completely healthy?

17. How do you feel after doing the visualization using the new golden threads only?

18. Which world do you want to inhabit? Are you willing to pay the short-term price for the long-term gain?

19. How would you respond to someone who claims that this process is akin to denial?

Chapter VI: Life as Metaphor

1. Did the story of Jane strike any familiar chords in you?

2. If so, describe their correlative nature.

3. Go to the Appendix and familiarize yourself with this shorthand description of the process used with Jane. Think of a single incident in your Life that has flared up. That has informed you of a thread that beckons you within. Briefly apply this process to see how it can assist you in holding yourself responsible for self-accountability. If you need more clarification, pair up with someone and practice the process. If you still need reinforcement, I suggest you get yourself a copy of Byron Katie's book, *Loving What Is,* and work your way through it.

4. How can you use Jane's story to part a veil of illusion that clouds your view from the divinity you are?

5. In what ways does change of perspective render one whole again?

Chapter VII: Turning Deeper Meaning Into Common Meaning

1. What is the purpose for which you came to Earth?

2. What is it that makes your heart sing?

3. Setting aside financial considerations, what would you like to do the rest of your Life beginning tomorrow morning when you awaken?

4. How did you do with your review of Jane's story? What further suggestions do you have for Jane? For Christo? For yourself?

5. As you read the examples of metaphor informing about spiritual condition, which ones resonated within? Share any personal examples that could inform others as well as inspire them to likewise share.

6. What could you do to become more aware of the influence of metaphor on your daily Life?

7. What could you do to become obedient to the Truth to which the metaphor points you?

8. What relation do you see between metaphor and illness? Can you describe some personal examples that now stick out in your mind? How can you use this information to lead you to the meaning that will relieve you of such impositions on your Life?

9. How single-minded can you be in this regard? Why is single-mindedness required?

10. If you were the representative of every cell in your body, what would be the tale you'd tell about what your voice is commanding your cell structure to do? Said another way, if you looked into every cell in your body, what directions would you see each one following? Those directions are the ones you continue to give, after all. Do any need to be changed? How would you go about changing the directions given? Give this exercise plenty of time to be perceived and to sink in. You may want to take several days to complete it properly.

11. How did the poem, "Life," strike you? Was any new meaning awakened in you? Were you put in touch with compassion? With the need to listen and reflect another's Truth back to them unadorned? With the need to refrain from "fixing" another?

12. In the context of spirituality, describe the difference between dependence, codependence, and interdependence.

Chapter VIII: Untying the Knots That Bind Us

1. Describe the main differences between force and power.

2. What are some synonyms for force? For power?

3. Given this context, which would you say the Apostle John is referring to in his Prologue of the Gospel according to John, force or power? How so?

4. What is the Gospel of John referring to? What is the entire Bible speaking to?

5. What is necessary if we are to eliminate the world of duality? How can learning to read spiritual meaning help? Of what use is learning to read the face of metaphor?

6. What is Life if not dreams portrayed in all their forms?

7. What's the essential difference between dreams viewed during sleep and those we call: "day dreams?" Between the latter two dream states and ordinary Life we view with our eyes open?

8. What language or tongue is common to all?

9. Define Life and how it operates on our behalf.

10. Describe the spiritual meanings of infinity and immortality. How does each affect our everyday lives? What relief, if any, do these spiritual perspectives give to the idea of death?

11. What meaning did the story of "stormy weather" have for you? How about the story about the woman who had issued blood for years, and the one about the two blind men?

12. In what tongue do you speak? Are you yet comfortable speaking in the tongue of metaphor? What can you do to buttress your ability in this regard?

13. Do you yet see the necessity for speaking and otherwise communicating in the language of the metaphor? For speaking spiritually? For speaking materially?

14. Are you willing to let go of literality and rationalism as the tongues you speak most often?

Chapter IX: Sending in the Troops

1. What connection do you see between Jesus, who used metaphorical meaning to define spiritual Life and you, who has done essentially the very same thing? Jesus is divine; so are you also divine by your demonstration in kind?

2. Have you not produced the identical results as Jesus is reported to have produced? If so, does this not render you with the same characteristics? Which just so happens to render you divine, as Jesus was divine?

3. Are you not divining precisely as Jesus did? By using essentially the same spiritual tools Jesus identified, albeit not by the same terms? Of course you do and are. Therefore, can you now feel your divinity a bit closer?

4. When we erase all the names that label us as this or that, what is left? Does this not place you parallel with Jesus? And God?

5. How large are you able to define your God? And you? If all is One, why should there be any real difference among those who compose One?

6. If we truly cannot describe God in words, how do you identify with God? How is God real to you? If you can identify with God, how is it you can if you are not at least a container for that very thing?

7. Conduct a survey of terms given to God and decipher those characteristics. Then place them in juxtaposition with those very same ones that you demonstrate. Any hints as to the correlative value between them?

8. Describe the relative power of objectification alongside subjectification. Which can be accurately attributable to all study and research—and thus to all levels of discernment?

9. Illustrate your understanding of the Law of First Cause by giving an example. How can the Law of First Cause be practically applied to Life's circumstances with ease?

10. Describe how one can be lead to utilize the Law of First Cause consciously as one's guide to fruitful living.

11. What course would you suggest for yourself so that you can step fully across the threshold to the seat of your divinity? What assistance would you like? How might you guide another in a similar manner?

12. At what depth are you valuing yourself as a spiritual being? In what ways are you devaluing yourself? What steps can you take to shift your perspective towards your full value—and towards the value of all else in Life?

13. How close are you in valuing yourself in comparison to the way God is depicting you in the song "In His Eyes?" In what ways are they the same? Different?

14. When you feel or see something that moves you, no matter in what way, of what does this inform you?

15. What meaning does the phrase "it takes one to know one," now have for you?

Chapter X: Coming Home to the Seat of the Immaculate Conception

1. Spiritually speaking, where is home for you?

2. What would it mean for you to be single-minded about something? Describe something that is highly important to your well-being and how you would be single-minded about it.

3. How is it that miracles can become commonplace?

4. How is it that miracles are made manifest?

5. For you, what are the basic differences between the perspectives on Life when using the old warp and the new warp?

6. Shed some light on the meaning of transcendence and resurrection in the context of spirituality.

7. What meaning does the term "immaculate conception" have for you? Are you capable of such a thing?

8. As you traverse the meaning of the immaculate conception and the birth of Jesus, what images resonate most deeply with you? How might you reconfigure the story metaphorically? How do you place this story in the context of your own Life?

9. Once again, how does the Law of First Cause relate to how you demonstrate Life?

10. Compare and contrast the basic messages of the Old Testament juxtaposed with those of the New Testament.

11. What perspective(s) have you wrapped in swaddling clothes?

12. How can the description of how Mary might well have raised Jesus apply to your own Life? Is there some way you can assist others in parenting in

this way? Would you be willing to learn how this can be done and give time to assisting in such a program?

Chapter XI: Home We Are

1. How do you feel when you sense the love Christo casts out to the participants? And when he conveys the full meaning of the greeting, Namaste?

2. Note the difference between the acceptance of your divinity and the meaning that you are God. What else is necessary so you can own and demonstrate what you really are?

3. Describe the means for achieving exactly that, and periodically assess your journey in that regard.

4. Does it really matter what you call yourself? *What* are you—really?

5. How do you feel about equating yourself to the image of the loving creator? Explain some ways that you demonstrate this vision for yourself in everyday Life.

6. What do you see your choices to be when confronted with what Life brings you each day?

7. How would you describe your theological mythology now?

Chapter XII: Tidying Up Before the Parting Gift

1. How might you be vigilant in monitoring your warp and its effect on your inner being?

2. What role might any personal ailments that show up play in discerning the condition of your spiritual perspective?

3. When you consider all the hype regarding the so-called "avian flu pandemic," how do you intend to deal with its potential in your own Life?

4. Given the context of your divinity, what designs do you have on how to treat your body, mind and spirit?

5. Describe the elements of toxicity in your Life. Outline how you might deal spiritually with each one. What are some of the considerations for regularly monitoring the implementation of a personal toxic waste program?

6. What meaning does inoculation have for you in the spiritual realm?

7. If you had just one story to tell about your Life in the spiritual realm, what would it be?

8. Preliminarily, what relations do you see between your spirituality and the world of work?

Chapter XIII

1. Describe your daily spiritual practice. What is its impact on your Life?

2. Permit yourself to initiate the three question prayer method over an acceptable trial period for you. Enter the results in your journal, or begin a separate journal for this purpose.

3. What has this prayer method produced in your Life? Does it work for you? What designs do you have for continuing its use?

4. Does this prayer method put you in closer contact with your divinity? Remember that you couldn't "hear" what is coming to you if you didn't have it in you, if it weren't already an integral part within you.

5. Within this context what is "the Word" to you?

6. Do you have any limitations you place on making a commitment to demonstrating the Word in every facet of your Life?

APPLYING INQUIRY TO AN UNDERLYING BELIEF

Write down a belief about a particular situation or person. Then follow this process of HONEST inquiry, for yourself only. The Truth for yourself is ALWAYS found within yourSelf. No one else can do this for you.

1. It is true?

2. Can I absolutely know that it's true?

3. How do I react when I think this thought? (How much of your Life is based on it? What do you do and say when you believe it?)

4. Can you see a reason to drop the thought? (Please don't try to drop it.)

5. Can you find some stress-free reason to keep the thought?

6. What would you be without the thought? How would you behave without it to exercise? How would you feel? What INsights show up? Enlightenment?

7. Turn the underlying belief around.

For example, if one were to say, "It's not right that my girlfriend has separated herself from me," some turnarounds might look like this: "It is right that

my girlfriend has separated herself from me." "It's not right that I have separated myself from my girlfriend." "It's not right that I have separated myself
from me. And from the God within me." "It's my thinking that has separated
me from my girlfriend, myself, and God"

This is making us responsible for self-accountability. Therefore it is not
what Life brings us, but rather how we see what Life brings us, that determines
our quality of Life. Now *that* is taking responsibility for our own Life! And our
Life expressed as victim falls by the wayside. We are thus free to express our
natural state of divinity once again. To love from that rich foundation which
nurtures all it touches. Transcendence has delivered you home once again.

Adapted from "Loving What Is," by Byron Katie

End Notes

The following is a listing of sources referred to, either directly or obliquely, in *A LABOR OF LOVE; Weaving Your Own Virgin Birth on the Loom of Life:*

- Katie, Byron with Mitchell, Stephen. *Loving What Is; Four Questions That Can Change Your Life.* New York: Three Rivers Press, 2002 (323 pp.).

- Dyer, Dr. Wayne W. *The Power of Intention; Learning to Co-create Your World Your Way.* CA: Hay House, Inc., 2004 (257 pp.).

- *The Holy Bible; Authorized King James Version.* Boston: The Christian Science Publishing Society.

- Hawkins, David R. *Power VS Force.* Carlsbad, CA: Hay House, Inc., 2002. (341 pp.).

- "In His Eyes," Music by Mindy Jostyn; lyrics by Mindy Jostyn and Jacob Brackman.

**Either we are seeing God *as* all
or we're not seeing God *at* all.**

—Jim Young, after a yogic saying

978-0-595-39931-4
0-595-39931-2

Printed in the United States
58053LVS00006B/256-273